AMERICAN THEATRE ENSEMBLES

VOLUME 1

RELATED TITLES

AMERICAN THEATRE ENSEMBLES
VOLUME 2
978-1-3500-5163-8
Edited by Mike Vanden Heuvel

MODERN AMERICAN DRAMA: PLAYWRITING IN THE 1930S
978-1-4725-7187-8
Edited by Anne Fletcher

MODERN AMERICAN DRAMA: PLAYWRITING IN THE 1940S
978-1-4725-7186-1
Edited by Felicia Hardison Londré

MODERN AMERICAN DRAMA: PLAYWRITING IN THE 1950S
978-1-4725-7142-7
Edited by Susan C. W. Abbotson

MODERN AMERICAN DRAMA: PLAYWRITING IN THE 1960S
978-1-4725-7220-2
Edited by Mike Sell

MODERN AMERICAN DRAMA: PLAYWRITING IN THE 1970S
978-1-4725-7175-5
Edited by Mike Vanden Heuvel

MODERN AMERICAN DRAMA: PLAYWRITING IN THE 1980S
978-1-4725-7246-2
Edited by Sandra G. Shannon

MODERN AMERICAN DRAMA: PLAYWRITING IN THE 1990S
978-1-4725-7247-9
Edited by Sharon Friedman and Cheryl Black

MODERN AMERICAN DRAMA: PLAYWRITING 2000–2009
978-1-4725-7147-2
Edited by Julia Listengarten and Cindy Rosenthal

STAGING AMERICA: TWENTY-FIRST-CENTURY DRAMATISTS
978-1-3501-2754-8
Christopher Bigsby

GOOD NIGHTS OUT: A HISTORY OF POPULAR BRITISH
THEATRE 1940–2015
978-1-3500-4621-4
Aleks Sierz

AMERICAN THEATRE ENSEMBLES

POST-1970: THEATRE X, MABOU MINES, GOAT ISLAND, LOOKINGGLASS THEATRE, ELEVATOR REPAIR SERVICE, AND SITI COMPANY

VOLUME 1

Edited by Mike Vanden Heuvel

methuen | drama
LONDON • NEW YORK • OXFORD • NEW DELHI • SYDNEY

METHUEN DRAMA
Bloomsbury Publishing Plc
50 Bedford Square, London, WC1B 3DP, UK
1385 Broadway, New York, NY 10018, USA
29 Earlsfort Terrace, Dublin 2, Ireland

BLOOMSBURY, METHUEN DRAMA and the Methuen Drama logo are trademarks of Bloomsbury Publishing Plc

First published in Great Britain 2021
This paperback edition published in 2022

Copyright © Mike Vanden Heuvel and contributors, 2021

Mike Vanden Heuvel and contributors have asserted their right under the Copyright, Designs and Patents Act, 1988, to be identified as authors of this work.

For legal purposes the Acknowledgments on p. xiii constitute an extension of this copyright page.

Cover design by Holly Bell
Cover image © Gem Lauris

All rights reserved. No part of this publication may be reproduced or transmitted in any form or by any means, electronic or mechanical, including photocopying, recording, or any information storage or retrieval system, without prior permission in writing from the publishers.

Bloomsbury Publishing Plc does not have any control over, or responsibility for, any third-party websites referred to or in this book. All internet addresses given in this book were correct at the time of going to press. The author and publisher regret any inconvenience caused if addresses have changed or sites have ceased to exist, but can accept no responsibility for any such changes.

A catalogue record for this book is available from the British Library.

A catalog record for this book is available from the Library of Congress.

ISBN: HB: 978-1-3500-5154-6
PB: 978-1-3501-8736-8
ePDF: 978-1-3500-5156-0
eBook: 978-1-3500-5155-3

Typeset by Integra Software Services Pvt. Ltd.

To find out more about our authors and books visit www.bloomsbury.com and sign up for our newsletters.

CONTENTS

Notes on Contributors		vi
Series Preface		ix
Acknowledgments		xiii

1 **Historical and Cultural Background**
  Mike Vanden Heuvel — 1
2 **American Ensemble Theatres, 1970–95** *Mike Vanden Heuvel* — 21
3 **Theatre X** *Curtis L. Carter* — 83
4 **Mabou Mines** *Jessica Silsby Brater* — 105
5 **Goat Island** *Nicholas Lowe and Sarah Skaggs* — 129
6 **Lookingglass Theatre Company** *Jane Barnette* — 151
7 **Elevator Repair Service** *Roger Bechtel* — 173
8 **SITI Company** *Scott T. Cummings* — 197

Notes	219
Bibliography	225
Index	240

NOTES ON CONTRIBUTORS

Jane Barnette is Associate Professor in the Department of Theatre and Dance at the University of Kansas, where she teaches courses in dramaturgy, theatre history, and script analysis, as well as seminars in theatrical adaptation and the performance of gender and sexuality. Her recent book, *Adapturgy: The Dramaturg's Art and Theatrical Adaptation*, explores the powerful alchemy of dramaturgically savvy adaptations for the stage. Barnette's research includes Chicago-based touring theatre practice at the turn of the twentieth century, American pageantry, and depictions of "witch" characters onstage as well as in popular culture.

Roger Bechtel sadly passed away not long after this work was first published and having recently retired from a twenty-year career in higher education, including stints as tenured professor and chair at Bowdoin and Carleton colleges, and director of graduate studies at Miami University, Ohio. He had returned to an earlier passion, working as a criminal defense trial attorney for the Minnesota Board of Public Defense. To satisfy his theatre cravings, he had remained active as a playwright. His first full-length play, *Private*, was the winner of the Portland Playwrights Competition, where it received a full production, and a revised version later received a staged reading at the New Frontiers Playwrights Festival in Alaska. He had recently finished his second full-length script, *The True Believer*.

Jessica Silsby Brater is Assistant Professor and Coordinator of the BA and MA in Theatre Studies at Montclair State University. Publications include *Ruth Maleczech at Mabou Mines* (Methuen Drama); chapters in *Women, Collective Creation, and Devised Performance* and *Contemporary Approaches to Adaptation in Performance*; and writing in *Aujourd/hui/Samuel Beckett Today* and *Theatre Journal*. Forthcoming publications include contributions to *The Cambridge Companion to American Theatre 1945–present, Analyzing Gender in Performance,* and *Great North American Stage Directors* (Methuen Drama). She holds a BA from Barnard College and a PhD from the Graduate Center, CUNY.

Notes on Contributors

Curtis L. Carter is Donald J. Schuenke Chair and Professor of Aesthetics in the Department of Philosophy at Marquette University and the Les Aspin Center for Government, Washington, DC. He is author of numerous works on aesthetic theory, most recently *Border Crossings: Aesthetics into the Arts* (2018); *Unsettled Boundaries: Philosophy, Art, Ethics East/West* (2017), and co-editor, with Liu Yuedi, of *Aesthetics and Everyday Life East/West*, 2014. His work on Jan Fabre and the Troubleyn Theatre (Antwerp) helped contextualize the group's work for American audiences. He is a former board member of Milwaukee's Theatre X.

Scott T. Cummings is past Chair of the Theatre Department at Boston College, where he directs plays and teaches courses in playwriting and dramatic literature. He is the author of *Remaking American Theatre: Charles Mee, Anne Bogart and the SITI Company*, and *Marie Irene Fornes*, as well as numerous performance reviews, journal articles, and essays on contemporary American theatre and drama. Scott's teaching, research, and professional interests center on contemporary American theatre, new play development and devised work, dramaturgy, and theatre criticism.

Nicholas Lowe is an interdisciplinary artist, curator, author, and teacher. Significant curatorial projects include *goat island archive—we have discovered the performance by making it* (2019) and *Roger Brown: Calif USA* (2010). His visual and performance works explore archival detail and museum display contexts as research-based iterative practices. Lowe joined the faculty at School of the Art Institute of Chicago in 2003 and is Chair of the Department of Historic Preservation. He was born in England where he received the Higher Diploma in Fine Art in 1989 from the Slade School of Art at University College London. His exhibition and teaching career include engagements in the UK, France, Germany, and the United States.

Sarah Skaggs is an independent administrator, producer, and curator based in Chicago. Currently she is the Company Manager for the performance art collective *Every house has a door* (Lin Hixson, Director; Matthew Goulish, Dramaturg). She was the registrar and curatorial assistant for the exhibition *goat island archive—we have discovered the performance by making it* (2019) at the Chicago Cultural Center. She completed her MA in Arts Administration and Policy at the School of the Art Institute of Chicago (2016) and graduated Magna Cum Laude from the University of Missouri with a BA in Art History and a BS in Business Administration (2007).

Notes on Contributors

Mike Vanden Heuvel is Professor of Interdisciplinary Theatre Studies and a member of the Classics and Near Eastern Studies Department at the University of Wisconsin-Madison. Author of *Performing Drama/Dramatizing Performance: Alternative Theatre and the Dramatic Text* (1991) and editor/contributor to *Modern American Drama: Playwriting in the 1970s* (Methuen Drama, 2018), his teaching and research are centered on modern and postdramatic theatre as well as theatre and science.

SERIES PREFACE

In 2006 Diedre Heddon and Jane Milling published a key text on the history and practice of devising, *Devising Performance: A Critical History*. Despite a laudable attempt to encompass work from the UK, Canada, Australia, and the United States, the authors overstated the case when they asserted that "[t]he relative scarcity of contemporary devising companies in the USA is all the more marked when placed beside the vibrant scene in the UK, where there are too many companies to mention" (247, f.n. 3). This repeats a line of thought initiated by Richard Schechner in *The End of Humanism* (1982) and repeated by Arnold Aronson in his *American Avant-garde Theatre: A History* (2000) that American artists, retreating from the counterculture ethos of the 1960s and seduced by the lure of individual success and the quickest route to Broadway or television, were by the end of the 1970s no longer interested in collective work (Schechner has since amended his view; see 2010). As for the comparison made by Heddon and Milling, it is not accurate and requires remediation. The misapprehension stems, in part, from the very different funding strategies pursued by artists in different locales. Support for devised work in the UK and Commonwealth nations is more centralized and overseen by national arts councils, which results not only in a relatively higher profile for ensemble creation but also provides a ready archive of the extent of its practice.

In America, on the other hand, without a central funding agency whose records define the true scale and range of such work, the practice of ensemble creation is scattered; much activity goes unnoticed, in part because most collectively created work is not, for reasons of aesthetic style and sometimes a textual animus, intended to be, or not valued sufficiently to be, published. It is easy to mistake that lack of hard evidence for lack of activity, but as research for this series has proved, there has always been a tremendous amount of collaborative theatre-making happening both on and off the radar in the United States, and this has been true since the 1970s.

The period selected for attention in this series was chosen, in part, to rectify this misinterpretation. Especially for the time frame of the first volume (1970–95) scant critical attention has been given with respect to collective creation, in part for reasons discussed in the introduction.

Series Preface

These include the general acceptance of what I refer to as the "declension hypothesis" and its conclusion that after the early 1970s creative collectives had all but disappeared. Another factor is the lack of primary materials and archives for such work. A vast number of companies that began in the 1970s are no longer operating and—with few exceptions—often had neither the means nor the desire to archive their activities, so the collective memory of this work is threatened. In the UK, by contrast, a relatively stable record exists made up in part by the archives from the state funding agencies as well as research they have supported. For instance, the project *Giving Voice to the Nation: The Arts Council of Great Britain and the Development of Theatre and Performance in Britain 1945–1995*, undertaken in 2009 by the University of Reading and the Victoria and Albert Museum, became

> a unique and, up until recently, unexplored resource for the study of theatre companies active in those years: materials include minutes of company meetings, funding proposals for projects, records of tour dates, statistics on box-office takings and audience attendance, newspaper and magazine reviews and publicity materials, as well as Arts Council memos, letters and records of meetings. (Bull and Saunders 2017, ix–x)

In addition, the UK online archive "Unfinished Histories" under the supervision of Susan Croft has gathered scholar- and practitioner-contributed research and interview material devoted to fringe companies, as well as placing hard copies of materials in central archives.

Meanwhile, in the United States, the remnants of the greatest part of the material archives of collective creation are dispersed and will require a massive commitment of time and resources if they are ever to be recovered sufficiently to produce a coherent historical account. While *American Ensemble Theatres* does not attempt such an epic project, the hope is that it might inspire others to contribute to imagining such an endeavor. The first case study in the series by Curtis L. Carter on Milwaukee's critically neglected Theatre X, complete with reflections from former company members and collaborators, provides an example of the kind of reclamation project that might fill gaps in the historical record and indicate the true extent of collective creation activity in the United States.

The two volumes of *American Ensemble Theatres* represent the first collection of critical assessments devoted to US companies who have created and self-produced theatre work collectively between 1970 and the present.

They both supplement and mark a departure from the compilation edited by James M. Harding and Cindy Rosenthal, *Restaging the Sixties: Radical Theaters and Their Legacies* (2007). While picking up roughly where that volume ends and extending the chronology of collective creation to the present, this series questions the assumption (indicated in its title) that what follows the work of the collectives of the 1960s in ensemble-based theatre must be seen in light of only those radical legacies. For this reason, too, the series departs from the approach used by Mark Weinberg in his *Challenging the Hierarchy: Collective Theatre in the United States* (1992) because his focus is on the continuation of the collective work of the 1960s rather than the diversification of collective practice represented in *American Ensemble Theatres*. The more recent trio of books on the longer and transnational history of collective creation edited by Kathryn Syssoyeva and Scott Proudfit—*A History of Collective Creation* (2013); *Collective Creation in Contemporary Performance* (2013); and *Women, Collective Creation, and Devised Performance* (2016)—more substantially reflects the orientation of this series with regard to historiography, chronology, and theoretical models. Recent work by Rachel Anderson-Rabern (*Staging Process*, 2020) and others has further elaborated this historiography and also questions the simple line of descent from the 1960s to the present. Yet the nature of legacy and succession is a complex one, and there is value in attending to the continuing dialogue between past and present.

Of course, eliminating the single criterion of direct legacy from the 1960s and opening up the history of collective creation to its many and diverse expressions means quickly becoming overwhelmed by the sheer number and variety of ensembles that merit attention. Thus, it is important to state at the outset that the series does not pretend to "cover" US ensemble-based creation over the last fifty years. A growing but scattered critical literature is emerging that addresses the many forms of collective creation and devised theatre in theatre for youth and young adults, theatre in education, grassroots and community-directed theatre, a wide assortment of applied theatre forms, a variety of constituency-directed theatres, game-based performance, immersive theatre and many, many more. While my introductions to the two volumes attempt to construct a partial ecology of these diverse practices and place many of these forms of ensemble creation within the larger trajectory of collective creation broadly conceived from 1970 to the present, I make no attempt to be comprehensive. Rather, the main goal is to establish contexts that scaffold the kinds of work represented in the series. With regard to the companies chosen for individual case studies, the aim was not to make them

Series Preface

in any sense representative of the variety and range of practices that fall under collective creation, a goal that would surely founder under the weight of evidence.

Instead, the guiding principles for selection directed focus toward the most prominent ensemble practices over the past fifty years, those that have helped to distinguish and define what is generally understood as modern and contemporary collective creation and devised theatre in the US context. As these definitions remain imprecise, the intent was to feature ensembles whose work was diverse enough to elicit a wide range of individual essays and approaches. Companies that have endured for long periods were particularly attractive, as these allowed contributors to begin at the founding date of the ensemble and track developments and the evolution of practices over many years and in changing contexts. "Significance" is always slippery concept on which to hang choices, but effort was made to find a balance between repeating material on companies that have already received substantial critical attention and recognizing that such consideration is a sign of an ensemble's vitality and importance. A special case arose with respect to the Wooster Group, whose singular importance to developments in ensemble theatre-making in the United States can hardly be overstated. Given their unique contributions to the field, it was felt that these would be better contextualized in the editor's introductions to both volumes rather than in a single case study restricted to one time frame or the other.

Even so, during the process of organizing the series it was impossible not to be sensible of what has been left out. From the "binders full of ensembles" with which the project began, many worthy companies could not be included, and my hope is that these two volumes of essays will pave the way for similar studies that broaden our understanding of the exciting work, past and present, that collective creation has contributed to American theatre.

ACKNOWLEDGMENTS

I thank the contributors to the two volumes in this series, whose acuity and obvious passion for the work they write about made this a most satisfying project. Mark Dudgeon, whose enthusiasm for theatre and scholarship first launched this series, has my respect and gratitude. Lara Bateman assisted at every stage of the undertaking and guided the project to its conclusion.

I gratefully acknowledge research support provided by the University of Wisconsin-Madison Office of the Vice Chancellor for Research and Graduate Education. The Howe-Bascom Professorship, bestowed by the Integrated Liberal Studies Program at UW-Madison, allowed me to conduct necessary research in New York City.

I dedicate these volumes to the memory of my father, Norbert, and younger brother John, whose company was taken during the completion of the project, but whose memories I cherish. Later editions of the series are also dedicated to Roger Bechtel, who sadly passed away soon after his essay was published.

To Tracy: my life's companion, adored G3, beloved playmate of Mr. Crowley and generations of pups, and consort in every adventure. T, M, D.

CHAPTER 1
HISTORICAL AND CULTURAL BACKGROUND
Mike Vanden Heuvel

It is no coincidence that American ensemble theatre-making is reborn and revitalized during one of the most volatile periods in American history. From its earliest manifestations with the Provincetown Players and Washington Square Players, where the idea of artist-led ensembles was first put into motion in the United States, collective creation has emerged when artists felt change in the wind and sought alternatives to mainstream practice. The period selected for the first volume of *American Ensemble Theatres* is no exception, although the 1970s have often been dismissed in general histories of the United States as a mere aftershock to the turbulent 1960s (with studies entitled *The Lost Decade* and *It Seemed Like Nothing Happened*, for instance), while the endpoint of this volume, 1995, carries no iconic resonance in American history as does, say, 1968, the millennium, or 9/11 (Hurrup 1996; Carroll 1990).

Yet the period between 1970 and 1995 marks a period of notable transitions. During these years the long-standing liberal consensus that shaped US economics and politics since before the Second World War gives way to a more conservative political landscape in which free-market principles clash uncomfortably with hot-button social issues. The Cold War continued to fuel extravagant spending on defense and ignited US military operations in Lebanon (1982), Grenada (1983), and Panama (1989). With the fall of Communism in 1991, the Cold War seemed poised to end until the rise of autocratic regimes, first in the former Soviet states and then worldwide, even as events in the oil-producing Middle East laid hopes of reduced tension to rest. The Arab nations and Middle East became an area of global conflict, and the United States was involved in numerous interventions there, as well as the Gulf War against Iraq (1990–1): the Afghan occupation continues to this day. Conflicts in the region would intensify after 9/11 in 2001. Ethnic wars and coups initiated American involvement in Somalia, Bosnia, and elsewhere.

Closer to home, second-wave feminism arrived fully at the outset of the 1970s and reshaped US labor, domestic and cultural sectors before encountering a fierce backlash in the 1980s and transitioning into new forms in the 1990s.

The AIDS crisis marked a signal moment in American consciousness and transformed political activism in profound ways, in addition to altering the landscape of American theatre. The groundwork for the tech revolutions of the 1990s was laid during the 1970s and 1980 as well. Perhaps most momentously, these decades see the full flowering of postmodernism and the onset of globalism and usher in a new neoliberal order that significantly impacts the arts in general and ensemble theatre in particular.

The year 1970 is significant if for no other reason than it marks the pinnacle of the first term of Richard Nixon's presidency, begun in the ferment of 1968. What followed, of course, has received more attention, as Nixon would be reelected for a second term following a landslide victory in 1972 only to be roiled by the Watergate scandal and its cover-ups. These would lead to the president's eventual resignation on August 9, 1974. By that time, however, Nixon had reshaped the nation and the presidency in important ways, laying the foundation for the resurgence of conservatism by demonizing the counterculture of the 1960s in the eyes of a "silent majority" set fair to raise its voice by the 1980s. In American theatre, by contrast, by 1970 the pinnacle of collective theatre-making appeared to have been reached as the major radical ensembles begin to disperse. The movement showed signs of receding slowly into the past, such that Arnold Aronson was led to report—focusing on the movement of collectivist theatre in New York City that gave rise to the Living Theatre, Open Theater, and the Performance Group— that "[t]he ensemble theatre movement had essentially disappeared by the mid-1970s" (2000, 102). Similarly, James Harding and Cindy Rosenthal framed and titled their collection of essays on "radical theatres" *Restaging the Sixties* (2006) to signal an endpoint to the surge of ensemble theatre activity defining that decade and demarcating it from what would ensue.

At the outset of the 1970s, then, bearing in mind these contexts, one might reasonably predict that the future would lie, politically, in the continued ascent of Nixonian conservatism and, artistically, in the waning of the collective, radical spirit that ignited theatre ensembles of the 1950s and 1960s: and in doing so, one would be at the same time very prescient and also quite wrong.

Politics

The main trajectory of US history in the final twenty-five years of the twentieth century is typically described as a drifting away from the liberal consensus, undergirded by Keynesian economic principles, which dominated the country after the Second World War toward the resurgence of conservatism and the rise of the New Right. While this accurately describes the main trajectory, it often leaves out the parallel transformation of liberalism itself in response to the rise of the Right, an important element of the story that assumes greater significance in the twenty-first century. The liberal consensus, of course, was neither particularly liberal when compared to classical liberalism (having asserted, during and after Roosevelt's New Deal [1933–9], a strong State role in balancing the economy and advancing individual freedom), nor especially consensual: conservative forces operated within both the Democratic and Republican parties even during Roosevelt's terms, and as the Cold War and anti-communism grew more intense in the 1950s, outlier organizations such as the John Birch Society retained credibility with parts of the electorate. Some historians claim that the civil unrest and countercultural activism of the 1960s accelerated the rise of this nascent conservatism, while others see the conservative Republican Barry Goldwater's overwhelming defeat in the 1964 presidential election as the humiliating low point of the ideology, after which conservatives learned to play electoral politics more effectively. In either case, as the 1970s dawned, many sectors of the industrial working class that made up the putative Democratic base were growing increasingly conservative, in part as a backlash to the directions taken by liberalism in the 1960s. But these changes also occurred in response to demographic shifts, first of "white flight" to the suburbs and then across the Southwest. But through all these decades, New Deal liberalism formed the dominant political ideology of the land, with the Democratic Party seen as its standard bearer and Republicans as the mostly moderating minority party whose role it was to advocate for business, federal fiscal restraint, and a strong national defense against Communist encroachment.

The slow crumbling of the liberal consensus that had bound Democrats and Republicans to a common set of principles after the Second World War (but which also allowed for the nationalist jingoism and technocratic establishment that the counterculture had defied since the time of the Beats) began in the 1950s and gathered force in the 1960s. Criticism of liberal policies and principles came, unsurprisingly, from conservatives, but now also from the coalitions that would eventually form the New Left in the 1960s. With a number of factors converging at the dawn of the 1970s—the catastrophe of the Vietnam War, the failure of the Civil Rights Movement to fully secure economic and social equality, the fracturing of the Democratic

Party following the 1968 election, the perceived rampant liberalization of culture, and a declining economy that would soon give evidence of the limits of State planning and intervention—liberalism as a basis for national consensus fell increasingly out of favor. The 1970s, as a result, are perceived as particularly unmoored as the nation struggled for its political identity: it is no coincidence that the period, which began with Nixon's dream of the Imperial Presidency, saw instead an unprecedented series of one-term administrations, with Ford, Carter, and, in 1992, George H. W. Bush, failing to win reelection. But by the end of the 1970s, and particularly with the election of the conservative Ronald Reagan for the first of his two terms in 1980, the United States as a whole began to shift notably to the Right. As the culture wars flared up throughout the 1980s and 1990s around issues like abortion, school busing, gay rights, affirmative action, and multicultural education, liberalism was constantly on the defensive. Meanwhile, once in power conservatives (including Reagan) struggled to maintain the purity of their own principles as they oversaw ballooning government agencies, climbing deficit spending, and a popular culture comfortable with electing them while generally ignoring their pleas for stronger traditional families, upright morality, and fiscal responsibility.

This tangled and decades-long narrative regarding shifting political sentiments has clarified only somewhat recently, displacing an older historiography that saw the 1960s and the dramatic rise (and eventual fall) of the New Left and counterculture as the fulcrum upon which these changes swung. As will be seen in the next chapter, this understanding of American history affects even the way that collective creation in theatre is said to evolve "out of" the dynamics of 1960s alternative theatre (a position I will contest). Formerly, the rise of the Right following the 1960s was seen as marking the end stage of a so-called declension hypothesis, one that emerged out of (using Allan Matusow's resonant phrase) "the great unraveling" of American liberalism ([1985] 2009). Following the pinnacle of the Great Society's domestic programs designed to use the powers of the federal government to combat poverty, racism, and inequality, Matusow's argument goes, the liberal program foundered on bad planning (for instance, by seeking to alleviate poverty by distributing funds and services rather than by politically and economically empowering the poor) and bad luck (the Vietnam War). Furthermore, the radical ideals of the New Left, which sought to undermine rather than rectify the fundamental principles of capitalism and traditional structures of liberal democracy, pushed moderate liberals further leftward. By 1968, the argument continues, all parties associated with liberalism were becoming unraveled and the spectacular results were on display in the streets outside the Democratic Convention in Chicago. In the 1970s, with both old and new Lefts in disarray, Matusow concludes, Americans became illiberal and divisive, turning inward and away from the public political sphere to pursue hedonistic goals. (These, conveniently, aligned with conservatism's desire to unstitch forms of collective identity to produce niche-buying consumers.) By 1980, Ronald Reagan arrived to sanctify that arrangement and to drive the final stake into the heart of the liberal, interventionist state.

This declension hypothesis gained credence in part because it is satisfyingly dramatic and well positioned to serve, for the Left, both nostalgia and indignation (one of the best accounts is Todd Gitlin's *Days of Hope and Rage*) and, for the Right, the basis for the then-out-of-the-desert-came-forth-a-savior myth that continues to shape the legacy of Reagan. However, it misrepresents this important political shift in American politics and culture in consequential ways. First, the hypothesis unrealistically foreshortens and encapsulates the process of transformation, disregarding both the important skirmishes between liberalism and conservatism that preceded the 1960s as well as the many ways that these continued in and beyond the 1970s. It also places undue weight on the 1960s by making it the lever for all subsequent transformations. The hypothesis also leads many to assume that the counterculture, so antithetical to both the traditional Left and Right, simply became collateral damage and disappeared after 1968 (or 1972 when America's role in the Vietnam War ended). This obscures the counterculture's continued vitality into and beyond the 1970s in movements like feminism, AIDs awareness, and activism for social justice—not to mention its value to capitalism itself as a harbinger of the principles of hedonism and self-actualization that would make everything from soft drink preferences to personal care philosophies an expression of individual identity and brand.

1980 and All That

By most accounts, the American political scene of the period was dominated by Ronald Reagan, first as a popular pitchman for conservative causes—his televised talk in support of Goldwater, "A Time for Choosing," became known "The Speech" and thrust him into political office—then as Governor of California from 1967 to 1975, followed by a failed run at the 1977 Republican nomination, and finally as a two-term president from 1981 to 1989. Not unexpectedly, a Reagan myth has developed that depicts him as an underdog who beat all odds to vanquish liberalism and "Make America Great Again." In fact, Regan was a consequence, rather than the origin, of America's shift to the Right: this movement certainly did gain momentum from the "great unraveling" of the 1960s, but it was driven as well by events having little to do with that decade, such as the economic downturns of the 1970s, developments in the Cold War, and the outbreak on the cusp of the 1980s of the culture wars. Mostly, a new generation of conservatives energized by Goldwater's humiliating 1964 debacle had become more proactive, engaging in organizing and outreach activities that included developing new media outlets, initiating new think tanks and publishing houses, and reconnecting with faith-based organizations by, for instance, bringing the formerly quietist evangelicals into their camp (Greenberg 2009).

When Reagan won in stunning fashion over Jimmy Carter in 1980, capturing forty-six states and over 50 percent of the popular vote as well as gaining the Senate for Republicans for the first time since 1952, Republican moderates were shocked, but liberals were confounded into disarray, self-denial, and a decade's worth of soul searching. Moderate Republicans, many as stunned as liberals that Americans at last expressed a belief that a conservative could govern, were soon won over by the new president's pro-business tax cuts and strong positions on defense—if not initially eager to wade into hot-button social issues such as school prayer and women's rights. Reagan's unwavering faith in supply-side, "trickle down" economics (which, despite numerous failures in balancing federal budgets—glaringly so during Reagan's two terms—continues to be, under the rubric of "Reaganomics," the de facto Republican economic philosophy) and his vocal criticism of forms of liberty and identity based in collective principles, provided a substantial boost to a nascent focus on individual prosperity that had been building throughout the 1970s. Buoyed by an improving economy—one that helped launch the dramatic wealth inequality that still dogs the nation today—and a more attractive environment for investment and growth, middle America generally grew wealthier and pursued new forms of private enterprise and gratification in what came to be called "the New Gilded Age." This would continue, through peaks and valleys, until the stock market crash of 1987.

The rise of Reagan under these historical conditions plays a significant role in his most lasting legacy, which was to reconfigure both the Republican and Democratic parties along the lines of his particular brand of conservatism. His election overthrew the notion, held since Goldwater had tested the thesis in 1964, that a staunch conservative could never win the presidency (based on this fear, former President Gerald Ford considered running again in 1980 after Reagan began dominating the Republican primaries). Over his two terms, Reagan would shift Republican moderates further to the Right such that when his vice president, George H. W. Bush, ran to succeed him in 1988, his formerly moderate positions on abortion and the Equal Rights Amendment more closely paralleled Reagan's than his own from a decade earlier. More tellingly, after he gained the Republican nomination in 1988, Bush passed over several strong moderates and selected the relatively unknown conservative Senator Dan Quayle as his running mate.

Similarly, after their defeat in 1980 the Democrats found themselves reckoning with significant shifts in demographics that showed core constituencies, such as labor, fading. Elements within the party began efforts to reorient the Democratic platform, first by reshaping its economic principles. Responding to the stagnant US economy of the 1970s, the so-called neoliberals sought to move away from the New Deal and Great Society principles based in economic fairness and a redistributive tax code and to shift policy toward rejuvenating capitalism through more efficient and open markets. Democrats nominated a neoliberal, Walter Mondale (who selected Geraldine Ferraro as his running mate, the first female vice presidential candidate in the country's history), in 1984, but following his rout at the hands of Reagan other solutions were pursued. The key player became the Democratic Leadership Council (DLC), made up largely of conservative Southern Democrats who took into their platform the neoliberals' market-friendly economic plans and joined these with a new emphasis on the sort of values—patriotism, family, entrepreneurship, responsibility—that were thought to have drawn off the "Reagan Democrats" to the Republican ranks. Their efforts produced some successes, as when in 1986 Democrats captured the Senate. However, their 1988 presidential nominee, Michael Dukakis, presented himself as a competent neoliberal manager but failed to convey a strong sense of such values and was painted by his opponent as a 1960s liberal holdover. After Dukakis was soundly defeated, the DLC continued to strive for a synthesis of existing New Deal liberalism, neoliberal pragmatism, and values-driven principles, and in the early 1990s they found their ideal candidate in Bill Clinton.

Aided by an economy hindered by the leftover Reagan deficits and deregulatory mania (as President Bush was forced to oversee a bailout of the savings and loan industry), Clinton defeated the incumbent and returned the Democrats to the White House for the first time in twelve years. He immediately encountered strong Congressional opposition that led to Republicans, with the conservative Newt Gingrich as their spokesperson, to enact a "Contract with America" that repeated Reagan policy promises (as well as slashing the National Endowment for the Arts [NEA] budget by 40 percent). The Democrats were badly beaten in the midterm elections and lost both Houses, and so Clinton's first term and a good part of his second were fought on the defensive. This, added to the several investigations regarding financial transactions and sexual indiscretions that dogged him throughout the election and into his presidency—and would lead to his impeachment by the House in 1998 (he was acquitted by the Senate the following year)—weakened his ability to enact even the moderate reforms he claimed to support as a pragmatic centrist.

During his two terms (1993–2001) the Democratic Party committed to a center-right platform based in economic principles that prioritized open global markets and free trade while also partially dismantling the social safety net (supporting, for instance, "welfare to work" legislation). Clinton and the New Democrats could still claim victory by virtue of a revived economy following the 1987 market bust, and for balancing the federal budget and creating a rare surplus. He accomplished this, in part, by deepening Reagan's deregulation of the financial sector (which some see as contributing the Great Recession of the early twenty-first century). But while overseeing an economic boom tied to the rise of Silicon Valley and the high-tech markets, Clinton also enacted tough-on-crime legal reforms, such as the "three strikes and you're out" sentencing guidelines that disproportionately victimized minorities and produced huge increases in the US incarceration rate (Serrianne 2015). Moving the party further toward the center-right, Clinton allowed himself to be maneuvered into signing both the "don't ask don't tell" bill that further stigmatized gay and transgender members of the military while allowing them to continue serving and the Defense of Marriage Act that effectively outlawed gay marriage and defined marriage as a legal union between a man and a woman. On a number of related fronts, Clinton and the New Democrats eased the party toward solidifying their appeal to what now seemed moderates while at the same breaking with some of their historical constituencies.

Despite the moderation of these liberal policies, the 1990s saw increasing acts of domestic violence launched against what terrorists believed were unconstitutional acts of government overreach. In 1993, the compound of the Branch Davidians, a separatist religious group in Waco, Texas, was stormed by federal agents and US military personnel and resulted in the deaths of seventy-four Davidians and ten agents. The year 1995 brought the most violent act of domestic terrorism ever recorded in the United States when Timothy McVeigh, a veteran of the Gulf War, bombed a federal building in Oklahoma City that killed 168 people. The Age of Terror was upon the country well before 9/11 and to this day domestic acts of terrorism far outnumber attacks by international actors.

Economy

The last quarter of the twentieth century saw the US economy go through some of its lowest and highest points, experiencing periods of stagnation, inflation (sometimes, as in the 1970s, at the same time), and recession while also enjoying periods of dynamic growth and expansion. On the one hand, deregulation and privatization accelerated after the 1980s, opening up new opportunities for investment and innovative international trade agreements. For organized labor, conversely, after the mid-1970s almost every decade brought further erosion as the manufacturing sector that provided the bulk of its membership declined and its political power weakened in the face of conservative economic policies and vacillation from liberals. Job growth occurred at opposite ends of the spectrum, in the service industries and in finance, representing symbolically the income disparity that would grow ever larger by the close of the millennium: whereas in the 1970s a corporate CEO might make fifty times as much as an employee, by 1993 that disparity had doubled, and by the twenty-first century it was not uncommon to see CEO salaries at 250 times the average employee's pay. Joined to supply-side economics and the ubiquitous Laffer curve, these disproportionate earnings were rationalized as the mighty heights from which wealth would trickle, and then rush down upon, the rest of society. The one steadfast fact of US economic life, however, was a federal deficit that, except for the brief hiccup between 1998 and 2001 when Clinton created a surplus, continued to balloon under conservatives, moderates, and liberals alike.

The roller-coaster ride of economic highs and lows that characterize the final twenty-five years of the twentieth century in the United States can be seen on a local level by looking at the fate of New York City during the period. Since the city was home both to many of the radical 1960s theatre collectives and to nearly half of those featured in this series, its fate is intimately tied to the fortunes of ensemble theatre. As will be shown across the two volumes, the 1970s established what Hillary Miller (2016) calls a "logic of austerity" and self-sufficiency for arts funding that has proved consequential for ensemble-created theatre. More momentous still, the economic shocks of the 1970s, which saw soaring unemployment and inflation that wiped out twenty years of prosperity and forced the country to devalue its currency, are now recognized as a sign of the impending new global economy. As productivity and quality declined, more foreign competition (from Europe and Japan) raised the trade imbalances and caused further declines in manufacturing. As these were centered mostly in the Midwest and Northern states, they hit urban centers hardest.

New York City, in particular, faced grave circumstances at the outset of the 1970s, stemming from the more widespread urban crisis that dramatically reshaped demographics and political power in the United States. As the industrial Northeast and Midwest suffered economic decline following the Second World War, American cities saw precipitous population declines sometimes approaching, as in Cleveland and St. Louis for instance, 50 percent. These shifts affected class and ethnic demographics, as millions of middle-class whites moved to the suburbs and, increasingly in the 1960s and 1970s, to the South and Southwest. In their place large numbers of lower-income migrants from the South and new arrivals from the Global South came seeking opportunity and cheap housing in the cities. In New York as elsewhere, with employment trends favoring the lower-paying service industries, falling rents created a drain on the tax base; these, coupled with often race-based policy decisions, left large swaths of the city infrastructure and its population bereft of social services. As the city fabric continued to deteriorate, more businesses left and further weakened the tax base, until New York was caught in a vicious cycle of economic downturn. Many studies point to the manner by which the city was represented during the 1970s in popular culture as a site of decay and moral anarchy, citing vigilante-themed films from the 1970s like *Taxi Driver* and *Death Wish* and the graffito-covered subway cars of the MTA. Broadway and the theatre district suffered as well, becoming home to peep shows, massage parlors, and porn shops.

Wedded to the sluggish national economy of the 1970s, New York's 10 percent unemployment rate and suspect financial accounting methods left the city ill-prepared when the United States moved into recession in 1974. The city famously came within a hair of declaring bankruptcy in 1975, eliciting the famous *Daily News* headline purporting to quote President Ford's response to the request for a bailout: "Ford to City: Drop Dead." Almost as seriously, the city's finances were turned over to State-appointed authorities who pursued austerity policies. Soon, power began to shift from the political parties and neighborhood councils to bondholders, and policies were often driven by the need to improve the city's economic profile and bond ratings rather than to address the fate of the commons or improve the city's decaying housing stock.

Historical and Cultural Background

In 1977 Ed Koch was elected mayor, and his platform of fiscal restraint, a tough stance on crime, and criticism of the social welfare system influenced the Democratic Party's national platform to begin moving to the Right. By the early 1980s, his austerity budgets balanced the city's financial books, and as Reagan began his first term by deregulating the financial industry, Wall Street was well positioned to lead the way to recovery and to fund the real estate boom of the 1980s. By the mid-1990s, New York had transformed into the financial capital of the world, bling was back, and Broadway was well on its way to becoming the gleaming altar to corporate power that it remains to this day.

Education

In 1983 President Reagan established the National Commission on Excellence in Education and tasked it with assessing the current state of US schooling. Among his motives was the desire to reform K-12 and higher education to move it away from the liberal goals of the Great Society and to staunch movement toward multicultural education that was gaining ground as new ethnic studies textbooks, courses, departments, and degrees appeared during the 1970s. As Sandra Shannon summarizes the conclusions of the bombshell report by Regan's commission, ominously entitled *A Nation at Risk*:

> it said the US educational system was not meeting the national need for a globally competitive workforce. The report, which warned that American schools were failing, alarmed elected officials, corporate executives and education leaders to the point that education reform shifted from a liberal left-of-center focus on school integration and civil rights to one concerned with setting national standards and building accountability systems. (2018, 16)

It was the first move that would lead, with the support of President Clinton and both Bush administrations, in 2002 to the first "No Child Left Behind" legislation, which cemented neoliberal education policy as the cornerstone of US educational standards.

Although neoliberalism was not yet a cogent alternative to the welfare economy that had prevailed since Roosevelt, education reform was a major step toward understanding and addressing social problems not with direct State intervention, but through market-based solutions. By shifting emphasis from the putative goal of educating students to serve the general welfare of the State, to preparing workers (and consumers) to succeed in the competitive job market, education reform recast educational institutions in the role of providers, not of some abstract quality of "learning" or "knowledge," but of credentials and skills necessary to contribute to the health and expansion of the economy as the first step toward gaining social mobility. This, in turn, directed centers of learning to compete for students by promising to deliver such skills as were valued in the market, including entrepreneurship, innovation, and flexibility with regard to skill sets.

At the same time, state and federal spending on both public K-12 and higher education came under scrutiny, and both became targets for disinvestment. On one level, this began the push for charter schools for young students and other privatization schemes, which would intensify moving into the twenty-first century. Also, as accountability standards became a litmus test for funding, schools began to "teach to the test" in order to raise their metrics, altering curricula promoting certain kinds of rote learning. For higher education, decreases in state support meant efforts to secure greater private support and higher tuition. As costs rose—tuition alone doubled between 1990 and 2000—public colleges and universities found themselves competing with one another and needing to justify the expense. This led many schools to focus on providing the skills most needed in the job market, which, while it did not much affect the historically vocational fields (law, medicine, engineering), decidedly altered training in the arts and humanities by emphasizing transferable skills like innovation and creativity. Especially after the 1990s, with many new theatre ensembles forming out of college and university training and collaborations, these changes would significantly impact the direction of devised theatre.

The Women's Movement and Feminism

The Women's Movement evolved through several distinct phases during this period, beginning in the mid-1960s and exploding across all areas of US culture in the 1970s. As seen in the next chapter, the focus on collective political action by second-wave feminists played a significant role in sustaining ensemble theatre practices in the decade. By the 1980s, some of the initial energy and hope for substantial change had begun to falter, particularly after the failure to ratify the 1972 Equal Rights Amendment (ERA) became final in 1982, and feminism entered a stage of critical self-reflection. This coincided, during the Reagan years, with an intense media backlash against the movement. Moving into the 1990s, pundits were proselytizing for "third wave" feminism that incorporated the new mantra of individual effort and success while retaining feminism's critique of the patriarchy, though now expressed more often with irony than with direct action. Eventually, "postfeminism" would emerge as a contested term moving into the millennium.

Despite this evolution, feminist activism remained constant throughout the period, though it tended to move from collectivist platforms that self-consciously identified as separate or alternative to mainstream culture in the 1970s toward individuals occupying hard-won positions of relative cultural power and speaking from those standpoints into the 1980s and 1990s. Early second-wave feminism, inspired by books like Betty Friedan's 1963 *The Feminine Mystique*, provided the basis for rendering patriarchy visible as a coherent set of interconnected social, political, and economic practices. Initially, these were contested through the National Organization of Women, which Friedan founded in 1966 to seek legislative changes pertaining to women's issues. This trajectory would lead to the appearance of hundreds of new college courses on women's history, literature, and gender politics by the end of the 1960s, and beginning in the 1970s, a growing number of accredited women's studies programs. Often students from such programs were radicalized and wished to press beyond the incremental changes that NOW pursued. A more militant tone was expressed by the women's liberation movement, which included a number of radical groups who took part in street actions and protests such as those at the 1968 Miss America Contest. By the 1970s, dozens of women-focused organizations were operating (the National Women's Political Caucus, National Abortion Rights Action League, the Combahee River Collective, the American Association of University Women) and second-wave feminism as a whole was characterized by group activities, not the least of which were the large number of feminist collective theatre ensembles that formed during the period. After publication of Kate Millet's *Sexual Politics* in 1970, some radical feminists began to argue for separatism, and a number of theatre collectives, such as At the Foot of the Mountain, voted to become all-female.

After a slate of legal and judicial victories, such as the 1972 Title IX Education Amendment outlawing discrimination in public schools and colleges and the landmark *Roe v. Wade* (1973), efforts focused on passing and then ratifying the ERA. However, under pressure from Phyllis Schlafly's STOP movement (Stop Taking Our Privileges, which focused on the threat to traditional gender roles), passage faltered as women's rights became increasingly a partisan issue and Republicans who once supported the amendment—but who at the time were beginning to create alliances with formerly politically quiescent but reliably conservative white evangelicals—began to voice opposition to the amendment. Hereafter, and especially when abortion rights became the key wedge issue later in the decade, the Democrats would be seen by many as the party of women's rights, and largely on that basis women later helped elect Bill Clinton to his two terms of office.

By 1982, when the ratifying period for the ERA lapsed, a focal point for organizing group activism and identity was lost and a period of fragmentation ensued. Divided by issues ranging from pornography to education and, most importantly, race, class, and sexual difference, the women's movement embarked on a period of self-reflection and critique. Some historians argue that this introspection fomented forms of identity politics that sent activists to address only their chosen constituencies, leaving the New Right to dominate national politics and culture. In theatre studies, Jill Dolan's formulation of the differences among liberal, radical, and materialist feminisms laid bare the significant disparities with respect to the founding principles and ultimate methods and aims of women's liberation (1988). Such differences were evident in feminist ensemble theatres as well, although the majority adopted radical and/or materialist positions since these placed greater emphasis on group solidarity and intersubjectivity. Due in part to these conflicts within feminism, but affected much more by external factors such as changes in funding schemes and public support, as well as the media backlash against feminism during the Reagan years, feminist theatres began to close in depressing numbers by the late 1980s.

The backlash was fueled by many factors, not least of which was the masculinist culture that developed under Reagan and its efforts to position liberalism, and especially 1960s liberalism, as effete and "feminine." The New Right gospel of manly self-determination acted as an acid on notions of collective endeavor and group solidarity. Just as importantly, after Paul Weyrich and Jerry Falwell successfully forged the Moral Majority, largely by recasting abortion as the cause for white evangelicals to engage with secular politics and form an important conservative voting bloc—one that Regan courted by disavowing his earlier support for abortion (he legalized it as Governor of California) and becoming pro-life at a crucial moment during the 1980 election—the New Right had a wedge issue that could tar feminism more broadly with the stain of self-indulgence and immorality. National mainstream media, many now run by conservative owners or corporations, relentlessly drew attention to issues like single (female) parenthood and a perceived rise in disruptive young people and welfare recipients. Often, they positioned themselves as supporting women, as when pointing out the pitfalls of the "dual career woman" striving to maintain balance between the domestic and work-centered worlds.

After a period of relative withdrawal, the women's movement was reenergized in 1991 when President George H. W. Bush nominated the conservative federal court judge Clarence Thomas to replace Thurgood Marshall on the Supreme Court. Already made anxious by Thomas's views on abortion, feminists rallied when an African-American law clerk, Anita Hill, testified to Congress that Thomas had sexually harassed her in a previous work environment. Hill's composed testimony riveted the nation, as did Thomas's bellicose response. Eventually, a Judiciary Committee made up entirely of males allowed the nomination to go forward, and Thomas was eventually confirmed by a small margin. For feminists, the confrontation not only dramatized how much work needed to be done but also revealed the way that race and gender intersected to shape unequal relations of social and political power.

Despite divisions within the movement and the insistent signs of backlash against it, feminism advanced in the 1980s through its mostly unified opposition to the anti-abortion movement (though disagreements arose with regard to whether it should be defended by reference to "choice" or "rights"), by evolving new perspectives on issues of difference, and institutionalizing the progressive gains made in the 1970s, as in the case of women's studies programs. Combined, these would help pave a route to the "third wave" or "intersectional" feminism that begins to develop in the 1990s.

AIDS

In 1981 doctors began reporting an outbreak of a rare cancer among gay men, in particular those living on the East and West coasts, which indicated failures in their immune systems. By December a male nurse in San Francisco diagnosed with Kaposi's Syndrome, Bobbi Campbell, had gone public via a newspaper column in which he described the onset of the disease, sometimes posting images of his lesions in the windows of local drugstores to alert other gay men. Of the first three hundred cases reported, more than a third died before the end of the year.

While public reaction was slow to gather, the gay community organized quickly, with Larry Kramer forming the Gay Men's Health Crisis in New

York City early in 1981 and Cleve Jones organizing what became the San Francisco AIDS Foundation later that year. By 1983, the "San Francisco Model of Care" for patients was being widely adopted, and the first gathering of the AIDS community took part in candlelight vigils in New York and San Francisco. Due in part to this response, researchers originally named the epidemic GRID (gay-related immune deficiency), which inadvertently spread the misconception that only gay men were susceptible to the disease (it was renamed AIDS in September 1983). Despite introduction of legislation to fund AIDS research that year, Congress failed to act and the first dedicated funding arrived only in 1986, and then in amounts only a fraction of which were being spent on less-threatening diseases.

Despite the virulent spread of the epidemic—by the late 1980s upward of 50 percent of all gay men in New York City were infected, with an even higher figure among intravenous drug users, and in 1989 deaths were averaging 4,000 per year—President Reagan did not utter the word "AIDS" in public until 1985. By 1986 William F. Buckley was calling for AIDS patients to be tattooed. Senator Jesse Helms led the fight to stigmatize the disease and defund scientific research, and Falwell's Moral Majority, aided by the activist Anita Bryant, pressured the Reagan administration to silence their own appointed Surgeon General, C. Everett Koop, on the subject for more than five years.

Since the Stonewall "riots" of 1969, gay Americans had pressed for a Constitutional amendment protecting the rights of gay and lesbian people. The first March on Washington in support of the idea drew more than 100,000 participants in 1979. The Gay Men's Health Crisis, although mostly directed at lobbying for increased scientific research on the disease, managed to push through local measures outlawing discrimination against gays pertaining to housing and employment in 1986. But Kramer and others sought more direct intervention against government apathy in the fight against the pandemic, and in 1987 the AIDS Coalition to Unleash Power (ACT UP) was formed. They demonstrated at the second Washington March in October and conducted die-ins in front of the Supreme Court building, and the media attention led other activists to return home to form local chapters. This was followed by actions on Wall Street against the price of AIDS medicines, at which numerous members were arrested. Their iconic "Silence=Death" posters (created by the art collective Gran Fury) marked a return to the radical activism of the 1960s but with a very 1980s sense of marketing savvy, in which the cool, abstract fuchsia pictograph (influenced by the work of the feminist art collective Guerilla Girls) inverted

Historical and Cultural Background

the orientation of the Holocaust's yellow triangle to suggest a rising action, while the stark sign of equivalence conveyed the true stakes of the crisis (Finkelstein 2017). It would appear at every succeeding protest, including those at *Cosmopolitan* magazine, the FDA, in the aisles of Saint Patrick's Cathedral in New York City, and in an action at the home of Senator Helms in 1991 where his house was encased in 15-foot-tall condom.

The arts were particularly affected by the disease, both in terms of the illness and death of numerous artists and in the artistic response to the outbreak. The death of star movie actor Rock Hudson in 1985, who went public with his sexual identity, brought both needed attention to the outbreak and also greater AIDS hysteria. Artists, including many working in the theatre, sought both to bring attention to the lack of funding by the Reagan administration and to make up the shortfall by presenting a host of fundraisers. Art Against AIDS, though only launched in 1987, raised both money and public awareness. By 1992 President Clinton had established an Office of National AIDS Policy and public opinion was turning toward support of government-sponsored research. Even so, the pandemic continued to spread, peaking in the United States in 1995 when 41,699 deaths were reported. Later in the 1990s, AIDS-related deaths began to drop dramatically (less so among blacks) as treatments improved with the introduction of antiretroviral treatments. Some historians (Aronowitz 1996) posit that the crisis, which exposed fault lines running under both liberalism and conservatism, was largely responsible for resuscitating collective activism after a long dormancy. It certainly provided momentum for LGBTQ ensemble theatres to begin forming, such as About Face Theatre in Chicago.

Race

Hard upon the disappointment at the failure of 1960s Civil Rights legislation to realize its goals, and in light of the subsequent forms of Black Power activism that arose as an alternative, the country remained a powder keg with respect to racial tensions. The match was struck in 1974, first when the Supreme Court ruled in *Milliken v. Bradley* that to address de facto school segregation, lower courts could order districts to use busing to desegregate schools. A fierce backlash ensued, centered in Boston but replicated across the nation, which quickly became violent. Beginning in the same year, the drawn-out case of *Bakke v. Regents of University of California* (resolved in 1978) eventually upheld the principles of affirmative action but weakened them as a matter of law. In both instances further division was sown between Left and Right, as the former increasingly staked its claim on the notion of "diversity" instead of the original goal of integration, while the latter continued to view the issues through a logic of eliminating remaining de jure forms of discrimination. Minorities in the meantime, which by the 1970s included activism among all peoples of color as well as LGBTQ citizens, grew more vocal in their demands as well as electorally more potent.

Reagan, when he addressed racial issues at all, often took a page from Nixon's playbook and used coded language to stoke racial resentments, most infamously with his contrived image of the "welfare queen" who cannily lived well off the misplaced guilt of white America (his administration calculated pretax yearly earnings of $150,000). Although Bush, Sr., sought to diversify his cabinet by appointing Colin Powell as the first black Secretary of Defense, his nomination of the ultra-conservative Clarence Thomas to succeed Thurgood Marshall on the Supreme Court sent a strong message, even before the accusations of sexual impropriety in the workplace were made by Anita Hill (Thomas was approved despite her testimony by a narrow 52–48 vote). When the Rodney King tape depicting the police beating of an unarmed black man in Los Angeles appeared on the national news in March 1991, Bush remained mostly silent, but when the verdict acquitting the white police officers was publicized he seemed to join many Americans in questioning "how the verdict could square with the video" (Fisk 1996). The Los Angeles riots broke out after the verdicts were delivered on April 29, 1992, lasting six days (while others broke out in Seattle, San Francisco, Atlanta, and other cities) and claiming sixty-three lives while causing more than a billion dollars in property damage. President Bush deployed 20,000 federal troops but did not address the nation until three days into the rioting. His vacillation may have weakened him in the 1992 election.

Clinton, in turn, was elected with huge majorities among black voters. Declared by no less a cultural icon than Toni Morrison to be "America's first black president" based on his upbringing in the segregated South, Clinton's actual record on race was quite mixed, given his "Third Way" policies on crime and welfare reform (Carter 2018). His stalwart support of affirmative action in the face of major resistance and rollbacks (as when Texas, Louisiana, and Mississippi effectively outlawed its use in college admission procedures in 1996) may have saved it from extinction, but his continuation and exacerbation of the Reagan "War on Drugs" policies often set him against minorities.

Arts Funding

The last half of the twentieth century saw revolutionary movements in federal arts funding that produced numerous positive results but also left the practice open to politicization and backlash, many instances of which occurred during the chronology of this volume. After the Republic went 176 years without any national funding for the arts, once the NEA was implemented in the 1960s, it assumed economic, cultural, symbolic, and political significance far surpassing its actual scale.

After the demise of the Depression-era Works Progress Administration and its Federal Arts Project unit in 1943, US politicians generally retreated from the issue of federal arts support for political and practical reasons. Prompted by the Ford Foundation's initiatives of the late 1950s to fund humanities and creative arts projects, the tide turned in the 1960s, and in 1965 the Johnson administration created the National Foundation of the Arts and Humanities. While the organization lagged due to funding shortages during the Vietnam War, Nixon ramped up funding for the foundation's endowment from $8.3 million in 1970 to $80 million in his final 1975 budget. By the close of Carter's term in 1979, this had reached nearly $150 million: collectively in real dollars the largest increases in the NEA's history. However, when Reagan launched his "First Hundred Days" legislative plans to reform federal spending (abetted by the first Republican Congressional majority in decades), the NEA, like many Great Society initiatives, was scheduled for deep cuts. Due to savvy media campaigns launched by the arts community and the NEA, these were held to just 10 percent, and throughout Reagan's two terms, they actually recouped that deficit. Nevertheless, the seed had been planted that the NEA was a liberal holdover, and all that was needed to undermine its work was a timely scandal.

This erupted in 1989, after George H. W. Bush had succeeded Reagan in office and named John Frohnmayer as NEA chair. Earlier that year, Andres Serrano's photograph, "Piss Christ" (featuring a crucifix floating in urine), was featured in the media and linked to indirect NEA funding. Soon after, it became known that an exhibit of homoerotic photographs by Robert Mapplethorpe had been cancelled by a Washington, DC, gallery for fear of distracting from the scheduled reauthorization of the NEA that year. Although not directly funded by the NEA, the situation caused an outcry both from conservatives and artists protesting the censorship of the work. Gathering steam, the funding of "obscene" art by the NEA became a *cause célèbre* among conservative politicians like Jesse Helms and Dana

Rohrbacher, who sought to include anti-obscenity language into the NEA's charter. Many moderate Democrats, including John Kerry and Arlen Specter, signed a letter demanding a review of the organization's procedures. Despite failing to defund and outright eliminate the NEA, the "Helms Amendment" led Congress to add a decency clause to the NEA charter itself and the agency chief, John Frohnmeyer, to insert language into grant applications that forced artists to pledge that they would not create obscene material. Frohnmeyer, himself, screened applications for content after they had passed peer review and rejected a number of them based on the obscenity clause. In 1990, four artists (the "NEA Four")—all performance artists, three of whom dealt directly with queer subject matter—were denied funding and thereafter sued. They won in the lower courts in 1993, but the case wound its way to the Supreme Court, which in 1998 upheld the decency clause.

The decision dramatically altered the methods used to disperse funding, for instance, eliminating direct grants to individual artists. Minority and disadvantaged communities were affected disproportionately. Overall, the decrease in federal support led to huge increases in individual giving, which by 2012 made of 42 percent of all arts funding (adjusted for inflation, this is a 67 percent jump since 1995). Earned income made up another 42 percent of support and private foundation grants accounted for another 13 percent, the latter up 56 percent since 1995. That left just over 4 percent coming from public coffers.

While the case continued, Clinton entered office when the issue was still running hot, and after the Democrats lost both Houses in the midterm elections, another attempt was made to eliminate the NEA: in fact, Gingrich moved to also cut the National Endowment for the Humanities as well as PBS (the Corporation for Public Broadcasting). Although all the agencies survived, in 1995 Clinton cut NEA funding by 40 percent, which reduced staff by half and forced the NEA to condense its funding categories from seventeen to four. Although funding would increase substantially under President George W. Bush, and despite the two terms of Barack Obama (during which the Great Recession entailed flat or reduced funding), calls under the Trump Administration to eliminate the agency continue, and the NEA operates, in real dollars, at a fraction of what it did in the 1970s, having decreased more than 25 percent since 1995.

CHAPTER 2
AMERICAN ENSEMBLE THEATRES, 1970–95
Mike Vanden Heuvel

A complete history of US ensemble-created theatre has yet to be written and would far surpass the scale of the brief introductions to the two volumes of this series. Unlike the generous scholarly coverage afforded the history and theory of British devised theatre, and significant work on Canadian, Australian, Western European, and Irish practices, no substantial study exists of ensemble-created theatre devoted solely to the American context.[1] Despite such forms of theatre-making becoming increasingly widespread and to some degree institutionalized, most ensemble-created theatre in the United States has been analyzed for the discrete styles of theatre it produces—variously Off-Off-Broadway, radical, guerilla, avant-garde, feminist, postmodern, applied, physical, site-specific, to name only a few—rather than the practices by which it is produced. This leaves its history dispersed and incomplete, with little sense of the continuities and evolution of its practices within changing historical contexts. Here in the first volume of *American Theatre Ensembles*, the goal will be to sketch a broad outline of how self-producing ensemble theatres sustained themselves and developed in the United States during the period in which the companies featured in the case studies originated and began forming their aesthetics between 1970 and 1995. Naturally, focus falls on establishing the contexts and influences that lead to the particular forms of ensemble-created theatre represented in the following chapters, which, though they exemplify a variety of styles, cannot stand as representative of the vast field, past and present, of collective creation in America after 1970.

The definitions of the central terms used throughout the series— "collective creation," "collaborative creation," "ensemble creation," "devised theatre"—are famously imprecise and problematic. To begin, "collective" creation carries obvious historical definitions and ideological assumptions that apply mostly but not exclusively to the more political international theatre collectives of the 1950s and 1960s, which explicitly organized under a Marxist, Maoist, or anarchist collectivist model. These include many of the best-known US collectives like the Living Theatre, San Francisco Mime Troupe (SFMT), and

El Teatro Campesino (ETC). Others, like the Open Theatre and the Performance Group, adopted a director-led, yet putatively nonhierarchical, structure similar to the *creación colectivo* practices of South and Central America.

But after the mid-1970s in the United States "collective" begins to take on less ideological underpinnings in the work of the succeeding generation of high-profile ensembles. Under changing historical and economic conditions, in America the overtly political expression of collective creation begins to fall out of general usage, indicating an important split within the practice that, although never absolute (many ensembles cross and recross these boundaries), nevertheless indicates several important distinctions. On the one hand, ensembles formed after 1970 that maintained specific ideological commitments to collectivity and particular constituencies carried forward many of the ideals of the 1960s companies, modifying creative processes and organizational structures to suit their needs: among these, feminist and ethnic-specific collectives are the most prominent, but many grassroots and community-directed ensembles also formed to create collectively (with and for those communities) using Forum Theatre techniques, Theatre of the Oppressed models, or practices derived from the radical 1960s companies such as environmental scenography.

But beginning slowly in the 1970s and gaining momentum through the 1990s, ensembles arrive that question and modify the legacies of the previous generation, including the notion of collectivity itself and the ideal of nonhierarchical creative processes. Terms like "collaborative" and "interdisciplinary" (and even the intentionally anodyne "group") begin to circulate in their place. These latter ensembles establish trajectories that lead to most of the companies featured in this series, which by the late 1990s are typically grouped under the more recent nomenclature, imported from the UK and Commonwealth nations, of "devised theatre." Even so, and despite what many see as an evolution from the strict practice of creating as a collective to the looser collaborations that make up devising, the terms continue to be used interchangeably in critical and journalistic discourse and elude stable definitions (Syssoyeva and Proudfit 2013a, 23).

To clarify these historical shifts, I use the chronology offered in the edited volume by Kathryn Mederos Syssoyeva and Scott Proudfit, *A History of Collective Creation* (2013a), which proposes three overlapping waves within the deeper chronological framework and transnational scale they adopt. The first commences in reaction to the rise of the modern director and runs roughly from 1900 to 1950; the second wave, running from around 1950 into the early 1980s, is characterized by "the utopic, communitarian ethos, antiauthoritarianism, and Marxist-inflected politics of the generation of '68 noncommunist states" (2013a, 7); and the third wave, emerging after a perceived decline in collective creation in the 1970s, gains force after that and culminates in the robust practice of devised theatre in operation today. The last wave is described as "in the main ... postutopic, dominated by an ethical imperative (over the ideological) and an interest in the generative creativity of the actor" (8), as well as more flexible in investigating relations with the institutionalized, professional, nonprofit theatre sector. For this series, the main focus will be on the US experience of the second and third waves (as well as the complicated relationship between them), although reference will be made to first-wave practices as needed. Another common chronology for American collective creation places, somewhat problematically, the utopian collectives of the 1960s and 1970s as a "first generation," with companies emerging in the 1980s as the succeeding generation and then those in the 1990s and 2000s as the third. Although I dispute the nature of that "generation," the terminology is useful in specific instances.

Earlier examples of US group theatres from the second-wave collectives, such as the renowned companies of the 1960s—the Living Theatre, SFMT, the Open Theatre, ETC, the Free Southern Theatre, Bread and Puppet Theatre, and the Performance Group (to name only the most often-cited)—assumed that the company structure, its political ideology, its relation to mainstream theatre, and its creative methods all aligned to produce a distinct and radical artistic identity. These often took the form of nonhierarchical company and creative structures, egalitarian decision-making processes, and an anti-establishment ethos committed to a social revolution aligned with discourses of participatory democracy (or, in the case of the Living Theatre, anarcho-pacificism) like those espoused by groups like Students for a Democratic Society (SDS). Critics and reviewers of the time generally followed suit and did not probe the term except, as in the first article-length study devoted to such work, "Collective Creation," by Theodore Shank in 1972, and in the first edition of Arthur Sainer's seminal *Radical Theatre Notebook* (1975), to reify and celebrate an idealized notion of collectivity. And while Mark Weinberg's pathbreaking *Challenging the Hierarchy: Collective Theatre in the United States* (1992) carefully parses the actual dynamics of creative collectives to locate points of tension and conflict in a number of companies, it nevertheless maintains that an anti-establishment ethos, community focus, and revolutionary political goals constitute the true ontology of collective creation. Indeed, just as the third wave of nonutopic devising companies arrive in the late 1980s and early 1990s, Weinberg sees true collective theatre "under siege" (1992, 232).

American Theatre Ensembles Volume 1: Post–1970

In the 1970s and 1980s, primarily under the influence of feminist theatre groups, notions of collectivity received more self-conscious and rigorous examination and reflection as these intersected with radical feminism's attempts to experiment with nonpatriarchal (and thus sometimes non-Marxist) collective structures. These too, as the work of Charlotte Canning (1996) and others show, struggled to sustain collectivity in the face of material and ideological conditions in the United States that rendered such configurations challenging. On a related front, community-directed theatres and various forms of participatory applied theatre (theatre in education, grassroots theatre, theatre for development, Theatre of the Oppressed, and the like), which exploded across the United States in the 1970s, often originated in collectivist principles even if many eventually modified these in practice. These all play a crucial role in sustaining collective practice in the United States but also redirect a good deal of ensemble energy into forms of applied and community-directed theatre which are not the primary focus of this series.

Meanwhile, companies not pursuing collectivity as an explicit political statement or in response to specific community needs felt free to experiment with different and sometimes more hierarchical organizational models, often featuring a strong artistic director and a rotating roster of artists. They maintained many of the methods for devising new material originating in previous forms of collective creation (the improvisational theatre games of Viola Spolin as well as the transformational acting exercises of the Open Theatre were mainstays) but did not promote themselves as models of cooperative, democratic, and nonhierarchical collaboration. Critical attention in the 1970s and 1980s, too, focused less on how such companies organized and practiced ensemble creation and more on the relation of the work to performance art, the degree to which it seemed to respond to postmodernism, and whether it maintained any connection to previous avant-gardes. An exception, and a critical study that plays a role in the revival of ensemble creation in the 1990s, is David Savran's *Breaking the Rules: The Wooster Group* (1986, 1988), which reported on and celebrated the company's alternative processes of ensemble creation.

As ensemble-created theatre emerged in the late 1990s as an increasingly potent player and attracted greater critical and mainstream attention (as well as inclusion in theatre training programs and crossover appeal for major regional theatres invested in new work), commentators became aware of how diverse its practices had become, not just across companies but even within particular ensembles. Some groups followed the 1960s model and created work collectively *ex nihilo* based on rehearsal exercises and research, while others improvised around existing texts and creatively adapted them using, for instance, physical theatre methods or scenographic writing to rework textual material. Other companies developed variations on the "Joint Stock model" (named after the UK company), which involved bringing in a playwright at some point of development. A long-standing company like Boston's Beau Geste Moving Theatre (founded in 1984) might traverse all these methods and range across physical theatre, dance theatre, and immersive performance as they experiment and evolve.

Most of the companies selected for this series have tried all of these, and myriad other methods, to create collectively, and as practices have proliferated, nomenclature has become more unwieldy, resulting in the turn toward "devised" theatre. While the term seems better able to accommodate a greater range of practices without insisting on egalitarian intentions or nonhierarchical creative methods, it also potentially muddies the waters, first by being too broad (an individual playwright or performance artist may devise performances) and second by emphasizing the craft of assembling a piece without regard for the collaborative nature of the creative process. But clearly the choice of "devising" also signals a turn away from the ideologically grounded connotations of collectivity and sheds the emphasis on nonhierarchical creative structures in pursuit of more variable methods and processes. Whether this shift in terminology signals a meaningful evolution of the methods, politics, and aesthetics of group-created theatre or arises out of market expediency or funding imperatives is still hotly debated and raises issues I address at the end of this introduction and in the second volume.

It seems significant, however, as we have moved through the 'oughts and into the second decade of the twenty-first century, that curators, critics, and practitioners with boots on the ground in the world of collective creation have begun to argue that all such taxonomies repeat just those connotations that contemporary ensembles have been trying to jettison. Many ensembles today eschew both "collective" and "devised" in describing their work, and it is often difficult to discern from a company's website and programs whether devising or collective creation is even being practiced. As Meiyin Wang, a former co-director of the Public Theatre's "Under the Radar Festival," wrote in 2011 in what might be considered a manifesto for these creative practices:

> There will be no titles of playwrights, directors, actors, designers, managers, producers. There will be theatremakers. That will be all that is allowed on a name card. "Theatremaker." People you meet will include a writer/designer. A director/electrician. A sculptor/actor. A film editor/musician. A cook/dramaturg. A plumber/poet ...

The notion of authorship, sole authorship, will change rapidly. Theatre will be made in duos—like Big Dance Theater's Annie-B Parson and Paul Lazar, in trios—like Alec Duffy, Rick Burkhart, and Dave Malloy in *Three Pianos*, in ensembles and collectives, like the Rude Mechs, Universes and SITI Company—where you will be not be able to see the edges of creation, generation, and execution. ("The Theatre of the Future" n.p.)

Similarly, Duška Radosavljević concludes, after exhaustively parsing numerous contemporary UK creative practices ranging from devising to adaptation, verbatim theatre, relational performance, and new writing, that "[m]y research into contemporary ensemble theatre has shown that the academically and politically defined distinctions between new writing, devising and live/performance are most definitely dissolved in those contexts where collaborative modes of theatre-making prevail" (103). She justifies the term used in her book's title, *Theatre-making: Interplay between Text and Performance in the 21st Century*, by recognizing, among other factors, shifts in training and practice:

> University education in Drama, Theatre and Performance Studies—as subjects which had emancipated themselves from Literature in British and US universities throughout the twentieth century—has in the latter half of the twentieth century produced multi-skilled, thinking artists capable of an integrated authorial practice which combines, writing, acting, composing, directing and design. Theatre-making is therefore capable of embracing multi-professionalization as well as process- rather than product-led theatre-making, and it may well soon call for a change to the current structures of professional theatre production. (194)

So perhaps it is time to admit that the confusing terminology should be utilized like the Buddha's boat: helpful for getting one across the choppy waters (and for floating a few signifiers), but too weighty and cumbersome to lug around once back on land. More pithily, Marc Masterson, artistic director of Pittsburgh City Theatre, cautions, "What name can you find to describe developments in new music? Or indie film? I would counsel us all not to worry too much about it" (Morris 2013, n.p.). One way to avoid the scrum among such terms is to place emphasis not on the ideological positions or the specific methods by which the work is made but on the self-identifications chosen and then embodied by theatre-makers, as well as the ethical consequences of their praxis. The title of this series carries over perhaps the oldest term ("ensemble") in the nomenclature of collective creation, one that evokes the foundational notion of an artist-centered company that assumes responsibility for all aspects of creation and administration. "Ensemble" can thus be applied generically to establish the biggest tent under which to gather like-minded creators while still respecting different intentions. For that reason, the main umbrella organization for many (but not all) devising companies in the United States is the Network of Ensemble Theatres (NET, created, in 1996): its membership of over two hundred companies includes a variety of theatre organizations, some of which do not regularly produce devised work but maintain a commitment to more traditional, resident-theatre models of ensemble *production* rather than ensemble *creation*. NET defines its members as "a group of individuals dedicated to collaborative creation, committed to working together consistently over years to develop a distinctive body of work."[2] By this definition (as NET intends), even productions based on existing dramatic texts can form the basis for an ensemble so long as the artists continue to work with one another "consistently over years." This is in fact the most common understanding of ensemble: a group of artists whose prolonged work together makes possible the manner they will produce and perform a preexisting score or script, using conventional creative hierarchies that feature specialists in each stage of production, even as the collaboration is enhanced by the increased focus and trust developed among the artists that only sustained group work may produce.

Ensembles of the type featured in this series, however, not only engage in collective creation but experiment with its processes and methods as a basis for creating new work. They utilize the ensemble in more open-ended and self-conscious ways, not in order to repeat creative practices "consistently over years" and thereby re-instantiate traditional hierarchies of creative labor, but to research alternatives and expand creative possibilities. As Ferdinand Lewis distinguishes ensemble practice,

> [E]nsemble theaters tend to be composed of *generalists* who create work in full collaboration, with each contributor directly responsible for a number of production and organizational elements, if not the entire production. The artists have their specialties of training and inclination, but they are generalists where the overall product is concerned. (2005, xii)

The choice to develop one's craft across artistic fields as a generalist and to collaborate with a like-minded ensemble has particular consequences and outcomes, which form the grounds for certain kinds of professional and ethical commitments. Most important in collective creation is a responsibility to support creatively all members of the group, perhaps as an extension of the improvisation credo to "say yes" to a partner. But this does not sanction an unrigorous "anything goes" ethos; in fact, these kinds of support usually entail constant checks on egos and authority and often lead to contentious encounters within the group that sometimes become sources of creativity but can also contribute to the notoriously short life of many ensembles (see Proudfit 2013). Most devising ensembles, too, have been nomadic and unattached to a facility or, in some cases, even a permanent rehearsal space. The ongoing narrative of SITI Company's failed quest for a permanent space and community, and perhaps the recent success of Mabou Mines to secure one only after more than forty years, suggests this is not always a preference: nevertheless, as a reality it obliges artists to commit to situations of itinerancy and uncertainty. Compounding that situation, many ensembles, particularly contemporary companies, have out of choice or necessity evolved membership structures that can lead to rapid turnover and reconfiguration; this confers an obligation to maintain and/or reorganize the ensemble and thus becomes, itself, an element of creative labor. Also, given the nature of ensemble creation, the time frame between gestation of a project and production can stretch on for years, making long-term and project funding difficult to obtain. This commits many ensembles to seek alternative funding or to generate alternative revenue streams, resulting in a wide variety of creative practices and styles. Finally, the choice to create with an ensemble often comes from a desire to engage with nontraditional forms of storytelling and to experiment with unconventional aesthetics that create new relationships with audiences. Commentators have remarked upon how difficult, and counterproductive it has been historically for creative ensembles to generate conventional dramatic writing (Heddon and Milling 2006, 222), and it is rare to find a devising ensemble that aspires to that goal. Thus, when artists dedicate themselves to ensemble creation they generally leave behind familiar performance structures and specific creative roles (as actor, designer, director) as they bind themselves to alternative practices and audiences.

There are, in other words, real commitments made when artists choose to create as an ensemble: to nontraditional venues, time frames, particular economies of scale, aesthetic directions determined partly by the mode of composition, forms of creative labor, and even particular artistic identities based in collaborative practices. As Sara Jane Bailes (2011) and Rachel Anderson-Rabern (2020) have argued, these generate an ethics grounded in process and a commitment to a certain kind of inefficiency that counters the models of productivity that govern conventional creative hierarchies in most US theatres. Given the nature of these choices to experiment with different forms of collaboration, perhaps "ensembling" might better describe this determinative act, designating a citational practice that repeats, with variations, over time to instantiate ethical commitments to a particular set of practices, relationships, and outcomes. As Kathryn Mederos Syssoyeva summarizes the definition arrived at by an ASTR working group on collective creation:

> There is a group. The group wants to make theatre. The group chooses— or, conversely, a leader within the group proposes—to make theatre using a process which places conscious emphasis on the *groupness* of that process, on some possible collaborative mode between members of the group, which is, typically, viewed as being in some manner *more collaborative* than members of the group have previously experienced. Process is typically of paramount importance; anticipated aesthetic or political outcomes are perceived to derive directly from the proposed mode of interaction. (2013a, 6)

This way of producing, and the kind of work fabricated, has a history, one that stretches back well beyond the formation of NET, beyond the beginning point of this series, and beyond the geographical borders of the United States. That longer global history is being uncovered slowly but effectively by current scholarship, and it is upon those foundations that I base this cursory history of the form from 1970 to present in the United States (Heddon and Milling 2006; Baldwin, Larrue, and Page 2008; Syssoyeva and Proudfit 2013a, 2013b, 2016). In the first volume it will be necessary to assess the relationship of post-1970s collaborative creation to its immediate forebears, the much more well-documented collectives that emerged during the "long 1960s" (roughly 1954–72). That legacy is more complex than has been assumed previously, but might yet, with some modifications, be helpful in rendering less tendentious the way that current, third-wave US devising practices are seen in relation to previous ensemble theatres.

Finally, this introduction will briefly contextualize the ensemble-created work during the twenty-five years between 1970 and 1995 by describing some of the more important of the many, and often overlapping, lines of flight that develop in collective creation after the 1960s, before refocusing on the trajectories that lead to the kinds of work presented in the ensuing case studies. While risking an unwieldy narrative in hopes of capturing as much of the field as possible in a relatively short space, the point must be made that collective creation survived the decline of the radical collectives after the 1970s by diversifying in ways that offered new practices, methods, and audiences and thus made the crest of the third wave possible in the 1990s. Recognizing that many worthy examples of ensemble creation must be left out in this brief overview, the hope is that by gesturing toward the breadth of ensemble practices between 1970 and 1995 and suggesting new contexts for their development, further research might be devoted to particular companies and alternative trajectories.

Histories/Historiographies

Second-wave ensemble-created theatre in the United States forms, as elsewhere, within the crucibles of alternative art practices. In America this means it partakes of a larger process of devolution from the commercial theatre sector associated with Broadway, a movement that begins with Off- and then Off-Off-Broadway in the 1950s and 1960s (Little 1972; Berkowitz 1997; Bottoms 2004). Off-Off-Broadway arose in the downtown areas centered around Greenwich Village but evolved in relationship with the concurrent regional theatre movement that created the resident professional theatre ecosystem now spread across all fifty states and overseen by professional associations like the League of Resident Theatres (LORT) and Theatre Communications Group (TCG). Most of these have been granted special tax-exempt status as not-for-profit (501[c]) organizations. The establishment of such noncommercial theatres promised to promote more stability for companies and producers by virtue of a repertory season model, deepen connections with their particular communities, and allow more risk-taking than in the commercial sector. However, the original notion of maintaining a resident ensemble of artists within specific regional theatres has largely foundered on economic grounds, and increasingly many of the regionals have developed business and production models similar to those in commercial theatre, such as staffing on a show-by-show basis. Significantly, almost all LORT theatres maintain the conventional division of labor in theatre production, which values a high level of specialist craft technique. Once a preexisting text is selected, and in the name of efficiency and short rehearsal periods, the theatre parcels out specific production roles along a hierarchy of authority made up of artistic directors, playwrights, directors, dramaturgs (in some cases), stage managers, actors, and designers. Oversight and scheduling of the process are handled administratively, and while there is artistic collaboration at every stage, it is quite specialized and serves, not the process of collaboration, but the efficient realization of the production.

Importantly, the New York "Downtown" experimental theatre that arose about the same time as the regional theatre movement was itself but one part of a more amorphous underground scene that would produce, alongside Off-Off-Broadway theatre, Minimalist and Pop Art, Happenings, Fluxus, and their offshoots, New Wave and Punk music, the New American Cinema of Jack Smith and Jonas Mekas, and the postmodern dance experiments centered around Judson Church (Banes 1993a, 1993b). The mix created a context for a widespread artistic avant-garde in the 1960s that featured an interdisciplinary and DIY ethos that encouraged experimentation with creative processes untethered to specialists working within conventional production hierarchies and time frames. This created an environment from which other and more diverse methods of art-making and collaboration might emerge, many of which have influenced the development of ensemble-created theatre. As well, the Downtown underground established important differences between connotations associated with the "alternative" of the regional theatre movement and Off-Broadway (which meant, increasingly, alternative only to Broadway) and the Off-Off-Broadway and underground scene (which conveyed alternative aesthetics but also unconventional politics, identities, communities, and lifestyles). The evolution of collective creation in the United States would often hew closely to its underground roots, but in recent years a rapprochement of sorts has brought the resident regional sector more closely into contact with devised theatre (Valdez 2013, 211).

These contexts and distinctions drove the original historiography that shaped the understanding of collective creation's revival in the United States during the 1960s in consequential ways. As argued by Richard Schechner (across several works, first in *The End of Humanism* [1982]) and Arnold Aronson (in *American Avant-garde Theatre: A History* [2000]) and cited and repeated across a number of other studies, this historiography depends on establishing the origin of modern US ensemble theatre-making in the work of the renowned avant-garde collectives of the decade of the 1960s and its particular ideological moment. Also, this perspective argues for an endpoint for collective creation, which is seen as declining in the early 1970s (with the closing of Joseph Chaikin's Open Theatre in 1973 a convenient reference point). As Aronson writes, "[t]he ensemble movement had essentially disappeared by the mid-1970s" (2000, 102). Following this fertile period in collective creation, the consensus historiography argues, avant-garde energy was dispersed into several interrelated trajectories: a second generation of less politically activist group theatres that retained vanguard status by virtue of their formal experimentation (such as Mabou Mines and the Wooster Group); a number of artist-auteurs (usually Meredith Monk, Richard Foreman, Robert Wilson, Ping Chong, Martha Clarke, and sometimes Charles Ludlam—and more recently Reza Abdoh) descended from movements in the visual arts and dance who carried forward the formalist emphasis of those forebears; and the many variations of performance art or live art, including solo performance, that would develop through the 1980s.

But depicting post-1960s ensemble-based theatre as belated—the sunken caldera that survives only to give evidence of the more spectacular eruptions of the previous radical work of the 1960s collectives—produces a number of suspect claims that affect our understanding of the evolution of collective creation. It flattens out the particular histories of the 1960s companies, conveying the sense that an essential method of collective creation emerged that all the radical 1960s companies practiced. It further assigns to the 1960s the origins of collective creation in the United States, ignoring the many and various instances of the practice during the "first wave" of international collective creation, some of whose legacies significantly impact developments after the 1970s. Along the same lines, it ignores influences from international ensembles from the second wave such as Ariane Mnouchkine's Théâtre du Soleil, Eugenio Barba's Odin Teatret, and the *creación colectiva* models created by Enrique Buenaventura and others the Global South in the 1950s (van Erven 2001). More concerning still is the way that the putative radicality and avant-garde status assigned to the 1960s collectives (but only in rare circumstances to later ensembles and almost never with respect to contemporary devising companies) leaves later developments seeming politically and aesthetically enervated and in a compromised relation to mainstream culture.

In unexpected yet illuminating ways, this conventional narrative closely matches the "declension hypothesis" created by the first generation of historians of 1960s America, described in the previous chapter. On a parallel track, histories of American ensemble-created theatre have delineated a decade during which avant-garde collectives, having shaken American theatre and culture to its core, eventually fell apart due to the implosion of the New Left and the counterculture. This then gives way in the 1970s and 1980s to a succeeding generation of companies, auteurs, and solo artists whose work (with a few exceptions) signals a decline into identity politics and an apolitical and inner-directed style that eventually diminishes avant-garde energy such that it is easily absorbed into the mainstream. Meanwhile, this narrative implies, ensemble theatre—as a mode of theatre-making—languished and eventually disappeared from view for over two decades after the end of the long 1960s. And so, when collective creation seemed to reappear out of nowhere in the 1990s as devised theatre, it could only be judged as a failed "revival" of the avant-garde of the 1960s.

The New Left consensus historiography was eventually challenged by perspectives questioning the centrality of the 1960s and its disproportionate influence on later historical developments. Similarly, a parallel revisionist historiography of collective creation has emerged out of which a less homogenous and more multi-vectored picture of ensemble creation materializes that divorces the practice from the single origin of 1960s companies and their intentions, organizational structures, politics, and aesthetics. In 1994 Alison Oddey published the first book devoted to devised theatre, focused on UK practices, *Devising Theatre: A Practical and Theoretical Handbook*. Even the fact that its title avoided reference to collective creation is noteworthy, as it suggests that the new terminology might be necessary to distinguish contemporary work from its predecessors (which in Britain references the fringe theatres of the 1970s, especially those with socialist foundations like Welfare State International, Red Ladder, and 7:84). Oddey followed the conventional line when she wrote that "[i]n the 1970s devising companies chose artistic democracy in favor of the hierarchical structures of power linked to text-based theatre"—thus positioning devised work both in the tradition of the Artaud-inspired line of the historical avant-garde and with the counterculture ethos of the 1960s. However, she finishes with an important caveat:

> [A]nd yet, within the last twenty years or so there has been a move from this standpoint to more hierarchical structures within many companies in response to an ever-changing economic and artistic climate. In the cultural climate of the early 1990s, the term "'devising" has less radical implications, placing greater emphasis on skill sharing, specialization, specific roles, increasing division of responsibilities, such as the role of the director/deviser or the administrator, and more hierarchical company structures. (1994, 9)

Since her work is primarily directed at the application and pedagogy of devising, Oddey does not devote much space to conceptual matters. But when Deidre Heddon and Jane Milling followed more than ten years later with *The Theory and Practice of Devised Theatre* (2006), they explicitly questioned the idealization of the 1960s and 1970s British fringe theatres and radical US companies and stated plainly that the time had come to dissociate the multiple trajectories of devised creation from the sole origin of the 1960s, stating that "devising is best understood as a set or strategies that emerged within a variety of theatrical and cultural fields, for example in community arts, performance art/live art, or political theatre" (2006, 2). More pointedly, they went on to critique the long-standing rhetoric, developed during the heyday of 1960s collective creation and supported by the consensus historiography, by which an idealized image of collective creation had been based: one that established "almost mythic status" for 1960s concepts like collectivity (the ensemble forming as "a practical expression of political and ideological commitment"), the "de-commodification of art," and an Artaud-inspired aggressive attitude toward the conventional priority of the dramatic text (4–5). Heddon and Milling specifically called out the rhetoric surrounding the notion of ensembles evincing strictly nonhierarchical forms of creation, questioning not only whether stalwarts of the "original" creative collectives— Judith Malina and Julian Beck (Living Theatre), Joe Chaikin (Open Theatre), and Richard Schechner (Performance Group)—were actually on equal creative and managerial footing with their companies, but also if the same pertains to the succeeding generation of ensemble directors such as Liz LeCompte (Wooster Group), Tim Etchells (Forced Entertainment), and Lin Hixson (Goat Island). Providing a key insight, Heddon and Milling set out to inquire "where these beliefs about devising arise from and whether they are accurate in relation to historical and contemporary practice, and sustainable within contemporary social structures" (5).

A number of studies appearing in and after 2010 picked up on these fault lines and began to explore new perspectives from which to view the relation between contemporary forms of devising and 1960s collective creation. The collection edited by Jen Harvie and Andy Lavender, *Making Contemporary Theatre* (2010), reported on the rehearsal and preparatory processes used by an international cohort of companies. They carried forward Heddon and Milling's critique of the collectivist ethos, calling out "decades of attempts at democratic practice which were at best sometimes frustrating and at worst grossly compromised" (2010, 4), and featured a number of ensembles with relatively hierarchical structures. Around the same time, an American

Society for Theatre Research (ASTR) working group devoted to the history of collective creation was founded by Kathryn Mederos Syssoyeva and Scott Proudfit. Out of their meetings, conference panels, and collaborations came the volumes *A History of Collective Creation* (2013a), followed in the same year by *Collective Creation in Contemporary Performance*. A third related volume, *Women, Collective Creation, and Devised Performance: The Rise of Women Theatre Artists in the Twentieth and Twenty-first Centuries*, was published in 2016.[3] In addition to an excellent contextualizing introduction penned by Syssoyeva that summarizes historiographical developments since Oddey's text arrived, the volumes provide both a much-enlarged time frame for collective creation's history and a transnational perspective on its differential global developments. The broad focus places American developments in wider contexts and makes evident that, although the radical companies of the 1960s play a significant role in the evolution of collective creation and devising in the United States, they are not the sole determinant of future developments nor the only point of reference for contemporary devising. Rachel Anderson-Rabern argues in her recent *Staging Process: The Aesthetic Politics of Collective Performance* that by the twenty-first century ensembles view the work of the radical 1960s collectives and their formalist successors in more nuanced ways, "sketch[ing] successorship as a tense product of pushes and pulls, alignments and resistances, rife with opportunities to dismantle and expose toxic power systems embedded in the cultural water of those forbears" (2020, 17).

What actually occurs, quite naturally, is a sort of inverse square law of influence: immediately following the 1960s, the legacy of the radical collectives is still relatively pronounced, but as that tradition propagates into the 1980s and 1990s the gravitational pull is dispersed. As the living memory of the earlier ensembles fades into anecdote and scholarly forms of remembrance, the nature of legacy and succession take on different forms. An adequate historiography, then, must reject the quest for an ontology of collective creation located in the origin or root (the other meaning of "radical") in favor of more nuanced historical consideration of the many different formations that it produces in changing contexts, and so it is to these that I now turn.

"The Sixties Never Died, Man… ": The Afterlives of 1960s Collective Theatre

[I]f collective creation does not in fact vanish with the fading of the radical politics and countercultural movements of the 1960s, to be reborn almost three decades later as devising, "something" happens in those years: if not an ending, then a fading from view; if not rebirth, then an evolution. (Syssoyeva 2013b, 13)

The new historiography of collective creation allows us to treat the period after the so-called collapse of the practice in the early 1970s with the sense that it offers new beginnings rather than a decline. An apt place to start is the simple fact that the actual number of established companies that truly collapsed by 1973 is relatively small: while the Open Theater officially disbanded that year, its style of work continued via other means, as described below. It is certainly the case that scores of smaller and less well-established 1960s ensembles folded for various reasons. Many of these—the Pageant Players, Mass Transit, American Playground, WITCH, Burning City, the Diggers, SF Red Theatre, and Berkeley Radical Arts Troupe— were guerrilla theatres that never intended to last beyond "the Revolution" (or its disappointing refusal to manifest). Nevertheless, even they created a template from which collective forms of performance, including street theatre and direct-action performance, would be revived at the height of the AIDS crisis in the 1980s by groups like Queer Nation, Gran Fury, and, later, the Lesbian Avengers. Several prominent, if smaller, ensembles outside New York, like the Firehouse Theatre (founded in Minneapolis in 1963), also fell on harder times but continued producing by moving to San Francisco, where they continued until they disbanded in 1974.

Yet, while these disappearances certainly signal a turning point in activist culture more generally, the valuable "legacy" essays in the James Harding and Cindy Rosenthal collection, *Restaging the Sixties: Radical Theaters and Their Legacies*, show clearly that most of the renowned companies featured there are still active, though each in significantly altered circumstances and having evolved different practices (2006). The Living Theatre survives mostly by doing street theatre in marginalized communities both in the United States and abroad: they have produced more than a hundred works across five continents since their "disappearance" following the infamous 1968 American tour (Solomon 2006; Syssoyeva and Proudfit 2013, 16). The San Francisco Mime Troupe won a special Tony Award in 1987, taking a step toward becoming what its former house playwright, Joan Holden, called "the most established antiestablishment theatre in the country" (quoted in Harding and Rosenthal 2006, 172; Mason 2006). El Teatro Campesino has become a conventional producing operation with its own theatre and no longer creates as an ensemble, though it still features the work of Chicano/a and Latinx artists (Huerta 2006). The Bread and Puppet Theatre left New York for Dopp Farm (Vermont), where it first ran its *Domestic Resurrection Circus* until it became too popular with tourists, and now tours across the country and internationally, spawning numerous circus and physical theatre offshoots both in the United States and abroad. Only the Open Theatre, Performance Group, At the Foot of the Mountain, and the Free Southern Theatre from among those presented in *Restaging the Sixties* folded, and all have had interesting afterlives (in the form of Schechner's performance theory and the formation of the Wooster Group, Martha Boesing's late solo work, and Junebug Productions, respectively).

Still, the narrative persists that, with the failure of the counterculture, collective creation disappeared from the scene. But with a broader view of ensemble creation, such established trajectories recede and we can see with fresh eyes the "second acts" of collectives that emerged beyond 1970. These include not just the continued work of the ensembles mentioned above, but newly formed companies that, in many cases, were founded on similar models of collective creation. The itinerant ensemble Squat Theatre, originally from Budapest, relocated to New York from 1977 to 1983 (Shank 2002). Influenced by the Living Theater's European tours but equally grounded in the surrealism of Witkiewicz and Kantor, the company lived communally and created collectively—always, they insisted, for practical rather than ideological reasons—in their storefront theatre in Chelsea. They achieved their considerable US reputation through three works: *Pig! Child! Fire!* (1977), *Andy Warhol's Last Love* (1979), and *Mr. Dead and Mrs. Free* (1981). Presaging to some degree concerns Schechner would pursue with the Performance Group (and which have returned in force in postdramatic theatre), Squat investigated the "irruption of the real" in performance (Lehmann 2006, 99). They often dramatically exposed the window of their storefront theatre in order to mirror the audience's viewing perspective by highlighting passersby looking in on the spectacle, thereby rendering spectatorship uncanny.

Many such ensembles formed in New York, but also increasingly elsewhere in the country in response to gentrification and rising rents in the city. This tendency is exemplified by, in addition to Milwaukee's Theatre X (see the case study by Curtis Carter), the Otrabanda Company, who formed in 1971 out of Antioch College in Dayton, Ohio. After investigating popular theatre traditions from the Lower Mississippi region as a vehicle for radical political sentiments, the company participated in workshops with the Flemish director Tone Brulin. Combining techniques derived from Grotowski's "poor theatre" with their previous training in vaudeville and circus, the company established itself through tours in the early 1970s before returning to the river with its Mississippi River Raft Revue. Despite a learning curve that apparently included the discovery that the screaming of open glottals, while on par for a Grotowski workshop, did not sit well with local audiences, Otrabanda remained a staple of summer community performance between St. Louis and New Orleans (as well as on other waterways) through at least 1984, while continuing to tour and perform into the late 1980s.

Similarly, United Mime Workers (1972–85), founded at the University of Illinois-Champaign, achieved international recognition through a series of uniquely creative works (some of which, like *Implication*, could open today at a devising festival without seeming dated) that combined corporeal mime with Kabuki and highly theoretical concepts from musical composition, systems theory, and cybernetics. These suggest interesting points of intersection, not only backward to the radical 1960s collectives but also forward to the formalist theatre of the Wooster Group, Richard Foreman, and Robert Wilson as well as to the "new vaudeville" movement of clowning and mime associated with Bill Irwin (who worked with the Pickle Family Circus in San Francisco and later as a solo artist) and further to such later crossover companies as Blue Man Group (Weinberg 1992, 254). Unlike these contemporaries, however, the Mime Workers developed, in the vein of 1960s ensemble theatres, a strictly collectivist model for both company organization and creative processes and also claimed an overt political position through their troupe name and affiliations with various labor organizations.

Histories centered on the collapse or disintegration of the best-known collectives also fail to report that in fact they usually broke apart only to multiply and evolve: in the case of the Open Theatre and El Teatro Campesino, fabulously so. In the first instance, not only did Chaikin continue to develop work with the Winter Project until 1983 (made up, in addition to Chaikin, of Tina Shepard, Ronnie Gilbert, Paul Zimet, and the dramaturg Mira Rafalowicz, plus a number of performers and musicians who worked more occasionally with the company), but former members of the Open went on to form a veritable phalanx of offshoot ensembles. Already these companies were moving away from strictly collectivist models and experimenting with various forms of collaboration, laying the pathway to the next wave of devising. Zimet and Shepard, in addition to their work with the Winter Project, joined with Ellen Maddow to form the Talking Band. Their early experiments in choral presentation of epic themes aligned with the better-known work of Andre Serban at La MaMa, and they collaborated productively with Otrabanda Company and the then relatively unknown Anne Bogart (who had studied acting with the Open Theater's co-director Roberta Sklar at Bard College) to perform *No Plays No Poetry*, based on the theoretical writings of Bertolt Brecht, in 1988 (for which Bogart won her first OBIE). JoAnn Schmidman left New York to form the Omaha Magic Theatre and was soon joined by playwright Megan Terry, who had similarly departed the Open Theater, first to write for the Firehouse Theatre in Minneapolis before decamping to Nebraska. OMT thrived as a woman's theatre based in collaborative creation until 1998, garnering awards and substantial critical attention (Fletcher 2016). Sklar would eventually join Sondra Segal and Claire Coss to found the influential Women's Experimental Theatre (WET) in New York in 1976. And it is sometimes forgotten that Open Theatre member Paul Boesing originally cofounded At the Foot of the Mountain (Minneapolis) with his then-wife, Martha, before leaving in 1976 when the company elected to become all-female. Equally little commented upon, Ray Barry (originally a member of the Living Theatre before joining Chaikin) formed the Quena Company, which operated between 1973 and 1983, often performing in jails and prisons (as had the Living and the Open). Alongside that project, Barry was involved with the Street Theatre in New York City (1975–80), made up of formerly incarcerated men.

Similarly, Arthur Sainer established the Bridge Theatre (later Bridge Collective), and Lee Worley helped establish Medicine Show Theatre Ensemble with Jim Barbosa and Barbara Vann before moving on to work with the Naropa Institute (out of which later third-wave companies, like Mugwumpin, would emerge). Medicine Show conducted some of the most extreme experiments with language and text, first by producing plays by Gertrude Stein and poems by Kenneth Koch, but also by devising adaptations which combined a number of disparate texts simultaneously in performance (not unlike many contemporary devising companies do). *Bound to Rise*, a more straightforward musical that nevertheless utilized environmental staging, garnered the ensemble an OBIE in 1985, and their several homages to the poetry and sensibility of Leonard Cohen remain popular. The company continues to produce following the deaths of Barbosa (2003) and Vann (2015). To round out the review of Chaikin's impressive artist's tree, the work of former company member Muriel Miguel, and her long-standing work with Spiderwoman Theatre, is covered below under feminist ensembles. Finally, Chaikin himself continued to collaboratively create with playwrights (Beckett, Sam Shepard) and companies: one of his final associations took place with Philadelphia's Pig Iron Theatre in 1999 (see the essay by Syssoyeva in Volume 2).

Feminist Ensemble Theatres 1970–94

Recent studies of collective creation have situated female teachers, theorists, and practitioners at the center of its history, particularly in its second-wave manifestations. While a simplistic gendering of male-as-hierarchical and female-as-collaborative is historically unsupportable (and essentialist), the intersection between collective creation as a resistant but marginalized practice within the sphere of modern theatre and the marginalization of women's roles within theatre history more broadly is difficult to ignore. Seeking to address both erasures, Syssoyeva and Proudfit write in the "Introduction" to *Women, Collective Creation, and Devised Performance* that "[t]he history of modern theatre is a history of collaborative methods and the history of collaborative methods is a women's history" (2016, 5). An important part of that history, and one that plays a significant part in sustaining collective creation in its more overtly political form, is the rise of women's theatre groups and feminist collectives beginning in the late 1960s, peaking throughout the 1970s, and declining in the 1980s.

Feminist ensembles often emerged from the creative collectives of the 1960s and thereby established a lineage with that work. But they also self-consciously asserted their power to refine and reform many of the creative and organizational practices of those groups to create even more radical alternatives both to mainstream and existing (and male-dominated) ensemble-based theatre. They exposed much of the mythologizing that surrounded notions of collectivity in 1960s America across New Left and countercultural movements more broadly. The marginalization and outright oppression of women in the anti-war and anti-draft movement ("Girls Say Yes to Boys Who Say No"), the Civil Rights movement, the folk music scene, SDS, and other leftist groups have been well documented, and as in those movements, so too even the putatively radical theatre collectives often acted as a microcosm of the inequalities, lack of opportunity, and overt sexism writ large in the culture. Many women thus left theatre collectives, even those touting nonhierarchical creation, in order to escape the gender hierarchies they saw becoming institutionalized there. As Canning shows, equally important was the positive desire to work with other women and to forge new practices of collectivity and collaboration that would address the inequities of existing collectives (1996, 65). Feminist collectivity, it was often argued, would avoid the sex-role stereotyping that hindered the disposition of skills and labor, as well as addressing the latent competitiveness in male-led ensembles that interfered with the actual practice of nonhierarchical creation despite idealized claims to the contrary. Moreover, collectivity would emerge organically from a shared history of gender oppression, rather than a strictly Marxist focus on class, thus linking its political existence to personal and existential concerns.

Seizing upon the methods utilized in consciousness-raising activities and variations on the "story circle," feminist ensembles experimented more robustly with democratic and participatory structures than the more acclaimed collectives. In some cases, as with female members who left the SFMT to form companies like Lilith (San Francisco) and Family Circus Theatre (Portland, Oregon), this meant mollifying the stricter Marxist definition of the collective (especially as this was inflected by Maoist practices of self-examination and critique) in order to reclaim forms of collectivity based in shared oppression that did not impinge on the individual's identity and history (Lewis 2013). Perhaps even more so than the 1960s collective theatres, feminist ensembles placed emphasis on the process of creating their performances in relation to their audiences, as the nature of the oppression they sought to address was so widespread and ongoing that productions often changed over time to address the audience's immediate responses.

Although susceptible to the same pressures and tensions that fractured the theatre collectives of the 1960s, often exacerbated by the precarious economic situation in which almost all feminist ensembles of the 1970s and 1980s operated, feminist companies succeeded in, among other things, keeping the flame of collective creation burning in the United States when cultural and political forces may well have driven it to extinction. In ways that would prove fruitful for later devising companies, feminist theatres of the period reformed many collaborative practices in ways that allowed them to be picked up and utilized by other companies well after feminist ensemble theatre declined following the backlash against feminism and funding cuts to local theatre companies in the late 1980s.

Rosemary Curb estimated in 1980 that "more than half the feminist theaters in operation today are organized as collectives" and that "about two-thirds of the theaters create some plays through collective improvisation" (64). Although we should attend to Canning's warning against looking back at the beginnings of feminist theatre as a purely grassroots movement without leadership or professional connections, the early explosion of ensembles remains a grassroots phenomenon. The first self-identified feminist ensembles were established in New York (although the Los Angeles Feminist Theatre opened around the same time) and included the New Feminist Theatre (1969, which did not operate as a collective), It's All Right to Be a Woman (1970) led by Sue Perlgut as an outgrowth of the guerilla theatre Women of the Burning City, the short-lived (1972–4) Women's Unit at Bard College headed by Roberta Sklar, and Westbeth Playwright's Feminist Collective (1970, essentially a playwright's workshop rather than a creative collective). By the mid-1970s there were dozens more operating in the city, including Cutting Edge, the Latinx company Medusa's Revenge, Women's Collage Theatre, Emmatroupe, and Women's Repertory of Long Island. But in relatively short order, additional feminist collectives sprang up in the Midwest, with Minneapolis especially active with the founding of Alive and Trucking (1971), Circle of the Witch (1973), Lavender Cellar (1973), and At the Foot of the Mountain (1974, as a mixed-gender company, after 1976, female-only). Chicago, undergoing an independent theatre renaissance in the 1970s, was home to Chicago's Women's Theatre Group. San Francisco, already a hotbed of radical theatre going back to the founding of the Actor's Workshop in 1954, produced not just Lilith, but also It's Just a Stage (1974), La Cucarachas (also 1974, founded by Dorinda Morena), and the Women's Ensemble Theatre in Berkeley (1975). Cities with major universities provided audiences for numerous companies; in Cambridge, Massachusetts, both Commonplace Pageant Theatre and Mermaid Theatre were founded, while Madison, Wisconsin, had Poor Sid. Seattle saw such a surge in feminist theatre companies that producing organizations such as Womyns Theatre quickly formed to support them. Companies were formed in Pittsburgh, Providence, New Haven, Ithaca (Mischief Mime Co.), Northampton (Chrysalis Theatre Eclectic, 1978), Washington, DC, Rhode Island, Tucson, and Schenectady. No region was exempt, as ensembles appeared in Connecticut (Theatre of Light and Shadows, 1977), Indiana (Womanshine), and even in the conservative South with Red Dyke Theatre and Womensong in Atlanta. Curb estimated that 80–100 feminist theatres were operating across the country by 1980, and Hayes lists 185 women's theatre groups (not all collectives) between 1969 and 1992 (Curb 1979; Hayes 1994).

Many of the ensembles were short-lived, and few had staff or resources to archive their work, so in-depth coverage of not just productions, but organizational records and rehearsal processes, is scarce. Dinah Leavitt's 1980 *Feminist Theatre Groups* focuses on the four Minneapolis companies named above. Influenced by the older historiography of collective creation (just taking shape after the publication of Sainer's *Radical Theatre Notebook* in 1975 and essays like Michael Kirby's 1975 "On Political Theatre"), Leavitt accepted the utopian radical premise of collective creation uncritically but made the point that "[w]hile feminist theatres borrowed from and were encouraged by the Radical Theatre Movement, they did not become a woman's branch of that movement" (6). Her careful contextualization, as well as plot summaries of important but unpublished works such as Alive and Trucking's *Battered Homes and Gardens* and out-of-print pieces like *Pig in a Blanket*, remain invaluable. Primary source citations from company-based publications such as internal histories, brochures, and artistic statements provide insight into the collectivist organizational structures and reveal the degree to which these were more rigorously instituted and followed than in the major 1960s collectives. Leavitt records how Circle of the Witch, for instance, extended collective responsibility for every aspect of running the company—including filing, touring van maintenance, and publicity— to all its members. With respect to creative collaboration, directing duties were rotated among the members across their repertory, and at any rate the role "was viewed as more of an artistic coordinator than controller" (55). Plays normally developed over anywhere from four months to a year interspersed with "basis-of-unity meetings" during which the company discussed personal and collective issues that bound the company together and provided material for workshops.

However, Leavitt's book was published before certain changes latent in second-wave feminism itself had become apparent that would later destabilize ensembles like AFOM and introduce fractures within other companies as well as across feminist ensemble-based theatre. First, feminist collectives confronted the same incongruity experienced in the radical collectives of the 1960s, as the utopian desire for nonpatriarchal structures of organization and creative processes ran up against pressure to institute more top-down methods (especially for ensembles with nonprofit status, which increasingly required boards of directors in order to solicit grants) to accommodate the individual skills and commitments of the artists and the necessity to centralize logistics and planning (Hayes 1994; Canning 1996). Of the four Minneapolis companies, Alive and Trucking and Lavender Cellar had become inactive (in 1976 and 1975, respectively). Both suffered the typical pressures of time and money, which are particularly consequential for nonprofessional companies with neither the means nor time to train or to develop more than niche audiences and reviewer interest (especially for the all-woman Lavender Cellar). But along with these challenges, the ensembles never managed to balance the desire for collectivity with the need for authority to find its place in the creative process and sometimes confronted situations where collective approaches actually forestalled both the theatrical and political force of the shows. As Canning and Hayes show across a number of ensembles (including Lilith, ATFOM, Red Dyke, and Sangoma [the latter founded in Brunswick, New Jersey, in 1988, under the aegis of the seminal African-American regional Crossroads Theatre]), internal divisions brought about by the difficulty in managing leadership issues caused as much or more instability than did economic issues (recognizing these are never wholly separate).

Often these tensions were exacerbated by internal fault lines within feminism itself. By the mid-1970s, long-standing issues of exclusion along the lines of race, class, and sexual preference began to roil the concept of "Woman," revealing that the reclamation of a common experience of oppression based in gender alone was flawed from the beginning. "The Combahee River Collective Statement" (1977) famously exposed the many rifts between mainstream and an emerging Black Feminism. Canning's 1996 study of US feminist theatres, appearing more than fifteen years after Leavitt's and from a relatively safe distance from the conflicts of the 1980s, devotes a chapter to feminist theatre collectives. As well as narrating the historical trajectory by which feminist ensembles came to define the first phase of feminist theatre, and carefully parsing the evolution of a specifically feminist conception of collectivity, Canning uncovers many of the reasons why this concept was difficult to sustain in practice as feminist theatre attempted to become more integrative and responsive to gender, class, and sexual differences. She examines case studies of four companies (Spiderwoman/Split Britches, Lilith, AFOM, and Seattle's Front Room Theatre Guild). In the first three cases, companies were riven by, and sometimes disbanded or reformed over, issues grounded in differences of sexual preference and racial and class inclusion and the attempts to remedy it by transforming ensembles into multicultural companies: only Patricia Van Kirk's Seattle-based (and nonprofessional) Front Room Theatre Guild successfully navigated the currents, though it closed in 1987 due to financial stress.

As the final multiplier, second-wave feminism encountered external pressures that increasingly made it difficult to maintain ensemble creation in particular given its longer devising processes. Funding had always been difficult—women's theatre groups sometimes had to decide whether to compete for small grants with rape crisis centers—and became increasingly so in the declining US economy after 1973. Along with other devising companies, feminist theatres suffered disproportionately as the NEA eliminated grant categories for experimental work throughout the 1970s. Also, by the end of the decade, with the country leaning fiscally and culturally rightward and preparing to elect Ronald Reagan to the first of his two terms, a palpable backlash against feminism formed in the media and other cultural institutions. Combined with significant cuts in federal funding, exacerbated by the Tax Reform Bill of 1986 (which disincentivized corporate and public giving to nonprofits) and fallout from the NEA controversies of the late 1980s and early 1990s, feminist theatres were folding at an alarming rate. Hayes writes that by 1992, only five all-women theatre companies that could be identified as feminist were still operating, with a tremendous drain in talent taking artists into stand-up, solo performance, higher education careers, and relatively more mainstream theatre.

All of these factors contributed to the relocation of some ensembles into forms of applied theatre after the 1980s: there, different funding structures connected to educational and community institutions, though meager, were more readily available, and the outreach and service intentions, always strong in feminist theatre, could more readily be attained by establishing direct connections to youth centers, educational institutions, and community development organizations.

On the positive side, the growing awareness of difference within feminism produced a small number of companies and forms of collective creation able to address these concerns and to continue to thrive through the Reagan years and beyond. Women's Experimental Theatre (WET) began producing in 1977 and only closed in 1986, surviving even the departure of Clare Coss in 1980. While *The Daughter's Cycle* (1977–80) remains their signature piece, works like *Electra Speaks* (1980) explored more flexible forms of collective creation by running workshops with hundreds of women on the theme of silence. Lilith, despite significant turnover that included founder Terry Baum's abrupt departure, continued to devise work in San Francisco until 1986. *Sacrifices* (1977) established their typical method of co-authorship, but the company was restless in their pursuit of different collaborative processes, at one point enlisting 80–100 women to devise *Fetal Positions* (1983–4) and *Breeding Grounds* (1984–6) (Canning 1996, 105).

The story of Split Britches evolving out of Spiderwoman Theatre is well known (Weinberg 1992; Hayes 1994; Canning 1996), and the argument has been made that it represented a critical turning point in feminist theatre history in which "the senses that feminism might provide an all-encompassing critique gave way to explorations by new, more narrowly focused activist groups" (Case 1996, 5). But rather than leading to the collapse of a major ensemble, the split engendered growth within collective creation and perhaps influenced the style of later devising ensembles with commitments to feminist principles and ethnic audiences conceived within an intersectional field of difference. In fact, both Spiderwoman and Split Britches were among the few feminist companies to openly address difference in their work, eschewing the more common function of "taking and displaying," in Elaine Aston's words, "the disenfranchised 'woman's part'" ("Feminist Theatre" n.p.). By "spoofing the gaze" of the white, heterosexual subject of address through Brechtian techniques and campy humor that put to rest the stereotype of feminist art being unfunny (though in uniquely different ways, Spiderwoman more often in reference to ritual and family dynamics and Split Britches by citing vaudeville, TV sitcoms, or film), both companies self-consciously referenced existing theatrical forms in order to bring focus to layers of identity that exist in a state of performative play. After the split, Spiderwoman focused more intently on representing Native American identities and issues in works like *3 Up, 3 Down* (1986) and their popular touring show *Winnetou's Snake Oil Show from Wigwam City* (1988). Split Britches, having established their international reputation with works such as *Dress Suits for Hire* (1987) and *Belle Reprieve* (1990), has pursued various combinations of solo performance and/or playwriting—usually with company member Deb Margolin—as well as devised and education-based performance, setting an early example for the more flexible forms of collective creation that characterize almost all devising companies today. More recently, Lois Weaver and Peggy Shaw have pursued solo work on both sides of the Atlantic (Dolan 1991; Harvie and Weaver 2015). Their work garnered substantial academic attention and formed the core of work in gender-based performance theory and criticism for two decades (Case 1996).

Also, Split Britches hosted the first Women One Women (WOW) theatre festival in 1980, which then transformed into a permanent East Village performance space that went on to become the leading venue for lesbian solo performance artists, including Holly Hughes and Alina Troyano (aka Carmelita Tropicana). The most important ensemble to emerge from WOW—although creative collaboration thrived there across companies and solo artists—was the Five Lesbian Brothers, who began performing there in *Voyage to Lesbos* in 1989. Their cabaret-style humor mocked popular culture and second-wave feminism alike, and the canny, vaudevillian self-referentiality of their performances helped launch the playwriting career (and style) of member Lisa Kron. As their audiences grew and attracted a non-WOW crowd at larger spaces like the New York Theatre Workshop, the company became somewhat more conventional in their theatricality and by the time of *Brides of the Moon* 1997 their work was being reviewed and anthologized. Perhaps sensing a drift into the mainstream, although still nominally a company, the Brothers haven't produced together since the 2005 *Oedipus at Palm Springs*. Moe Angelos, another Brother, performs regularly today with the Builders Association.

Ethnic-specific and Constituency-based Ensembles

From the vantage point of the third decade of the twenty-first century, collective creation and devised theatre in the United States appear to have developed predominantly among middle-class white artists—as much today as at any time since the 1960s and 1970s.[4] Victoria Lewis recounts a fascinating interview with SFMT member Dan Chumley, in which the practice of Maoist self-criticism in the ensemble was being discussed: Chumley responded with this telling anecdote concerning one of the few black members from the early years of the company:

> Lonnie Ford came in and said, "In order for criticism/self-criticism to work, we all have to be equal, see. And ain't one of you equal to me. Ain't one of you come up from where I come up, you don't know shit about my life, and you can't say … anything to me as an equal, so this shit's over." And it was over. (2013a, 187)

Although SFMT would address issues of race head-on in works like *The Minstrel Show: Or, Civil Rights in a Cracker Barrel* (1965), the somewhat cavalier and not particularly subversive use of blackface indicates the state of racial representation in collective theatre of the time. Within the mainstream, the decentralization of American theatre during the 1960s and 1970s produced a number of major African-American regional professional repertory companies, many launched through funding by CETA (the Comprehensive Employment and Training Act, signed into law by Nixon in 1973), such as Penumbra (Minneapolis), Crossroads (Brunswick, New Jersey), Freedom Theatre (St. Louis), and Oakland Ensemble Company. The period also saw the founding of organizations like the Black Theatre Alliance and, later, the Black Theatres Network, along with festivals such as the Black National Theatre Festival. Among the political group theatres of the 1960s, the Free Southern Theatre stood out for its status as a cultural arm of the Civil Rights Movement and for establishing a model for grassroots-based principles that would significantly influence later developments in applied theatre. However, none of these initiatives featured ensemble creation as a primary or sustained practice, although Gil Moses, a cofounder of Free Southern Theatre, created workshops in 1965 out of which community-based shows (*The Jonesboro Story* and *The Bougalusa Story*) emerged.

Black theatre companies founded in the 1960s and 1970s, ranging from those built on integrationist politics (the Negro Ensemble Company) to the more nationalistic and Black Power-based ideologies of the Black Arts Movement—the New Heritage Players under Roger Furman, the Afro-American Studio, Barbara Teer's National Black Theatre of Harlem, the New Lafayette Theatre under Robert MacBeth (with Ed Bullins as playwright-in-residence), and Amiri Baraka's Black Arts Repertory in Harlem and Spirit House in Newark, New Jersey—mostly supported playwriting and did not regularly create collectively or form sustained creative ensembles (Olsen 2011). Some of the ritual-based "revivals" cowritten by Teer and Charles Russell, such as *A Ritual to Regain Our Strength and Reclaim Our Power* (1970), were scripted through workshops and allowed for a good deal of improvisation and audience participation, as were the rituals convened by MacBeth at the New Lafayette that utilized Africanist performance modes. Similar events at the Kuumba Workshop in Chicago and the staged chants at Baraka's Spirit House certainly approximated forms of ensemble creation that would be carried over into community-based theatre, but they did not yield self-producing ensembles who continued to work together.

Thus, surprisingly, no notable, sustained black-led collectives emerged into mainstream critical view from this dynamic period. Companies like Theatre X and Castillo Theatre, among many others, addressed local issues of race and formed as, or became, multiracial organizations. Especially in the 1990s, ensembles like Target Margin Theatre begin to form with diversity and inclusivity as guiding mission goals. Nevertheless, the lack of companies led by artists of color is an issue notably absent in existing histories of collective creation and has been largely overlooked in studies commissioned by the Theatre Communications Group, NET, and other umbrella organizations to research the support and development of ensemble theatres.[5] Charlotte Canning and other historians of feminist theatre have pointed to the lack of ensembles of color among the initial wave of women's theatre groups, citing only a handful (including Onyx Women's Theatre in New York—which featured deaf minority and lesbian actresses—and Black Star in

Cambridge, Massachusetts) and concluding that "[w]hile there were many women of color doing theatre in alternative groups, solo performances, or more mainstream theatres, they usually did not choose to become involved with the feminist groups. When they did, their experiences were often highly negative" (1996, 121). While it is almost certain that there have been plays by authors of color produced through some form of devising, the significance here lies in the aversion to self-identifying the work as the product of collective creation. The disturbing implication is perhaps that the term has become so attached to a predominantly white practice (one that could be seen, moreover, as recuperating elements of traditional African oral performance traditions) that many artists of color are uninterested in being identified with it.

Economics also likely plays an important role in the lack of ensembles of color, either negatively charged in the sense of driving artists away from the precarious career of ensemble theatre-making (though many past and contemporary ensembles are multiethnic) or positively in the sense that economic injustice calls out to artists of color to address those inequities by choosing to conduct their work in the communities most vulnerable to them, leading many to create ensemble work in applied theatre and community-directed forms. Meanwhile, African-American-led movement ensembles like the Bill T. Jones/Arnie Zane Dance Company (founded in 1983 in Harlem) and the Urban Bush Women, established the following year, have been at the forefront of ensemble-created work for decades yet typically define themselves as dance companies. As a measure of the lack of black ensemble-made theatre, the index to the 2019 *Routledge Companion to African-American Theatre and Performance* contains no direct reference to devising or collective creation.

However, we again see that tracing collective creation post-1970 solely from the model of the 1960s radical companies can lead to blind spots. An often-neglected source of inspiration for ensemble-based creation in the United States is the "poemplays" of female playwrights within the Black Arts Movement such as Sonia Sanchez and Barbara Molette (Forsgren 2020). Based in the performative dimensions of oral poetry, pieces such as Sanchez's *Sister Son/ji* and Molette's *Roselee Pritchett* feature multilevel narratives, audience engagement, disjointed movement and sound design, and improvisation, testifying to the fact that authors (especially those drawing on Yoruba and other African performance traditions) may devise work that remarkably aligns with ensemble-created aesthetics. Sanchez and Molette (along with J. e. Franklin's musicals) are often seen as precursors to

Ntozake Shange's choreopoems, which, in their own startling resemblance to a variety of contemporary ensemble-created theatre forms (dance theatre, physical theatre, interdisciplinary or postmodern theatre), signal that more attention is due toward understanding how certain forms of experimental playwriting have influenced the evolution of devised theatre. (Appropriately, in March 2019, students at Princeton University devised a production entitled *Choreopoem*.)

Shange had no overt connection to the avant-garde collectives of the 1960s, but her work emerged from a thriving number of Bay Area feminist collectives as well as her dance training with Raymond Sawyer, Ed Mock, and the choreographer Paula Moss. Although never having worked in a sustained manner with a collective, Shange's essay "unrecovered losses/ black theatre traditions" reads today like a clarion call for the formation of African-American devised theatre based in the interdisciplinary application of jazz improvisation to every element of theatre-making (Morris Johnson 333–4). Omi Osun Joni L. Jones and others have uncovered a parallel line of development originating in the Sounds in Movement Harlem dance studio created by Dianne McIntyre (2010). In the 1970s, the studio incubated talents such as Shange but also hosted workshops by Jowale Willa Jo Zollar, who would found the Urban Bush Women in 1984. Jones's own work with Sharon Bridgforth and Laurie Carlos utilizing the principles of the jazz aesthetic has been influential in contemporary queer devising practice (see Volume 2).

But it is not until the formation of companies in the 1990s, such as the short-lived Pomo Afro Homos (1990–5), the much longer-running and still active Universes (formed in 1995, and so referenced in the second volume), and recently formed ensembles like Chicago's Thick Routes Performance Collage (now Honey Pot), that inroads by black-majority companies are made into the predominantly white sector of ensemble-created theatre. Pomo Afro Homos (originally formed of Djola Branner, Brian Freeman—a former member of SFMT—and Eric Gupton) emerged at the nadir of the AIDS crisis to produce two notable pieces before they ceased performing as an ensemble (Gupton died in 2003). *Fierce Love* premiered in 1991 in San Francisco before touring to major cities and ending up at the Public Theater in New York. That show toured alongside *Dark Fruit* until 1995. Their "Pomo" credentials were made explicit by the critique of mediatized representations of black gay culture (notably the black comedy series *In Living Color*) as well as a queering of black gay identity into a multifaceted and intersectional formation that resisted easy essentialisms. Their performances appeared at a crucial time in the evolution of LGBTQ civil rights, caught between the 1991 announcement by the (heterosexual) black basketball star Magic Johnson that he had contracted AIDS and the continued rise of a neoconservative right that used the 1992 presidential primaries to demonize both blacks and gays (particularly the Republican candidate Patrick Buchanan, who directly called for defunding the NEA on the grounds it supported queer black art). A Pomo Afro Homos performance was certain to be topical—*Strange Fruit* opens with the performers representing Jacob from *La Cage Aux Folles*, Paul from John Guare's *Six Degrees of Separation*, and Belize from Tony Kushner's *Angels in America*—and fiercely devoted to its community while also welcoming (but never pandering to) white and/or straight audiences. The ensemble encountered controversy both from the majority culture (the mayor of Fairbanks, Alaska, sought to ban ads announcing their performance) and within the black arts community when they were not invited to the Black Theatre Festival in 1991, inciting charges of homophobia. Yet the ensemble also played at Lincoln Center and in many ways acted as a gateway company for spectators encountering the performance of black queer culture for the first time.

Although the origins of modern Asian-American theatre lie primarily in companies established to support playwrights and acting ensembles (East West Players, Asian American Theatre Workshop, Northwest Asian American Theatre) rather than collective creation, the presence of established companies like the Fiji Company (later the Ping Chong + Company) and a number of short-lived performance art crossover ensembles like Thought Music established a foothold in the 1970s. Chong's practice combined a natural auteurship that originated in his earliest work as an installation artist with a strong desire to collaborate with both his company members and associated artists: he claims he is "not so much a creator as an editor" (Gussow 1997, 17). Although always concerned with issues of alienation and otherness, he did not begin to explore identity themes explicitly until the early 1990s, when *Deshima* (1993) and *Chinoiserie* (1995) appeared after he had disbanded his original ensemble. *Kwaidan* (1998) initiated a series of works centered on Japanese ghost tales. Since 1992 Chong has collaborated with a number of artists as part of the *Undesirable Elements* series, a quasi-documentary format that allows the company to work with particular communities whose stories are perceived to be ignored or distorted in order to maintain them as marginal. His attention has shifted dramatically to issues of social justice (such as the extrajudicial killing of unarmed black men), yet his style remains abstract with its trademark combination of dance, music, puppetry, and media. Never uniquely an ethnic artist (Frieze 2006), like George Coates his work could also be aligned with the forms of ensemble creation that, especially in the UK (with exemplary companies like Station House Opera) and Canada (Robert Lepage), are designated as "visual theatre," which would influence later Asian-American companies like 2g (founded in 1997).

Similarly, Jewish theatre in America has a venerable tradition of playwriting, actor training, and ensembles but has produced few companies engaged in collective creation. (Chaikin's signature production of *The Dybbuk* in 1977 was for the NY Shakespeare Festival and not an Open Theater production, though many company members were involved.) A notable exception was A Jewish Traveling Theatre, which produced between 1978 and 2012 and became one of the founding members of NET. They created more than two dozen devised pieces, including *Coming from a Safe Distance*, *The Last Yiddish Poet*, and *Heart of the World*, and collaborated with companies abroad and in the United States (with Chaikin, Dell'Arte, Roadside, and others).

The outstanding exception to the lack of diversity in second-wave collective creation, of course, is Chicano/a theatre and cognates such as Latinx and Nuyorican spoken word performance. Unlike African-American writers and practitioners in the 1960s influenced by the Black Arts Movement, Chicano theatre-makers, like Luis Valdez with ETC, had few available literary or dramaturgical traditions on which to base their work, which helps to explain the turn toward popular, collectively created performance forms like the *actos* and *mitos*. But Chicano/a theatre was also inspired by movements in group-devised political theatre from the Global South in support of decolonization, such as *creación colectivo*. ETC was hardly the first Hispanic company in the United States to explore these traditional forms, as ensembles had been providing performances in urban neighborhoods since the beginning of the twentieth century, and the explosion of activist theatre in New York in the 1960s brought forms of collective creation to the fore. Supported by new producing organizations like the International Arts Relations (INTAR), Duo Theatre (as in bilingual) produced collaboratively authored work on folkloric themes in the late 1970s, eventually becoming one of the repertory theatres hosted by La MaMa. Similar collaborative methods were utilized by Teatro Orilla, Teatro Jurutungo, Teatro Guazabara, and Teatro 4 (sometimes Teatro Cuatro), the latter a mixed company of Puerto Ricans as well as Central and South Americans that hosted the first festival of Hispanic theatre at the Public in 1976 (the year of the American bicentennial). Such companies establish the link to the Nuyorican spoken word and performance scene that gathered

American Ensemble Theatres, 1970–95

in 1973 around the Poet's Café located in Alphabet City on the Lower East side (and would provide one of the launching pads for Universes). Although mainly a crucible for solo performance, Raymond Barry of the Open Theater led workshops there to introduce encounter sessions and transformational performance methods.

Nevertheless, after the meteoric rise of ETC (they were awarded an OBIE in 1968), the model of the *teatro* spread well beyond audiences of workers. In 1971 ETC published their first edition of its most popular *actos* and offered newly formed *teatros* production rights without charge. In the same year, the El Teatro Nacional de Aztlán (National Theatre of Aztlán), or TENAZ, was established and began to hold festivals, conferences, and, most importantly, workshops in collective creation techniques across the country. Soon these included representative ensembles from Latin and South America such as Enrique Buenaventura's Cáli Experimental Theatre that established a fertile intercultural exchange that characterizes Chicano ensemble-based creation to this day.

Teatro de la Esperanza, formed by Jorge Huerta in Santa Barbara, California, in 1971, exemplifies the trajectory of many Chicano/a companies of this period. Their ensemble-authored *Guadalupe* (1973) paved the way to their transformation into a true collective after Huerta's departure, which would then go on to create and produce *La victima*. But a European tour of the show fractured the company, and while rebuilding they turned mostly to theatre for youth productions (*hijos*) that could be funded through CETA grants. The ensemble struggled in the late 1970s due to the regular need to bring in directors to stage what were essentially collaboratively created texts (a not-uncommon issue in devised theatre today), and this sometimes caused friction. They also suffered, like many Chicano troupes, from funding shortfalls as civil right initiatives were rolled back over the decades and found themselves having to make the difficult decision whether to create and perform for more affluent audiences and form alliances with the professional theatre. But they remained active and devoted to the goal of becoming a true Marxist collective into the 1980s, hosting Latin American and Cuban companies as well as the TENAZ Festival and touring in Mexico and Cuba. As local arts funding dried up in the 1980s, the company took advantage of a spike in interest by the Ford Foundation in Hispanic theatre (created in part by the success, in theatre and film, of Valdez's *Zoot Suit*, the first Hispanic play ever to reach Broadway) and used a grant to relocate fulltime to San Francisco in 1987, hoping to find a permanent base. Exemplary of the experience of many politically motivated companies, Esperanza encountered difficulties in addressing varied publics and increasingly found itself compromising the collective spirit by turning over text creation to a single individual, seeking out topics and issues not relevant solely to their immediate community, and the like. On top of this, as San Francisco, and its Latino population has grown wealthier during the rise of Silicon Valley, the anti-capitalist basis of their work is less well received than in the past.

But dozens of Chicano/a devising companies continued to appear. Su Teatro formed in 1972 at the University of Colorado-Denver. After a decade of creating devised skits and agitprop performances, they found a permanent home in Denver (El Centro de Teatro Su) and opened it with *Chicano Studies 101*. The show marked a novel, but across activist ensembles a not uncommon, shift toward full-length plays, and this one gained notoriety by playing at New York's Public Theater. With its growing reputation, Teatro Su developed an interdisciplinary Latino cultural center featuring film festivals and a cultural arts training institute.

Later, Culture Clash, a cross between a stand-up comedy troupe and performance art (which they term "irreverent Chicanismo"), formed in 1984 (on Cinco de Mayo) in San Francisco. After performing cabaret-style comedy sketches that often echoed the humor of *actos* and the form of *carpas* in which song, dance, and poetry mix within a narrative, their first full-length play, *The Mission*, toured broadly in 1988 and played at the Los Angeles Theatre Center, where they established a base. *Bowl of Beings*, which introduced the ensemble's willingness to mock even the Chicano movement of which they were a part, played there in 1990 and a made-for-television version was broadcast in 1992 on PBS. As they extended their tours across the country (sometimes supported by Rockefeller grants), the ensemble initiated forms of community outreach that generated new material via local interviews touching on the experience of a wider array of minority cultures. *Radio Mambo: Culture Clash Invades Miami* (1994) addressed the experiences of the local Cuban population. Culture Clash performances are more highly improvised than most ensemble-created work, and so printed scripts make up only the skeletal framework for what actually happens onstage and in the group's regular interactions with the audience. Much of the humor derives from Brechtian play with the gap between performer and the various personae built up throughout the show, which often cross barriers of race, ethnicity, and gender through drag scenes and a vaudevillian pace of transformations and inversions. As they moved into the twenty-first century, Culture Clash became something of a Latino institution, performing regularly at campuses and receiving reverential reviews from both professional and academic critics (though also criticism for celebrating patriarchal and even homophobic elements of *la raza*). They have nimbly navigated changing notions of political correctness, in part by mocking them mercilessly but on occasion—such as foregoing the use of drag by bringing in a female performer (Eileen Galindo) for the first time to perform the female (as well as several male) parts in *Chavez Ravine* (2003)—by acknowledging changing cultural contexts. While they continue in the line of ETC by creating politically charged performances, their willingness to ridicule even the sacrosanct figures of Chicano/Latino culture (including Valdez himself), along with a postmodern sensibility with regard to the fluidity and performativity of identity, set their work firmly within the third wave of collective creation. Their success has spawned a number of similar comedy-based ensembles (Chicano Secret Service, ChUSMA, SalSoul, Latino Comedy Project), who often perform with similar groups such as 18 Mighty Mountain Warriors representing, for instance, Asian-American communities.

Gay and Queer Ensembles

Even if one considers Charles Ludlam's Theatre of the Ridiculous to have engaged in ensemble creation—while ample room existed for company members to improvise in performance, texts were assembled by Ludlam and he was careful to establish copyright over them—gay theatre in the 1970s was mostly playwright based. John Vaccaro's Play-House of the Ridiculous collaborated with Warhol's Factory but never produced classically ensemble-created work. Theatre Rhinoceros, founded in San Francisco by Allan Estes in 1977, did not regularly create collectively, instead producing plays by Harvey Fierstein (including what would become his *Torch Song* Trilogy) and others; however, in 1984 Estes organized more than twenty Bay Area playwrights to devise *The AIDS Show*, the first theatrical work to address the crisis (it was not produced because Estes died of AIDS that year). The San Francisco Gay Men's Theatre Collective staged *Crimes against Nature* (1977)—"a play by faggots about survival"—devised by collecting personal narratives from gay men struggling to articulate their identities (and thus vamping off the recent success of *A Chorus Line*). It toured for two years and was revived in 1997 by the New Conservatory Theatre. Diversionary Theatre formed in San Diego in 1986 at the height of the AIDS crisis, devising adaptions of texts by Fassbinder and others, although primarily supporting playwrights. Like many regional theatres today, however, they have begun to book devised work such as the Civilians' *This Beautiful City* in 2018.

Companies like the Hot Peaches (in New York) and the Cockettes (in San Francisco, with their founder, Hibiscus, returning to New York with Angels of Light in the early 1970s) composed their revues collaboratively, and most of the music was composed within the company, following the tradition of forebears like The Jewel Box Revue, which began in 1939 and persevered until 1975. The Cockettes formed in 1969, initially performing unscripted and mostly improvised takeoffs on B movies, but as their fame grew and they began performing shows monthly, the composition of the performances became slightly more coherent and allowed individual performers to devise short skits that would be shuffled and rearranged, Happening-like, from show to show. By the time they produced the full three-act performance of *Pearls over Shanghai* (replete in a cache of costumes lifted from a travelling Beijing Opera company), Divine and John Waters were regular contributors. They disbanded by 1972, although many individual performers continued to form similar groups (such as Ze Whiz Kidz in Seattle) and the outstanding vocalist Sylvester would find fame as a disco singer (Weissman and Weber 2002; Mailik 2017). Their work establishes a trajectory followed by solo performers such as Taylor Busch, Bradford Louryk, and Taylor Mac (Edgecomb 2007).

The notion of making ensemble-created theatre during the height of the AIDS crisis staggers the imagination, given the challenges of maintaining a company over long periods to develop and devise under the exigent circumstances in which the gay community found itself after 1981. But in 1991 Michael Rohd organized his Hope Is Vital program in Washington, DC, which featured local youth devising with HIV+ men, and by 1999 there were over one hundred groups operating across the country (Rohd published *Theatre for Community Conflict: The Hope Is Vital Training Manual* in 1995). Collective action also meant political action, and ACT UP and other organizations (Queer Nation organized in 1990) took inspiration from the radical guerilla theatre collectives of the 1960s to stage memorable interventions: converging on FDA buildings wearing white lab coats and with hands painted with blood, chaining themselves to the pews of Saint Patrick's Cathedral in New York (where one activist removed the Communion host placed on his tongue by Archbishop O'Connor), and interrupting the *CBS Evening News*.

By the late 1980s and early 1990s, AIDS activism was diversifying and LGBTQ ensembles began to form. Some, like Boston's The Theatre Offensive (founded in 1989), emerged from guerilla theatre groups (in this case United Fruit Workers, which formed in 1985) involved in AIDS protests. About Face Youth Theatre formed in Chicago in 1995, becoming an Equity company premiering new writing, performance installations, and ensemble-created work. Following the hate crime murder of Matthew Shephard 1998 in Wyoming, they inaugurated About Face Youth Theatre, which devises its own work (Johnston and Paz Brownrigg 2019). This model, of a major Equity house presenting mostly text-based work while an outreach program develops devised work, would fast become popular in other locales. It signals both the practicality of maintaining devised work as part of a theatre's programming and also the desire for ensemble performance to engage with the social turn in art (see Volume 2). In many instances, it is the outreach programs hosted by the major devising companies in the United States that maintain the idealized notions of collectivity and radical cultural politics from the 1960s, and in many instances these have welcomed LGBTQ artists and youth to participate in various forms of applied theatre practice.

Applied Theatre

Although not all community- and development-based or educational theatres are rooted in ensemble creation, these sectors lend themselves well to such practice, particularly when political and/or pedagogical goals form the primary intention to create. Ensemble-building itself is, of course, a form of community practice, and the decentered creative structure common to devising invites varying levels of participation from professional and nonprofessional contributors at every stage of development. The longer history of collective creation in the United States and elsewhere is deeply intertwined with community activism, social art, and education, and all of these feed into the collectives of the 1960s. Because of ensemble creation's long-standing connections to popular theatre and to workers' theatre, settlement house performance, theatre in education, theatre for young audiences, *creación colectiva*, and other cognate genres that featured collective and participatory forms of creation during the transnational "first wave" of collective creation (1900–50), it was inevitable that these political concerns would carry over to the succeeding second and third waves. Although the appellation "applied theatre" does not circulate widely until the 1990s and find regular use in the United States until after Phillip Taylor published *Applied Theatre: Creating Transformative Encounters in the Community* in 2003, the term can be applied retroactively to subsume a number of practices.

Theory and practice mutually and self-consciously enrich one another in theatre directed toward community cultural development and outreach.

The 1970s saw the flourishing of the "open classroom" movement (named after Herbert R. Kohl's 1969 book of the same title) that directed educators to develop curricula in which students participated more directly in the discovery of knowledge. At the same time, and linked to the constructivist theories of John Dewey and Jean Piaget, Paolo Freire's more radical education reforms laid out in *Pedagogy of the Oppressed* (1968; English translation 1970) entered US theatre discourse, often via the Forum Theatre methods of Augusto Boal (*Theatre of the Oppressed* was published in 1973 and translated into English in 1979). Critical pedagogy models were quickly passed along through workshops and incorporated into a number of ensembles working with marginalized communities in prisons, men's and women's shelters, at-risk communities, and youth organizations.

At the peak of the second wave during the 1960s, an important element determining the "alternative" status of the renowned collectives of the period was their intention to address countercultural communities and to use theatre as an agent of social, political, and cultural change. The Harding and Rosenthal *Restaging the Sixties* shows how the 1960s companies that survive into the present do so by drawing upon their earlier interests in audience interactivity, shared creativity, and participatory politics in order to connect more closely with communities. Thus, grassroots and community-based theatres that formed during the 1970s and beyond often reference as important influences the Living Theatre, SFMT, the Free Southern Theatre, Bread and Puppet, and ETC. Because of these continuities, grassroots, community-based, and educational forms of theatre most emphatically continue the 1960s utopian rhetoric of anti-hierarchical creation, anti-Establishment intentions, and egalitarianism. These ensembles were likely to evoke notions of ritual and *communitas* during the 1970s and 1980s that were muted in the profiles of contemporary mainstream devising companies. Indeed, it is increasingly clear that the major influence of the 1960s collectives was on the historical development of the various forms of ensemble-based applied theatre, including grassroots community theatre, forum theatre, and theatre in education, rather than on the trajectory that feeds into the work of the nonutopian, third-wave devising companies who do not identify with particular communities (bearing in mind that these are by no means mutually exclusive). When critics describe how American ensemble theatres turned away from politics and specific ideological positions after the long 1960s, they really are selecting from a narrow tranche of practice and neglecting the vast (and expanding) field of applied theatre. This trajectory will substantially affect directions that devised theatre takes moving into the new millennium.

Thus, in contradistinction to the existing narrative of American collective creation, that it went into decline because identity politics blew apart the desire for communality and collectivity that characterized the 1960s companies, we can see how the rise of identity politics actually spurred greater interest and diversity in how ensemble-based theatre might connect with specific communities in more direct and local ways. Against the grain of the tired stereotype of the 1970s and 1980s as the "Me Decade" (Thomas Wolfe), the "culture of narcissism" (Christopher Lasch), or a period of rampant hedonism, real data shows that Sam Lovejoy's explanation is closer to the mark: "The movement did not die. It did the most intelligent thing it could do; it went to find a home. It went into the community. It's working, unnoticed, in the neighborhood" (quoted in Miller, Douglas 1996, 139). Not surprisingly, after 1968 many former counterculture activists translated a questionable notion of total political revolution and liberation into grassroots activism focused on a search for meaningful community and social justice. In addition to the scores who flocked to professions in teaching, social services, law, and medicine, many activists pursued careers as applied theatre-makers: and many of these formed ensembles that maintained some of the utopian energy of the 1960s collectives.

Thus, the line from 1960s activist theatre to the forms of applied theatre that emerge after the former's loss of preeminence mark not a decline, but a rethinking of the aims and methods of realizing the 1960s dream of forging direct and substantial connections with the audience and the larger community or underground. As Jan Cohen-Cruz explains:

> By the late 1970s, a localized impulse manifested itself as identity politics, with artists, too, clustering around communities of ethnicity (as, Latino), circumstances (as, elderly) sexual orientation (as, gay). Dell 'Arte supporter Peter Pennekemp identifies this as a move from opposition to affirmation, citing Bernice Johnson Reagon's insight: "Remember when you first recognized injustice? And thought that of you saw it you could change it? Joined with like-minded people, worked at it for years, and eventually felt somewhat defeated? You know what was wrong with the way we approached it? We went out to do battle every day to win, rather than because it was the right way to lead a life." The result is what Lucy Lippard calls "the lure of the local," less about fighting injustice generally than providing alternative voices on the local level. (Leonard and Kilkelly 2006, 11)

Cohen-Cruz points to a critical mass of grassroots community-directed theatres arising in the early 1970s. From companies forming in the very small and remote towns of the country (for example, the Road Company in Johnson City, Tennessee in 1970) to others taking shape in dense urban areas to address the aftermath of civil unrest (precipitated by issues like the school busing riots that followed implementation of the 1971 Supreme Court ruling addressing school desegregation), forms of theatre intended not only to intervene in different communities, but to make them active co-creators of the work, appeared in impressive numbers. Supported by funding streams both old (Johnson's 1964 Economic Opportunity Act) and new (CETA), by the mid-1970s grassroots theatre was on the rise, particularly in the South. The Alternate ROOTS (Regional Organization of Theaters South) formed in 1976, representing dozens of individual artists and arts companies, devoted to social change across fourteen states and Washington, DC.

Many of the earliest applied theatre companies of the 1970s utilizing collective creation were offshoots of the guerilla theatre movement of the 1960s such as the Pageant City Players and the City Street Theatre (New York City), Boston's Street Player's Union, the Black Power group Concept East (Detroit), San Francisco Red Theatre, The East Bay Sharks (out of Berkeley), Bodacious Buggerilla in Los Angeles, and the feminist Liberation News Service (comprised of members of Women's International Terrorist Conspiracy from Hell [WITCH]). As the politics of guerilla theatre gave way to the less confrontational goals of applied theatre, a number of collaborative ensembles arose to rebuild fractured communities following flashpoints like the race riots in Watts (1965), Newark, New Jersey (1967), and, in the wake of Martin Luther King's assassination in 1968, across the country but most violently in Baltimore and Detroit. Chicago's Free Street Theatre, still in existence, came into being following the rioting and community breakdowns that followed the Democratic National Convention in the city in 1968.

With political and countercultural ferment waning in the large metropolitan centers following Nixon's election, the movement began to splinter and many activists and artists sought both escape and new forms of community by relocating to rural areas, while others already living outside urban centers directed their efforts toward social justice within their own neighborhoods. After training with Jacob Moreno in psychodrama, Maryat Lee left her pathbreaking SALT street theatre company in New York in 1970 in order to return to her native Appalachian region, settling in West Virginia. She launched her EcoTheatre in 1975 as a means to investigate "indigenous theatre," in which all facets, from stories to performers to audiences, must have deep connections to the place of the performance, often staged in site-specific locales (French 1998; Swedberg 2006). In the first years, the ensemble received small state grants that allowed Lee to hire, train, and make use of nearby summer youth program students for performers. Lee struggled to present work with nonprofessional actors (and reported on her methods in the pages of *TDR* on several occasions), a flashpoint in applied theatre more generally. Although mostly celebratory of the lives and stories that the company gathered, improvised around, and then set to texts (which often changed following audience responses), works like *A Double-threaded Life: The Hinton Play* also ask the community to question its history and present situation: the play ends with the line "A door opens," suggesting the necessity to confront change. Lee's EcoTheatre produced until her death in 1989.

Carpetbag Theatre Company (incorporated in 1970) was established in the African-American and working-class communities of Knoxville, Tennessee, and is associated with the historically black Knoxville College. Like many grassroots ensembles, they have not promoted themselves as a collective but never had to do so, necessity shaping that structure organically. The company has always used forms of the story circle as well as documentary and/or investigative methods to gather the histories and experiences of their community, which are "woven with original music and dance, drawing from vernacular traditions of gospel, blues, funk and other African-American forms" (Leonard 2006, 51). Like many grassroots companies, Carpetbag uses collaborative creation to reawaken local history. *Red Summer* was based on the Knoxville race riots of 1919, while *Dark Cowgirls and Prairie Queens* investigated the marginalized black women of the American West to comment on similar forms of invisibility in the present. The collective creative structure provides opportunity for multiple viewpoints to be presented, a feature of their Boal-inspired politics.

Other such community-based ensembles forming in the 1970s include Doug Paterson's Dakota Theatre Caravan, whose long association with that state is detailed by Mark Weinberg (1992). Cornerstone Theatre, too, originally produced community-inspired work as a traveling ensemble in the Dakotas in the late 1980s before opting for a multiethnic base in Los Angeles beginning in 1992, joining a host of ensembles addressing urban issues. Cornerstone built upon past forms of guerilla and street theatre with their "rapid response theatre" after the 1992 Rodney King riots and also inaugurated the "bridge shows" that cast members of different communities (often those in tension) in a single show. They are best known for their multiyear production cycles devised around related themes such as "Faith,"

"Justice," "Hunger," and "Change." Sonia Kuftinec's 2003 monograph on their work initiated an important critical examination of community-based theatre by both celebrating the company's achievements and also drawing attention to the difficulties of conducting an ethical ethnography of diverse communities.

Across the country, Pregones Theatre, founded in 1979, has provided a link to the traditions of Caribbean and Latin American ensemble creation (*colectivos*) from their base in the South Bronx. Initially a traveling troupe performing across the Northeast, they eventually established a permanent home in the Morrisania neighborhood. They were among the first to receive funding from the Mellon/Doris Duke Ensemble Theatre Program (and cofounder Rosalba Rolón is a 2019 recipient, along with Muriel Miguel of Spiderwoman, of a Doris Duke Artist Award). Because the company includes both Nuyoricans raised in the United States and Spanish-speaking artists arriving from Puerto Rico and other Latin American countries, their style is heavily visual and often weaves music into the devised pieces and adaptations they feature. After many years of collaborating with other community-based devising companies like Roadside and Junebug, Pregones recently merged with the even more established Puerto Rican Traveling Theatre.

WagonBurner Theatre Troop [*sic*] was founded in 1993 in Iowa City to represent the voices of Native Americans. Their work takes place on reservations such as Rosebud, South Dakota, and in Native American urban communities and features a mix of satire and social critique. *Indian Radio Days* (1993) was originally penned by WagonBurner director LeAnn Howes and the late Roxy Gordon but developed further in each performance by the company as humorous "commercials" were added. Most pieces are developed in conversation with local communities and adapted to the particular challenges they face.

Though not strictly an applied theatre company, Bloomsburg Theatre Ensemble, also a founding member of NET, formed in 1978 after students at Northwestern University decamped to Eagles Mere, Pennsylvania, to study with Alvina Krause. She ran a summer theatre in which students fulfilled every creative and administrative task, similar to the Winedale (Texas) program that would produce the Rude Mechs in 1996. While not the first company to originate out of a theatre training program, they are characteristic of the trend that saw much of the 1960s counterculture's idealism find refuge in American institutions of higher learning in the 1970s and 1980s and pay forward their practice in new forms of activist theatre and art. Krause died in 1981, but the troupe continues in its mission—notably without ever naming an artistic director but instead electing a rotating "Ensemble

Director"—to carry forward the example of Harold Clurman's Group Theatre by maintaining a creative ensemble of artists who produce both canonical, "universal" drama in the same season they offer ensemble-created work responsive to its rural community (such as *Mimescape* during their founding year and *Hard Coal: Life in the Region*, 1999). In 1980 they took up residence in a renovated cinema, now renamed the Alvina Krause Theatre, from which they tirelessly promote ensemble-based community theatre.

Documentary theatre crosses over a number of applied theatre formats and has a long history within the longer trajectory of collective creation (Favorini 2013). The use of testimonials, verbatim material drawn from documents and archives, and interviews conducted by company members often form the basis of an ensemble's creative process and sometimes, particularly in community-based theatre, the primary content of a show. Although it was rarely highlighted, many of the 1960s collectives used documentary sources as material around which to build improvisations, as for instance the Open Theater's use of newspaper and TV accounts of the Vietnam War in *Viet Rock* and the Free Southern Theater's use of Martin Duberman's *In White America* as the basis for their first production of *In White America: A Documentary Play*. With the status of documentation and its relationship to objective truth increasingly under suspicion in our heavily mediated age, the focus of much contemporary work is directed toward highlighting the forms of mediation that take place in any act of reportage. This highlights the "contradictory multivocality inherent in historic event" (Favorini 2013, 109), a quality enabled by collective creation and one reason why creative ensembles have been drawn to the form. Moisés Kaufman's Tectonic Project (formed in 1991) is built around "Moment Work" that involves group improvisations and development that constitute a form of performance writing (though Kaufman is always listed as the playwright and director). In their early years, the company performed site-specific versions of Kroetz and Beckett, but in 1996 they initiated their first collaboration with a living playwright, Naomi Iizuka, who participated in the company's Moment Work while writing *Marlowe's Eye* (1996). Sometimes, as in their best-known work *The Laramie Project* (2000), credits are recorded for writer-directors, associate writers, and numerous dramaturgs in recognition that some of the verbatim material is drawn from company members' reflections on the interviews they conducted. The outstanding success of the show helped bring documentary theatre back as a platform for devised work after a long period when the genre was linked exclusively to playwrights (like Emily Mann) and solo performance artists (Anna Deavere Smith). Tellingly, more recent companies like the Civilians, sensitive to the suspect connotations of the "document," opt for the more equivocal term "investigative theatre" (see the essay by Sarah Freeman in the second volume).

Physical Theatre

Although the terminology, here as elsewhere in relationship to collaborative creation, is sometimes slippery, in general "physical theatre" describes practices unique to collective creation and distinct from forms of physical expressiveness used conventionally to interpret a preexisting text. Training in physical theatre typically prepares the performer in creative improvisatory techniques of the kind nurtured in collective creation. The creative, rather than interpretive, use to which physical training is put in ensemble creation is one of the most significant attributes of its aesthetic, opening up an interdisciplinary practice that incorporates dance, clowning, *commedia*, puppetry, mime and mask, and placing the body (and embodiment) on an equal footing with text in the creation of form, meaning, and affect: "Indeed, it has been argued that any account of contemporary forms of body-based theatre is at the same time a history of devised work generated through the various models of collaborative practice" (Murray and Keefe 2016 [2007], 23; see also Chamberlain 2007, 151–6).

The sources of physical training that feed into developments in ensemble creation are myriad, a fact sometimes distorted by the singular focus on Artaud's theories and Grotowski's contributions to the collectives of the 1960s. Both were certainly grounded in the body and explored somatic processes for creating meaning on stage but differed in significant ways from mime training and carried certain theoretical and spiritual investments not usually associated with the great traditions of corporeal mime, nor with other important methods such as Laban analysis, Feldenkrais, Michael Chekhov, and more recent arrivals like Viewpoints, Williamson Technique, Rasaboxes, and Lucid Body. Other sources of inspiration and training arrived with new mime-dance ensembles like Pilobolus (founded in 1971), the Flying Karamasov Brothers (who started busking in Santa Cruz, California, in 1973), and Mummenschanz, the latter touring America from their base in Lugano, Switzerland, beginning in 1972. The extravagant shows that the Quebecois *nouveau cirque* company, Cirque du Soleil, brought to American in the late 1980s inspired new modes of storytelling founded on spectacular physical performance that would be picked up by Lookingglass and other ensembles.

American Ensemble Theatres, 1970–95

Most vital to the continued development of ensemble-based physical theatre in the United States was the growing familiarity with the *autocours* training employed by Lecoq's "creative theatre," which features improvisatory, nonhierarchical ensemble creation (Murphy and Sherman 2013; Thompson 2007 and 2013; see also the chapter on Pig Iron Theatre by Kathryn Syssoyeva in Volume 2). Centers for corporeal mime expanded after the long 1960s and included Tony Montanaro's Celebration Mime Barn, founded in 1972 in South Paris, Maine (which continues to train performers for immersive theatre), as well as the Leonard Pitts Mime School established in Berkeley in 1970. Building upon the reputation of SFMT, mime-based ensemble theatres proliferated in the 1970s and 1980s, opening in Wichita, Kansas (Actor's Mime Theatre), New York (Margolis Brown Adaptors, Kupperberg Morris Movement Theatre), Ohio (Invisible People Mime Theatre), North Carolina (Touch), and New Hampshire (Kitchensink Theatre). Many of these ensembles were committed to sharing their training, and so complemented their public performance work with educational and applied theatre outreach programs, a model still followed by contemporary devising ensembles. A number of American artists have participated in Ariane Mnouchkine's Paris seminar, including recently some members of Pig Iron Theatre; their own new Advanced Performer Training school, in conjunction with the University of the Arts in Philadelphia, offers an MA in Lecoq-inspired devising practices.

One of the earliest American ensembles to import physical theatre to the United States, the Dell'Arte International School of Physical Theatre (originally the Dell'Arte School of Mime and Comedy) formed as a hybrid community-based/international touring company devising original work first in Berkeley (1971) and then, after 1975, in Blue Lake, California (population 1,200). Essentially, in the early years the school and community-based work served as the platform on which to create the professional work of the touring company, with popular theatre forms that can be learned or enjoyed at both nonprofessional and professional levels as common ground (Canavan 2013). The company could apply for small local, state, and even federal grants based in community development as one of the few rural professional ensemble theatres in the country and thereby forge an indigenous audience for what they call "Theatre of Place," which emphasizes local stories, histories, and crises as theatrical material. Meanwhile, their international tours took place within an ecology of festivals and alternative venues in countries with more robust traditions of physical theatre, and so they were able to connect with established practitioners and audiences there.

Finally, the school became an important source of future performers trained in mask, *commedia*, acrobatics, contact improvisation, and the like which generated trained professionals to spread the word and sustain American interest in the form. Among its luminaries, Robert Francesconi established the influential physical movement-based training program at the University of North Carolina School of the Arts, active since 1978. Today, Dell'Arte oversees both a small (114-seat) indoor theatre and a larger (350-seat) outdoor theatre and maintains an ensemble of close to twenty regular members who run the school for a full year-long term as well as short-term summer intensives. Dell'Arte has established a number of outreach programs with local schools and campuses and hosts the Mad River Festival of cabarets and experimental performance. Like many companies who have survived this long, they have devolved from a strict model of collective administration to a more flexible and layered one that "ensemble members call the 'Hub.' This structure defines how power is shared through several specific people, emanating outwards to include all who associate with the organization" (Leonard 2006, 102).

Theatre de la Jeune Lune, founded by Lecoq students who relocated to Minneapolis in 1978, combined physically expressive productions of classical plays with occasional ensemble-created work (*Goodbye Paradis Can Can* [1983], *Children of Paradise: Shooting a Dream* [1992], *Description of the World* [2001], among others). They raised the visibility and stature of physical performance considerably, garnering the Tony for Best Regional Theatre in 2005 and thereby helping to establish the form as a viable platform for mainstream audiences in the United States and collective creation as an effective means to capitalize on the blend of mime, clowning, dance, and even opera featured in the work (Thompson 2007). Their focus on epic storytelling through physical means would influence the work of SITI, Lookingglass, and Pig Iron as well as later ensembles like Theatre Movement Bazaar and immersive theatre companies like Third Rail Projects in Brooklyn. The company endured until funding dried up following the Great Recession in 2008, one of a number of companies (as well as regional and for-profit theatres) that folded due to economic exigency.

There had been pockets of mime-based ensemble theatres outside New York and California. Stacy Klein's Double Edge, established as a feminist theatre in Boston in 1982 before relocating, in 1994, to a former dairy farm Asheville, Massachusetts, developed a visceral and visual style based on Klein's training with Rena Mirecka, a founding member of Grotowski's Theatre of 13 Rows in Opole, Poland. The company produced a series of five devised cycles, beginning with the Women's Cycle in 1982 and continuing through today with the Latin American Cycle, many of which have toured internationally. From the beginning it was run as an art cooperative with members contributing to creative and administrative duties. Over the years the company has incorporated puppetry and voice training, which they now offer through a year-round training program. Beginning in 2002, Klein initiated a Summer Spectacle, often site-specific and based on well-known fictional texts but serving as a springboard to investigate identity and the nature of democracy. Stein herself was awarded a Doris Duke Performing Artist Award in 2013 in recognition of her sustained and significant influence on both physical and community-based theatre, and the company's work is featured in both an award-winning documentary (*Theatre on the Edge*, directed by Julie Akeret 2012) and an American Theatre Wing "Working in the Theatre" online video.

Touchstone Theatre (formed in Bethlehem, Pennsylvania, in 1991) adheres to Lecoq-based somatic forms of expression over verbal dialogue in order to connect more directly with its communities through street performance and staged work. In alliance with Lehigh University, they sponsored a festival in 1994 celebrating and featuring Lecoq's own company. Often picking up ensemble members trained at Dell'Arte and Double Edge, Touchstone, like other physical theatre companies, has been forced to adopt a looser notion of ensemble as the historically itinerant artists of the form tend to move on to other challenges. This is particularly taxing for a community-based physical theatre, whose artists ideally form lasting connections in the area in which they perform. Also, their work was at the center of debates at the turn of the millennium regarding the relative radicality of community-based theatres whose work must operate in uncomfortable proximity to local power in order to secure funding, permits, and permissions, an issue that stalks applied theatre in particular but alternative theatre more generally (Brady 2000; Jackson 2011).

The late 1980s saw several circus-based street theatres forming, including the still-active Circus Amok (formed in 1989), which combines drag elements from Ludlam's Theatre of the Ridiculous with postmodern dance and mask performance. Influenced by the Bread and Puppet Theatre, they are renowned for presenting queer spectacles on the avenues and in the parks of New York City. Amok turns the circus "freak show" into a platform for destabilizing gender assumptions, while also commenting on social issues such as income disparity and the mechanization of labor under late capitalism.

Several companies pursued hybrid performance configurations that featured corporeal mime, dance/movement, and text, often accompanied by brilliant visual design (sometimes inspired by workshops and seminars with Mnouchkine in Paris). Stemming from the work of Foreman, Wilson, and West Coast companies like George Coates Performance, Snake Theatre, the Modus Ensemble, and Alan Finneran's Soon 3, this American version of what is termed in the UK "visual theatre" is often helmed by an auteur but sometimes engages in forms of collaborative creation. This multidisciplinary work crosses a number of categories and provides many examples of postmodern theatre, multimedia and intermedial theatre, site-specific performance, and immersive theatre. An important influence was German *tanztheater*, brought to the United States in 1984 when Pina Bausch's Tanztheater Wuppertal appeared at the BAM Next Wave Festival.

Perhaps the best-known contemporary company to emerge from these influences is Big Dance Theatre, established in 1991 under artistic director Annie-B. Parson (who also worked with the Brooklyn-based Irondale Ensemble, which formed in 1983) and collaborator Paul Lazar. Their work has gained an international reputation based on its quirky treatment of canonical texts—highlighting how dance theatre has embraced text and thus indicating a significant break with the radical 1960s ensembles—and its infusion of dance and scenography. Like many third-wave companies, Big Dance maintains a loose affiliation with scores of associate artists working across movement, music, and design, allowing them to explore a wide variety of styles and to tour extensively overseas: next to the Wooster Group, they are likely the most sought-after and commissioned ensemble for the EU fringe festival circuit (and have even performed at London's Old Vic). The company has earned numerous Bessie and OBIE awards, and Parson was awarded a Guggenheim Fellowship in 2007 and a Doris Duke Performing Artist Award in 2014, making Big Dance one of the most high-profile ensembles of the twenty-first century. They are among the leaders in breaching the long-standing divide between devising companies and major regional theatres and have toured to Hartford Stage, Berkeley Rep, and other venues. As will be seen in the second volume of *American Theatre Ensembles*, visual theatre (in its most hybrid definition) makes up a significant percentage of contemporary American mainstream ensembles, and many have felt Big Dance's influence.

Postmodern Ensembles

Among companies whose ensemble work did not attach itself to a particular community, constituency, or training regimen, two—Mabou Mines, formed in 1970, and the Wooster Group, producing since the mid-1970s and incorporated under that name in 1980—are regularly featured as exemplary of a second generation of American collective creation marked by both continuities and departures from the radical work of the 1960s. Sometimes that engendering is portrayed as an oedipal break, especially when the Wooster Group's split from Schechner's Performance Group is the focus, and in other cases, the succeeding generation is seen as emerging from different sources and precedents, as when Mabou Mines was linked with the theatres of Richard Foreman and Robert Wilson in Bonnie Marranca's *The Theatre of Images* (1977), and Aronson (2000) chose to treat the Wooster Group alongside performance art. What seems clear, referencing the porous border between what Syssoyeva calls the second and third wave of international collective creation, is that the work and the influence of these companies provide the main conduit through which devised theatre develops in the United States. Their complex response to the companies of the 1960s sets up a rethinking and revision of the legacy of collective creation that carries into, and helps shape, developments for the remainder of the millennium and into twenty-first-century ensemble theatre.

After the counterculture energy of the 1960s began to disperse after 1968, the idealized utopias and revolutions imagined and sought after by activists came into question. With reference to the overtly political collectives, Jan Kott's "After Grotowski: The End of the Impossible Theatre" (1984) detailed the manner by which much of the radical theatre of the 1960s was compromised by its own extreme commitments to embodiment, presence, the liberation of consciousness, and various idealizations of freedom. His despondent conclusion evoked both Artaud and Jonestown, implicating not just Grotowski but the Living Theatre and Peter Brook and other adherents of a "holy" theatre in the unintended consequence of pursuing impossible utopias in which the pursuit of the most primal impulses provided not the release of anarcho-pacifism or participatory democracy, but obeisance to charismatic cult leaders and the devastation of the plague. As a result of these and other factors, the work of creative ensembles in the 1970s began to take on the shade of the third wave's postutopic wariness, dampening the extreme liberatory promises of performance and authenticity in general and collective creation in particular. As seen above, this drove politically active ensembles who sought to maintain some of the 1960s collectives' ideals into grassroots and constituency-based theatres to pursue more measured progress off the mainstream radar. What emerged among higher-profile companies pursuing artistic goals was a practice that sought inspiration and influence from a wider variety of sources than only the radical American theatre groups: even when the latter were evoked (as with Lookingglass's and Pig Iron's initial interest in Grotowski's ideas and training in the late 1980s), they were revived mostly absent the cultural context in which their underlying utopian programs originally resonated.

When second-generation US ensembles are placed within their own historical contexts, critical studies point to the influence of postmodern ideas on new forms of collaborative creation (Savran 1986; Vanden Heuvel 1993; Kaye 1994; Auslander 1994). Heddon and Milling make a strong case that "devising processes match contemporary [postmodern] critical concerns, making it the ideal means to explore and embody those concerns in practice. … a layered, fragmented, and non-linear 'text,' one specifically courting various perspectives and viewpoints, perhaps lends itself more readily to the group devising process" (2006, 192). Significant in this regard is the influence of movements in visual art, dance, and cinema that arose in the 1960s alongside, and often intersecting with, the radical theatre practice of 1960s collectives. As much as the new generation of collaborative theatre-makers were turning away from the utopian projects and earnest search for forms of authenticity that characterized the 1960s collectives, they were also drawn to the radical aesthetic experiments of the 1960s underground scene: Minimalism, Pop Art, Body Art, and Happenings, as well as to New Wave and Punk and the early postmodern explorations of Cage's aesthetics of chance and indeterminacy as these were explored in Happenings and in dance at Judson Church (McLeod 2019). Aronson (2000) draws a number of these threads together as he marks the shift from the last gasps of modernist theatre in the work of the 1960s collectives and the emergence of the recognizably postmodern practice of Robert Wilson, Richard Foreman, Meredith Monk, and Martha Clarke.

Even before the discourse around postmodernism had fully developed, the work of new ensembles like the Wooster Group, Mabou Mines, and Ping Chong's Fiji Company was often said to be engaged in collaborative (rather than collective) creation, using interdisciplinary and intercultural methods that combined dialogue and dramatic action with dance, mime, puppetry, Asian movement or acting styles, media such as televisions and tape recorders, and a shifting relationship between character and performer. This aesthetic of hybridity in every element of performance marked the greatest shift in sensibilities from the collectives of the 1960s, which in most instances were dedicated to some Americanized variation of a "poor theatre" ethos; that is, the stripping away of every inessential component of theatre that rendered its authenticity suspect. This grounded the actor training of the period and its focus on distilling the performer's essential presence, provided impetus for the experiments with audience participation and the tactics of guerilla theatre, and undergirded everything from the use of rituals in performance to the aggressive stance toward the authority of preexisting dramatic texts. In contrast, interdisciplinary and intercultural performance, rooted in aesthetic experiments that privileged intertextuality, multimedia, and structures of layered composition that invited multiple points of view, was constructed to mitigate purity and presence. As Nöel Carroll has argued, "Happenings were gestures against an essentialist view of the fine arts whereas the work of the Living Theatre and of Joseph Chaikin's Open Theatre, given their emphasis on the craft and process of acting over the literary dimension of drama, were motivated by a search for the real essence of theatre" (Carroll 1990, 73). Moreover, the focus on authenticity allowed the radical collectives to maintain the avant-garde's historical distance from mass culture, which was deemed irredeemably false and, worse, the bearer of false consciousness. Postmodern performance reconfigures that relation and mines popular and mass culture for its imagery and power to evoke not deep, metaphysical connections but the associative responses and cognitive dissonances that late capitalism has made our habitus. When "everything is in the center," that location becomes a site not of pure presence but a dynamic surfeit of competing signifiers.

Ensembles of the post-1960s generation absorbed and revivified the various crossovers of visual and live art performance in a different register than their forebears—one that did not prioritize authenticity—and thus derived other inspiration. As this hybrid art-performance work was often grounded in anti-essentialist principles and working methods, it found common ground with evolving theories of postmodernism emanating from literary studies, the social sciences, cultural studies, and the emergent field of performance studies. These ideas often undermined Enlightenment notions of the liberal humanist subject as the ground for authentic being and thereby interrogated the basis for much of the radical and utopian theatre of the 1960s avant-garde (Fuchs 1986). Perhaps aligning with the widespread sense of limitations Americans felt owing to the oil crisis and other historical circumstances, the utopianism of the earlier collectives (less so among the line of applied and constituency-based theatres discussed above) gave way to a harder-edged cynicism and that helped lead to the shift toward the nonutopic ethos of the succeeding wave of devised creation.

American Theatre Ensembles Volume 1: Post–1970

Jessica Silsby Brater's essay on Mabou Mines in this volume provides a comprehensive overview of their work spanning the entire chronology of this series. Pertinent to my presentation here is, first, her recognition that the company originally formed as (and remains) a collective even as the members and associates have experimented with every known form of collaborative and devised creation. This both establishes continuity with the collectives of the 1960s and also marks the shift toward a less ideological expression of collectivity, one based in a democratized creative practice rather than a political statement regarding the superiority of collectivity itself. Also significant is the Mines's self-conscious decision to stage their earliest work in galleries rather than conventional theatre spaces, marking their alignment with both visual art and performance art practices. Even when they turned to staging Beckett's work, they concentrated on the dramaticules and late prose (which are bereft of, and often point to the absence of, the kinds of presence pursued by the 1960s collectives) and often staged these in nontheatrical spaces. Although impressed by both the Living Theatre and Grotowski, they nevertheless remained open to other, equally important influences, such as intercultural theatre and experimental film, and evolved from those multiple origin points.

As will be evident from a number of the case studies across both volumes, the Wooster Group plays a singularly important role in the development of American ensemble creation. Under director Liz LeCompte, they have evolved a body of work, a set of creative practices, and an ethos of collaboration that has propagated rhizomatically across US alternative theatre to help produce the dense ecology of ensemble practices that operate today. Their work exemplifies both the continuities and breaks with the previous generation of ensembles—a subject explored explicitly in their own 2004 piece, *Poor Theatre* (see Savran 2005)—and established trajectories for the third wave of devised creation in US theatre. Moreover, their contributions have generated a substantial body of critical writing, which in complex ways has itself proved productive in the development of later ensembles. Alternative theatre-makers and performance artists of the 1970s and 1980s in general, and ensembles in particular, were notably cool to academia's attempts to align new theatrical developments with postmodern theory (Richard Foreman is a notable exception). But as these theories coalesced into a confederation of critical approaches by which to rethink performance, gender, representation, the body, and other fundamental theatrical concepts, they altered disciplinary formations in the academy, making the study of marginalized forms of performance a discipline unto itself (in the case of performance studies) or a topic that might be encountered in any number of art- and humanities-related disciplines. This affected the manner by which students after the mid-1980s first chanced upon the histories, contexts, and practices of alternative theatre in general and ensemble creation in particular (featured in texts like Theodore Shanks's *Beyond the Boundaries: American Alternative Theatre* by his coverage of first-generation companies like Living Theatre and SFMT and second-generation collaborative ensembles such as the Wooster Group, Mabou Mines, and Squat Theatre). Also, higher education institutions began to host residencies, commission work, and hire artists as guest and permanent faculty (Banes 2000). As the fame of ensembles like the Wooster Group grew, alternative forms of practice circulated in academic as well as conservatory-based training, further institutionalizing forms that would feed into the third weave of devised creation.

But it was the Wooster Group's ensemble practice itself, and the growing national and international acclaim it created, that kept the spirit of collective creation intact and aligned with radical practice after the dispersion of the 1960s collectives. While no single feature of their work comprehensively distinguishes their style as postmodern or marks new directions in collective practice, certainly their interest in proceeding collaboratively, but without a semblance of a predetermined intentionality or meaning, establishes an important break from the work of the 1960s. While those companies were invested in process, and made room for indeterminacy both in collaboration and in performance, the prevailing ethos of authenticity and presence (again, strongly evident in the Performance Group owing to Grotowski's influence) conveyed a clear intention of realizing moments of various kinds of truth: political awareness, consciousness expansion through somatic effort, and the presence of the actor as a unique human being encountering the audience in real time and without the mediation of the fourth wall or the authority of the playwright. As John Freeman (2007, 124) points out, when Adrian Heathfield sets out to specify the collaborative process of Goat Island—who "do not set out to deliver the meaning of their work, but rather they undertake a process of the discovery of meaning *in* their work, and implicate the spectators within this process"—he is recognizing a practice first explored theatrically by the Wooster Group (along with auteurs like Robert Wilson and ensemble directors like Lin Hixson during her time in Los Angeles with the Hangers) and then uniquely developed by Goat Island and other third-wave ensembles. This notion of absenting predetermined goals and sources of presence develops in part from the "landscape" aesthetic of Gertrude Stein (and, from a more *belle lettres* perspective, from Beckett) who, although common reference points for 1960s ensembles, were seldom appropriate models for theatres built on a desire for presence understood in metaphysical terms. The presence or awareness pursued by Stein, Foreman, the Wooster Group, and many ensembles today has more to do with achieving moments of perceptual dynamism that enable productive confusion and/or synesthetic effects, stimulating associative affective and cognitive responses that are powerful but transient. Indeed, the anticipation of groping about with absolute freedom to devise theatre in an unformed vacuum of desires and potentialities, and positioning the spectator in a similar state, is often mentioned as what draws contemporary artists to the practice in the first place, and the Wooster Group is often acknowledged as a model.

Three Places in Rhode Island, the group's first trilogy staged between 1975 and 1980, established them as an important ensemble exploring new combinations of text, dance, media, scenography, and task-oriented acting, all quite unique at the time. While carrying forward elements of 1960s performance, such as environmental staging, these were always modified to better capture the pulse of a changing society. For instance, while Schechner's environments were intended to facilitate embodied audience interactions and ritual enactments, the Wooster Group's scenography was, and remains, predominantly frontal and famously mediated by the use of taped music, sound environments, and TV screens (later digitized and sometimes connected to live-feed video), which rarely synchronize to the action or emotional moments performed live. One "environment" sets up the potential for an authentic moment or encounter, while the other screens the action so as to deflect and defer such idealized moments.

Whether the group may have found widespread acclaim eventually through other means, the scandal that erupted around the use of blackface in the 1981 *Route 1 & 9* (which caused them to lose 40 percent of New York State Arts' Board funding) thrust them into an uncomfortable spotlight from which they have never escaped. The show was featured (along with the 1984 *L.S.D. [… just the high points …]*) in a documentary that accompanied their tour of the UK in 1987, drawing the attention of Tim Etchells from Forced Entertainment and introducing the group's work, via bootlegged tapes of the show, to many other British ensembles. *Route 1 & 9* also opened Savran's *Breaking the Rules* when it was first published in 1986 (the trade version arrived in 1988), and by starting with this work rather than chronologically with the Spalding Gray-centered first trilogy, Savran imprinted upon a generation of readers the notion that the ensemble was primarily engaged in deconstructing canonical dramatic texts. By coincidence, this was just as the initial third-wave ensembles were forming in America (Irondale Ensemble Project [1983]; Goat Island [1987], Lookingglass [1988], the Neo-Futurists [1988], Elevator Repair Service [1991], and SITI Company [1992], among others), many of whom had direct or indirect connections to the Wooster Group (Collins 2013). This suggests that LeCompte's company (sometimes via Savran's book) not only provided new performance strategies that future devisers would welcome, but had also raised the stakes for artists drawn to dissident and experimental work to consider once again ensemble theatre as a means to achieve these ends: an important consideration, given the preference hitherto shown by many artists during the period to explore solo performance art instead.

By the chronological endpoint of this volume the Wooster Group had cemented its international reputation by mounting four more major works: *Frank Dell's The Temptation of Saint Anthony* (which rounded out the second trilogy in 1988), *Brace Up!* (the radical adaptation of Chekhov's *Three Sisters*), *The Emperor Jones* (1993), and *Fish Story* (1994). Although often strapped for funding (and able to continue mainly because it owned the Performance Garage), the company now financed its new work primarily through its European and Asian tours. In 1985 they received a NEA "Ongoing Ensembles Grant" (a significant source of funding in the revival of collective creation, since terminated) and in 1991 an OBIE for sustained achievement—the same year that LeCompte was recognized with a Lifetime Achievement Award (she received a MacArthur "genius" award in 1995). The ensemble was until this point relatively stable, excepting the departure of founding member Spalding Gray in 1985 and the arrival of Willem Dafoe (formerly with Milwaukee's Theatre X) and Kate Valk in 1980. More rapid turnover will characterize the company after 1995. As a final metric of their influence, Marianne Weems (former dramaturg and assistant director) now heads The Builders Association, while John Collins, a sound designer for the Wooster Group, helms Elevator Repair Service. Similar filial connections include Richard Maxwell (New York City Players) and Richard Kimmel's Cannon Company (Mufson 2004).

Heddon and Milling (2006) provide a wide-ranging chapter on devising and postmodern performance that features the work of the Wooster Group as well as European and Australian companies. Rather than repeating their analysis here, I will first consider a few lesser-known US ensembles whose work investigates similar concerns to show how widespread the connections were to postmodern ideas, before concluding with some reflections on the nature of ensemble moving toward the close of the millennium.

American Theatre Ensembles Volume 1: Post-1970

Herbert Blau's KRAKEN company (1971–81), housed first at Oberlin College in Ohio, emerged out of a distinguished line of ensemble theatre practice. Blau first directed the non-devising Actor's Workshop in San Francisco, which featured as members Ronnie Davis (founder of SFMT) and both Lee Breuer and Ruth Malaczech of Mabou Mines. After penning the incendiary *The Impossible Theatre: A Manifesto* in 1964, Blau became, along with Jules Irving, the co-artistic director at Lincoln Center from 1965 to 1967. Blau eventually went to Oberlin and formed KRAKEN (it included Bill Irwin and Julie Taymor), founded on an intensive actor training regimen based in psychophysical exercises, *ta'i chi*, and advanced critical thinking. Their signature productions included the ensemble-created adaptations *The Seeds of Atreus* (1973) and *Elsinore* (1976) as well as the devised *The Donner Party, Its Crossing* (1974). While the actor training seems much in line with the work of the 1960s collectives, Blau unequivocally critiqued, through performance and his substantial theoretical writings, the pursuit of presence and the notion of overcoming intransigent binaries such as mind/body or being/becoming (Diamond 2018). In fact, coming to the postmodern thought of Barthes, Derrida, and Foucault in the 1980s, Blau insisted that "what appealed to me in poststructuralist thought was that it seemed to be theorizing what we were doing" (Blau 2000).

Snake Theatre formed in Venice, California, in 1972 (originally as Beggar's Theatre) before relocating to Northern California. Their work was featured in Shank's *Beyond the Boundaries* under the heading of "environmental theatre," revealing the lineage that connects physical theatre with its antecedents in street performance (co-director Christopher Hardman had worked with Bread and Puppet), ritual performance traditions, Schechner's evolving theories of environmental theatre, installation/environmental art, and what would come to be known as site-specific performance. Once a permanent core of artists was formed by 1978, Snake became famous for their use of Javanese mask dancing and vocal music in their found environments, such as the Fort Cronkhite Beach setting of *Somewhere in the Pacific* (1978). But when the composer Larry Graber died in 1980, Snake disbanded and Hardman formed Antenna Theatre while his co-director, Laura Farabough, founded Nightfire. Antenna was among the earliest to expand the range and scale of environmental theatre by incorporating portable acoustic media worn by spectators (the "audients"), who moved through installations and site-specific environments both listening to ambient sound and responding to instructions for completing basic tasks. An important step toward ambulatory, interactive, and immersive theatre, Antenna, like Shunt, Third

Rail, and Punchdrunk today, created environments not in order to absorb the spectator, but to activate the potential for decentered and emergent meanings.

Another company to originate in the mid-1980s under the auspices of postmodernism and to successfully evolve into the present, Castillo Theatre exemplifies some of the transitions taking place in ensemble creation as the second wave gives way to the third. Still under the influence of the radical 1960s collectives, Castillo negotiated the slippery terrain between explicitly political intentions and the post-politics atmosphere of the 1980s, as a "political theatre without an ideology" (Friedman 2000, 6; Olsen 2008). Such hybridity manifested in their productions through devising with divided communities, using Brechtian models to motivate audiences to form their own critical positions, and overtly referencing African performance modes to address rising racial tensions in New York City in the 1990s such as the Crown Heights murders. As the company built an impressive community of followers, it both broke the mold of ensemble theatre-making by purchasing its own theatre (on Theatre Row, no less) and also followed the post-1990s trend of developing a youth-based outreach program, "The All Stars Talent Show," in the inner cities of several metropolitan centers.

At least according to Frederic Jameson, Los Angeles constituted the epicenter of American postmodernism, with the lobby of the Hotel Bonaventure as its hyperspatial ground zero (Jameson 1991). The source of a good deal of US pop culture and a metropolis famously addicted to the image, transience, placelessness, and life-as-performance, Los Angeles was by the late 1970s the seedbed of West Coast performance art. Rachel Rosenthal was completing coursework at CalArts where Nam June Paik and Dick Higgins taught (and which, in 1971, instituted a separate feminist art program under the direction of Judy Chicago that featured performance art), the Judson dance soloist and choreographer Rudy Perez was offering his "Art Moves" workshops, and the L.A. Contemporary Exhibitions (LACE) center hosted the new *High Performance* magazine under Linda Frye Burnham (Apple 1991). Lin Hixson began a succession of collaborations, first with the Hangers collective and then with a number of writers, dancers, filmmakers, and designers, before quitting Los Angeles in 1987 to return to her hometown of Chicago (where she would cofound Goat Island later that year). Hangers produced a series of interdisciplinary works between 1979 and 1982 that confused the lines between performance art and theatre in much the same manner as the Wooster Group, about whom Hixson had read but had not yet seen. And, like their New York counterparts, Hangers became a source for numerous important performance art and theatre companies across the

1980s. Writing and composition were shared, and the members rotated roles between director, choreographer, and performer. They investigated nonlinear composition and different forms of duration influenced by multichannel TV viewing. A characteristic strategy involved quoting shards of pop culture (particularly 1950s films) alongside representations of "proper" mainstream culture. Often the quotidian movements were paired with projected media, creating tension between moments hovering on a momentary presence between performer and audience and the mediated images. As Jackie Apple describes *Flatlands* (1983), the text consisted of "excerpts from *The Great Gatsby*, the flight log of a Florida plane crash, personal anecdotes, and one-sentence news headlines of unidentified disasters were juxtaposed without giving any one category of information greater weight or significance than the others. This leveling out of fact and fiction, tragedy and triviality, severs events from their consequences, as history is cut loose from memory" (1990, 30). Hixson's work with Hangers culminated with the large-scale *Birds on Pedestals with Bomber Ladies* (1981), after which she ceased performing and concentrated on directing, the role for which she was unanimously elected to perform with Goat Island.

Ghost Road Company formed in 1993 and represents the succeeding generation of CalArts graduates who turned to devising following coursework. Their premiere show, *Eloise: A Ghost Play*, was performed in Los Angeles and then at Dell'Arte in Blue Lake. The first installment of an ensemble-created adaptation of *The Orestestia* (*Orestes in El Lay*) toured to the Edinburgh festival, while the second entry (*Clyt at Home*) saw the Ghost Road's director, Katharine Noon, move over to Theatre of NOTE (founded in 1981) to rehearse, devise, write, and direct with that company in Hollywood. In 2007 Ghost Road landed a residency at Loyola Marymount College, which allowed Noon and the company to work with students on the last entry in the trilogy, performed in Santa Monica. Peripatetic, motivated by circumstances and creative opportunities to share resources and projects with diverse presenters, collaborators, and academic institutions, Ghost Road is paradigmatic of the post-1990s world of devising to be covered in Volume 2 of *American Theatre Ensembles*.

And yet, by way of conclusion, it is worth considering how and why collective creation, founded on the ideal of sustained ensemble art-making and revived in the 1960s as a demonstration of communality and participatory democracy—principles often observed more in theory than practice, but instrumental nevertheless—should find itself pursuing into the next millennium this transient mode of existence. (By the early 2000s one begins to hear artists speak of "temporary ensembles" and to voice suspicion about long-standing companies and the compromises they must have made to remain ensembled [Proudfit 2013].) But if explicit ideological positions petered out among most ensembles, this cannot mean that ideology itself ceased operating on the evolution of collective creation. Rather than thinking only in terms of how third-wave companies responded to their more overtly ideological predecessors in an ahistorical aesthetic bubble, we should consider as well the material influence of changing notions of labor that began to infiltrate American culture beginning in the 1980s. For instance, due in part to the increased presence of information technologies in the workplace, but later as a consequence of the Reagan era's mantra of deregulation and dismantling the liberal welfare economy, massive reorganizations in white-collar businesses and corporations were undertaken throughout the 1980s and 1990s to generate greater flexibility in skills requiring integration with technology. As John Ehrman describes it:

> What this meant, in practice, was that job classifications were consolidated so individual employees could do a wider range of tasks. Workers often were reorganized into teams, given greater responsibility for product quality, and paid according to new incentive systems. They were expected to be more productive, take more initiatives, make more decisions, and keep their skills up-to-date. Firms also sought flexibility by making more use of temporary and contract workers. (2005, 102).

Because of the transparent correlations between these workplace practices and the rise of a neoliberal economic order, such transformations are seldom—given the typical left-leaning character of American art in general—consciously linked to new forms of devised theatre that emerge in America around the same time. But increasingly, devising companies will adopt (and adapt) principles of "post-Fordist" labor into their looser organizational structures and creative processes, celebrating attitudes such as "entrepreneurship," "flexibility," "innovation," and "transferability of skills" in their practice and thereby linking themselves, whether more or less consciously, to the contemporary discourses and labor practices of neoliberalism. Alex Mermikides has analyzed the increasing use by creative ensembles of the "core and pool" structure, "in which the director (often supported by an administrative team) forms the permanent 'core,' drawing from what [Katie] Mitchell calls 'a constellation of performers' and other collaborators for individual productions" (2013, 57). She argues that the structure often promotes "individual authorship rather than group authorship" while also establishing the director or artistic director's brand at the expense of the collaborative processes by which the work is devised (57).

Also, with many contemporary ensembles forming out of shared college and university-based training and collaboration, we cannot ignore the transformations that have taken place in higher education more broadly, which have been radically reshaped by a market-based ethos. Liz Tomlin, analyzing the effects of New Labour's neoliberal reforms of the mid-1990s on British university arts training, describes a "circle of commodification" by which

> [v]anguard practice now emerging from the universities has a ready-made market that can quickly name, authorize, and validate it as the next generation of the consecrated avant-garde. As a consequence, not only are university departments and lecturers drawn ... to encourage students to make the kind of work that will meet the particular demand of that market but that same market can now also supply the academic interest in vanguard practice with the work the market has authorized and validated. (2015, 279)

Already in their 2006 study, Heddon and Milling expressed anxiety that an "identifiable 'style'" of devised theatre might be emerging, and one finds evidence for this in the journalistic shorthand that reviews work by new companies as "like Big Dance" or "Woosterish." Some have gone so far as to claim of contemporary ensembles that "their formalism, like their content, is recycled, paraphrased: Builders Association has adopted the Wooster Groups technophilia, Elevator Repair Service (ERS) shares the Group's love of non sequitur dancing, all are suckers for Formanesque soundscapes and effects" (Garret 2001, 47). Richard Schechner, struggling to contextualize contemporary devising in light of 1960s avant-garde collective practices (an exercise, as I've said, that remains problematic), denominates it as a "conservative avant-garde" that revels in "excellence" rather than "innovation" (2010, 895, 899).

Nevertheless, the consequences of creating work under present conditions are always complex and we must avoid simply laminating neoliberal ideologies onto the practices of collective creation: on the one hand, the myriad ways that labor is distributed in today's devised theatre may come to look something like the gig economy, which would seem to introduce additional forms of precarity into the practice of ensembling. On the other, since neoliberalism is itself based in logics of austerity and precarity, collective creation may find itself in a unique position to speak from that position and, by virtue of its organizational structure, "slow" and "inefficient" collaborative practices, and ethical commitments to process, embody forms of resistance to an advancing globalism and neoliberalism (Syssoyeva 2013b, 26; Anderson-Rabern 2020). Such ambiguous positions, to be explored more fully in the introduction to the second volume of *American Ensembles*, return us to the notion of collective creation as an evolving form and to more contemporary devised creation as a thoroughly hybridized, and thus potentially compromised, practice.

CHAPTER 3
THEATRE X
Curtis L. Carter

Theatre X, as one of the longest living experimental theatre projects in modern times, began in Milwaukee in 1969 and extended its life of some thirty-five years of active theatre to American cities including New York, San Francisco, Baltimore, and other venues across the nation and throughout Europe.[1] A highlight in Theatre X's career was a ten-year collaboration with Ritsaert ten Cate at the Mickery Theatre, Amsterdam, from 1975 to 1985. The approach to exploring the career of Theatre X here will examine the activities performed in the processes of creating Theatre X's contributions to experimental theatre. The focus will be on the activities that constitute the life of Theatre X as a living form of theatre evolving during the second half of the twentieth century.

Theatre X was officially formed under the leadership of Conrad and Linda Bishop (now Elizabeth Fuller) in 1969 by a group of faculty and students at the University of Wisconsin-Milwaukee. Their inaugural production of *X Communication* by faculty and students of the University of Wisconsin-Milwaukee's theatre program took place at the Village Church located in downtown Milwaukee. My own first encounter with Theatre X occurred shortly after arriving in Milwaukee from Boston this same year of 1969. Having enjoyed experimental theatre in Boston and New York, I was curious to find the announcement of Theatre X's *X Communication* taking place in Milwaukee. The performance consisted of individual segments based on the actors' concerns with contemporary societal issues. Soon after, a 1970 production of Bertolt Brecht's *The Measures Taken* held at the first International Brecht Symposium in Milwaukee received acclaim from critics and scholars. Subsequently, the name Theatre X began to appear in various European theatre journals.

The X in the company's name refers to the mathematical symbol "*x*," which alludes to the unknown or an element of change. Initially, according to the original bylaws, Theatre X operated under a collective consisting of some twenty-two member-directors, each with equal voice. Three of the collective participants were designated as co-managers responsible informally for artistic and administrative management. The initial co-managers were Conrad Bishop, Ron Gural, and Dan Desmond, all of whom eventually moved on elsewhere to successful careers in the theatre. Initially, Theatre X functioned as a democratic collective with each company member entitled to one vote on artistic decisions affecting the choice of productions and their development. The decision-making structure was modified later, depending on the understanding of the company leadership and a board of directors that was added later and which included both Theatre X company members and community leaders.

Among the early artistic contributors to Theatre X was Willem Dafoe (1975), who began his acting career with the company prior to moving to the Wooster Group in New York, followed by his rise to top billing in film and Off-Broadway theatre. Victor De Lorenzo (1976), later a founding member of the band the Violent Femmes, was also a member of Theatre X. Flora Coker (1970), John Schneider (1971), John Kishline (1972), and later Deborah Clifton (1976) became the core members who remained with the company until shortly before its ending in 2004. In 1973, Theatre X became a company of seven people replacing the original home company of twenty-two in order to focus on its national and international touring while also maintaining its base in Milwaukee.[2] Paring down the company size reflected in part a focus on the ensemble's developing national and international opportunities.

The mission of Theatre X from its beginnings was both to create and to present original theatre works that emerged out of the experiences of the artists as they researched and reflected on the nature of theatre and its experimental possibilities for examining contemporary personal and social issues. Its productions aimed at creating a "total theatre," which employed multimedia as well as verbal and physical performance. The range of Theatre X's activities encompassed seasonal productions in Milwaukee, a national touring program touching down in American cities and towns to present "on the road" performances, and performances in the theaters of major American cities. In 1973–4, for instance, the company performed some 250 performances with bookings at colleges and universities and small theaters across the country. The company's international touring program began in 1975 and included productions in the Netherlands, Germany, Sweden, Great Britain, and Japan.

The audiences for Theatre X productions consisted of artists and members of the public with a taste for reaching beyond the repertories of traditional theatre productions. In the words of artistic director John Schneider, speaking of Theatre X's Milwaukee audiences in 1989, "the audience includes a wide variety of people, including the Mayor of our town and most of its other artists ... feminists, gays and lesbians, and young people looking for ideas and experiences they won't find in any other theatre in town frequented the performances" (Schneider 1989).

Theatre X and Experimental Theatre

As this is the first case study in the volume, some background on the origins of Theatre X and companies like it may be helpful. Experimental theatre as presented here is a continuation of the avant-garde arts as they continued to unfold and develop throughout the twentieth century. Experimental theatre, broadly speaking, evolved through and beyond the various forms of modern representational and expressive theatre. The basic theatre experiences in Theatre X performances, as in all theatre, were formed by the encounters between performers who initiated a relationship among themselves and their audiences, aiming to engage with the audience in exploring feelings, ideas, and the means to critique contemporary social and historical issues. But like many ensembles emerging out of the 1960s, Theatre X was experimenting with these encounters.

By 1969 when Theatre X was born in Milwaukee, experimental theatre had already appeared in many forms. To cite only a few precursors, Antonin Artaud (1896–1948) had tested the boundaries of representational theatre in his "Theatre of Cruelty" with its preference for kinetic images, rituals, and magic over realism and narration. The Living Theatre, a creation of Judith Malina (1925–2015) and Julian Beck (1925–85), championed social cooperation in lieu of competition in their productions. In their search for cooperative methods for creating dance theatre, artists at the Judson Dance Theatre (1962–4) such as Yvonne Rainer and Trisha Brown sought to alter traditional forms of theatre through innovative dance performances (Banes 1993a). Similar developments abroad could be seen, for instance, in the Belgian experimental theatre artist and founder of the Troubleyn theatre company, Jan Fabre (1958–), who would interact significantly with Theatre X and challenged virtually all theatre conventions in his individual and group performances (Carter 1993).

The contributors to experimental theatre each chose a different path for examining the art of making theatre. Each aimed at reflecting on new possibilities for theatre experiences with a fresh view on altering its means.

What is common to these endeavors? Perhaps it was the desire to introduce new ways of understanding theatre itself and to have an impact on a changing culture. Were there still possibilities for a fresh approach to theatre at the point when the founders of Theatre X began their venture in 1969? Relying on their own desires and creative abilities, a talented core of Theatre X writers, directors, and actors committed themselves to the task. They shared with other experimental theatre artists a commitment to innovative and socially relevant theatre. Extending the perceptual capabilities of audiences, as well as those of the company members, beyond the offerings available in traditional theatre was central to their goals. What took place in a Theatre X performance is separate from the worlds of low and high culture that reside beyond its presentational spaces. It existed on the fringes of a culture, which it often sought to critique or subvert.

Theatre X, then, founded in the same decade as La MaMa in New York, belongs among developing forms of twentieth-century experimental theatre. Like other instances of the form, however, Theatre X abandoned, or used selectively and in different ways, the existing conventions of theatre. Experimental theatre reconstructs both the world of theatre and in varying degrees recasts the relation of performers and audiences. As in other examples of experimental theatre, Theatre X exposed what is capable of being representable within otherwise hidden or enclosed spaces of culture. It created theatre spaces where the underside of culture is exposed and experienced. Its significance depended on disclosures of personal and societal reality that may otherwise evade discovery.

Methodology of Theatre X for Creating Plays

Like the artist John Cage, who once said, "I can't understand why people are frightened of new ideas. I'm frightened of the old ones" (Kostelanetz 1986), Theatre X held no fear of new ideas. But the projects of Theatre X also showed no fear of older ideas. Rather, their repertory engaged past artistic themes while giving them fresh interpretations, as well as striking out in their own directions. From its beginnings, Theatre X's aims centered on the use of theatrical artistry (scripting, directing, performing, stage design) as a means of communication, first among the company members themselves and then with diverse audiences found in their respective local, national, and international platforms. The company did not endorse a particular creed with respect to theatrical practices.

Rather, it employed a variety of theatrical means including ensemble scripting, storytelling, physical-based performance forms, light, media, and film design, music and dance, experimental uses of technology, the space and architecture of the staging space as inspiration for new ideas, unexpected casting choices, and deep research and long development periods to articulate and implement ideas generated collectively through interactions among company members, with other artists, and with other theatre companies. Trial and error in the development of the art and a place where artists can fail was built into the operations of Theatre X (Schneider 1989, 5). Underlying the process of making theatre at Theatre X was to regard "x' as the unknown and to foster artistic research and critical thinking.

Succinctly expressing the mission of Theatre X, John Schneider offers this statement:

> We aim to create multiplicities of anti-realities. In other words, we mean to resist the manipulated and manipulating descriptions of the real offered by the social environment and the mass media. We embrace the idea that reality is constructed largely by the language and symbols that saturate our culture, the interplay between them, and the positions of power they affirm, conceal, or make possible. (1989, 2)

Schneider explains the company's approach to creating a new work thus: the seed of the idea that the play develops is discovered in the collective unconscious of the company members and is then further identified and agreed upon by the entire group. Research in conjunction with improvisation, and ongoing discussion among the company members, follows in an effort to identify more fully a theme for the play and its potential audience interest. Then follows the company's experiments in the search for form, style, design, and theatrical means suitable for presenting the topic. In a workshop mode, the company develops the acting model and identifies the skills and training necessary to implement the production. At this point in the process, a company resident playwright (in this case John Schneider) writes the script reflecting, but not copying the body of work done in the previous improvisational stages of creation. Then follow the customary design and construction of sets and costumes, and decisions concerning music and other elements of the production. Of course, the process does not end here, as rehearsals and performances invite continuous rethinking of the text and production aspects (1989, 6–7):

> The plays are personal. They represent individuals in the company, but our concerns are philosophical, aesthetic, social. We write for the actors in the group. We choose subjects about which we feel deeply. We try to make our lives (also our working lives) and the times we live in more vivid and understandable to ourselves and our audience.
>
> We champion no style; the plays are "total theatre" experiments ... We consider the form of a play, the process through which it is created, and all aspects of its presentation to the public to be at least as meaningful as its subject matter. (Schneider 1989, 5)

The subjects of Theatre X plays were grounded in the present experience of America and included, among others, gender roles and sexuality, civil rights, the impact of consumerism and the commodification of art, the role of the automobile, television, and the daily news, group dynamics and dysfunction, and violence in contemporary life.

Following a revamping in 1975, the company reaffirmed its commitment to the creation of original plays, which reflected the artistic and personal concerns of company members.

Its first original play under the new structure, *The Unnamed* (1974-5 season), featured experimentation with light and darkness, aiming to evoke an experience of "dread and cataclysm" informed by stories of H. P. Lovecraft (1989, 5). *The Unnamed* was followed by *Razor Blades*, both of which played by invitation at the Mickery Theatre in Amsterdam in 1975-6 and in Baltimore at the 1976 New Theatre Festival. The 1977-8 season resulted in a New York production of *A Fierce Longing* based on the Japanese writer Yukio Mishima. Theatre X's production of *A Fierce Longing* received an OBIE Award for its multimedia production design (still to this day the only such award garnered by a Wisconsin theatre company).

A secondary aspect of the company's mission was to explore both new and old theatrical forms in order to advance the shape of innovative theatre. Their efforts in this respect included revisiting and bringing fresh insight into existing texts that would not otherwise be available to its audiences, while defining and perfecting a unique style that could be identified with Theatre X. Examples would include Bertolt Brecht's *The Measures Taken*, 1969-70; Dylan Thomas's *Under Milkwood*, 1981-9; Samuel Beckett's *Happy Days*, 1987-8; and Truman Capote's *A Christmas Memory* (featuring Flora Coker, which became a seasonal favorite in Milwaukee).

Cultural Diversity and Theatre X

Throughout its history, Theatre X consistently aimed to address cultural diversity both with respect to its audiences and its productions. One aim of its audience development was to address "a variety of somethings" in their work: these included the experiences of diverse young adults that varied in race, gender identities, cultural preferences, and social and political views. During its thirty-five years of performance history, Theatre X explored a wide range of culturally challenging issues. These issues include among others Native American tribal and African-American issues, women in the theatre, and the 9/11 bombing of the Twin Towers in New York.

Native American–Themed Productions

While social justice, cultural diversity, gender, and sexuality issues are present throughout the repertory of Theatre X, its productions also addressed these issues in particular works. In 1994, the company collaborated with the Potawatomi Indian Nation to produce *Bode-Wad-Mi: Keepers of the Fire*, an original theatre work written with the performers, which for this piece included five American Indians who worked with Theatre X to devise the show. The performance portrayed storytelling around an intimate campfire setting, with actors reciting tribal documents pertaining to land transfers between the Potawatomi tribal communities and the United States government. *Bode-Wad-Mi* was performed both in Milwaukee at the Theatre X Black Box and also in Canada at a gathering of seven tribal divisions of the Potawatomi Nation, which had been dispersed.

African American-Themed Productions

As it evolved, Theatre X incorporated into its program projects to address societal issues and works by African-American and Latino writers, directors, and performers, including the African-American playwright Reggie Finlayson. The company's production of *Jazz* in 1999 focused on the lively African-American jazz culture that had existed in the Brownsville neighborhood of North Milwaukee during the 1920s. This production carried a social edge as it recalled an era of success for the African-American culture of Milwaukee located in a section of the city which was literally wiped out in the 1960s by an expansion of freeway construction that cut through and effectively demolished this thriving community.

Women in the Theatre

The position of women in US theatre was a theme that carried throughout the work of Theatre X. Flora Coker and Deborah Clifton each held central roles in the company as leading performers. They were also key contributors to Theatre X's ongoing creative and administrative processes and co-authors of its production, *Desire of the Moth for the Star* (1989). Others, including Elizabeth Fuller, who was active in the early stages of Theatre X, and long-time company member Marcie Hoffman held important roles in the ongoing operations.

A number of Theatre X productions focused on issues relating to or representing women's role in the theatre and in society. For example, the company's 1994 "Blue Stockings" series focused on the Women's Suffrage Movement. The company's annual "Theatre Women" series featured original performance art by diverse national women artists and was an important part of Theatre X's projects, especially during 1994–6. The Women's Series also included a production of Garcia Lorca's *The Shoemaker's Prodigious Wife*. *Imagining Brad*, another of the plays in the Women's Series, took place inside the Wisconsin Taycheedah Women's Correctional Facility, April 29, 1996, before the facility's inmates and staff. A 2001 production of *Arabian Nights*, John Schneider's adaptation of the classic, focused on issues of gender in the writings of feminist author Judith Butler.

Theatre X's National Outreach

Plans for Theatre X soon expanded beyond the productions introduced to Milwaukee audiences to include performances in cities and towns across the United States. Beginning in the 1970s, Theatre X established an impressive national presence through its performances in US cities including Baltimore, Boston, Chicago, Denver, Minneapolis, New Orleans, New York, Philadelphia, Pittsburgh, San Francisco, St. Louis, and Washington, DC. As a traveling company, Theatre X found it necessary to adapt its performances to many different kinds of theatre spaces—from its changing home bases in Milwaukee to a variety of theatre spaces in cities such as New York, San Francisco, and Baltimore. In the beginning, the opportunities for road shows meant adapting to university settings and whatever local spaces might emerge as the players endured rigorous road schedules. Company director John Schneider recalled that Theatre X had 250 performances across the country in 1973–4. These performances included bookings in colleges and universities, small experimental theatres, and churches in states across the nation. Among these national sites of Theatre X performances were residencies at Chicago's The Body Politic Theatre, 1974–5; the Baltimore Theatre Project, 1975, 1976, and 1986; New York at the Performing Garage, 1978; Seattle's New Theatre 1987; and Chicago's Goodman Theatre, 1987. During this period, Theatre X traveled to numerous other sites across Indiana, Ohio, Iowa, Massachusetts, and Oklahoma. Revenue from touring provided the main source of income for the company during this era.

Of their national touring projects, two are especially noteworthy. As mentioned above, the 1979 *A Fierce Longing* with script by John Schneider and directed by Sharon Ott played in New York and received an OBIE for its stage design featuring projected scenery. The other involved *A History of Sexuality*, a three-year collaborative project created with the New City Theatre of Seattle (1987–8) with John Kishline, Julia Romanski, John Schneider, and David Schweizer contributing to the project. The production was based in part on ideas found in the writings of French philosopher Michel Foucault as expressed in *The History of Sexuality*. The San Francisco Bay area's Critics Association viewed this theatre piece as an outstanding achievement of the American stage. After premiering in Seattle, *A History of Sexuality* played in Milwaukee, Stockholm, Sweden, and Munster, Germany.

Theatre X and Its International Productions

Concurrent with the development of its national touring projects between 1969 and 1975, Theatre X began to explore select international engagements. Central to the international dimension of Theatre X's development was its eleven-year collaboration (1975–85) with Ritsaert ten Cate, director of the Mickery Theatre in Amsterdam. After experiencing Theatre X's productions of *The Unnamed* during a visit to Denver, and a subsequent performance of *Razor Blades*, ten Cate invited the company to perform with him there. Ten Cate was a major catalyst for advancing experimental theatre worldwide.

Although their initial collaboration at the Mickery with *Folter Follies* turned into what ten Cate termed a theatrical failure, the discussions between ten Cate and Theatre X members resulted in a continued collaboration between the Mickery and Theatre X (Austria 1987, xv). The outcome of this collaboration resulted in a stream of Theatre X performances including *Sweet Dreams, Beauty and the Beast* (a John Schneider collaboration with the Mickery), *Half My Father's Age*, and *Scenarios for the Living/for the Dead*. All of these productions included experiments with video and live music. The work at the Mickery also included noteworthy collaboration on other in-house projects including *Rembrandt, Hitler, Or Me* (later made into one of Mike Figgis's early films) and numerous others. This collaboration brought the company into contact with the best of experimental theatre from around the world and challenged Theatre X to achieve accordingly.

The collaboration with ten Cate and the Mickery undoubtedly proved to be a high point in Theatre X's thirty-five-year history. It brought untold opportunities to develop their work among the leading experimental theatre companies from across the world who brought their performances to the Mickery. The collaboration between Theatre X and the Mickery ended in 1985 (ten Cate 1989, 11–12). Intermittent international productions of Theatre X continued alongside its Mickery performances in the Netherlands, Sweden, West Germany, Wales, and England. The company also performed at the Toga Mura International Theatre Festival at the invitation of Tadashi Suzuki at his company's home in Japan.

Theatre X in Milwaukee: Finding Space

While developing its national and international profiles, Theatre X also retained its base in its home city of Milwaukee. After performing in sporadic spaces throughout the city, including the Village Church, a coffee house, a jazz club, and the Haggerty Museum, Theatre X acquired a ninety-nine-seat space for its performances in a former toy factory in 1972 at 1247 North Water Street. It opened with it its own version of *Alice in Wonderland* featuring some forty puppets designed by company members. Following this opening, the company launched their staging of Samuel Beckett's *Endgame* and one of the first American productions of Peter Handke's *Offending the Audience*. These productions followed Beckett's and Handke's scripts closely, distinguishing this practice from the collaborative creation featured in *X Communication* and continuing throughout the company's history.

When the Water Street building was sold in 1980, Theatre X's Milwaukee productions moved to a gymnasium space in the basement of Lincoln High School, billed as Lincoln Center for the Arts, and began again with a black box construction. Soon this arrangement proved unsatisfactory for the work being undertaken by an experimental theatre. The company's tenure at Lincoln Center ended with the production of *My Werewolf* in the 1984–85 season. Departure from Lincoln Center was followed by a lengthy period of touring, which included performances in Baltimore and Great Britain, except for occasional performances around the city at such places as the Haggerty Museum, Milwaukee Repertory Theatre, and other local spaces.

Despite the nomadic existence, Theatre X continued to represent the cutting edge in Milwaukee theatre. Among the notable theatre events of this era was a controversial performance in 1981, *Theatre Written with a "K" Is a Tomcat* by Belgian visual artist and theatre artist Jan Fabre and his experimental theatre group, Troubleyn, from Antwerp, Belgium. The group's performance included a portrayal of simulated sex that drew the attention of the Milwaukee police and generated a media blitz in the Milwaukee news media. Objections from the theatre community and members of the public over the response of the Milwaukee police and the media on this occasion generated productive discussion over the content future of theatre performances.

Fabre also presented in Milwaukee two years later the eight-hour theatre piece *This Is Theatre Like It Was To Be Expected and Foreseen* (1982) together with Theatre X in Milwaukee's Skylight Theatre. These two works together with a third piece by Fabre, *The Power of Theatrical Madness* (1984), each performed in Milwaukee in conjunctions with Theatre X, formed a trilogy, which became legendary in twentieth-century theatre history.

Although much of Theatre X's work took place in national and international venues, the company continued to the end with its full seasons in Milwaukee and with ongoing efforts to attract local audiences and support. In 1985, the company began performing in another ninety-nine-seat black box theatre at 158 North Broadway. This site also became the home of the Skylight Theatre and Milwaukee Chamber Theatre and was named the Broadway Theatre Center. Theatre X performed its regular season in this space until its closure in 2004.[3]

Indeed, several of its most memorable productions focused on Milwaukee- or Wisconsin-related events. Among these is *Sketches from a Life* (1991), based on the life of Milwaukee-born power diplomat and author/scholar George Keenan, and selected for performance by Theatre X at the request of Milwaukee Mayor John Norquist. *Success*, scripted by

John Kishline and presented in the company's 1990 Milwaukee season, continued the company's interest in portraying individual personas of note in contemporary Milwaukee life. This work was based on a series of interviews with influential Milwaukee leaders including Mayor Norquist, investment banker Sheldon Lubar, CEO Max Samson, attorney Brendan Comer, and advertising executive Dennis Frankenberry.

Also reflecting its substantial engagement with Milwaukee area social issues is Theatre X's 1996 production, *The Line*. The show featured a failed strike by union workers after a two-year labor dispute between the Cudahay Packing Company and its meat-packing union workers. The performance of *The Line* was based on interviews with company representatives and union workers conducted by University of Wisconsin Milwaukee professor Michael Gordon and John Schneider (who prepared the script).

Extending its efforts in Milwaukee in 2002 by attending to current social and political issues, Theatre X explored the philosopher-anarchist Noam Chomsky's libertarian views in *Chomsky 9/11*, examining his perspectives on the Vietnam War, global economic power structures, and problems relating to pending terrorist attacks.

Conclusion

The question of endings for a vibrant experimental theatre project must be met with mixed feelings. Feelings of lament are common as the ending impacts the lives of those who have invested significantly with their commitment of ideas, emotions, and years of dedicated interaction with a community. It is interesting to note that the question of endings appears in the reflections of Ritsaert ten Cate as he pondered this question at the end of Theatre X's ten-year collaboration with the Mickery in 1989.

> So, there was a beginning with Theatre X. Is there an end? it is a fascinating aspect of mutually inspiring and beneficial relationships to not only see how they start, but also how they separate again, how at a certain point in the road, participants take different turnings. (ten Cate 1989, 11)

Perhaps a similar reflection might also serve to bring closure, though under more painful circumstances and with deeper personal and institutional investments at stake, when the time to close off the future to any further realizations of Theatre X came in 2004.

There seems little doubt that the ideas driving the accomplishments of Theatre X have more than brought to fruition a positive outcome far beyond the time frame allotted to most experimental theatre projects. Theatre X did not hesitate to explore both the new and the old alike in its creation of theatre works. It freely produced new works while also adapting existing scripts and giving them new meaning. Civil rights, the place of women in the arts, gender roles and sexuality, social violence, labor unions and worker's rights, and testing the boundaries of theatre in the same pursuit are among the issues addressed in the productions of Theatre X. African-American jazz culture, Native American tribal issues, and the influences of media (television, computers, internet, and news media) in a changing twentieth-century culture are all present among the issues represented in the company's thirty-five-year endeavor, which produced scores of original scripts and some four thousand performances.

The recognition given the work of Theatre X is noteworthy. Invitations to perform in the major experimental theatres across the nation and the world such as the ten-year residency with the Mickery, one of the leading experimental theatres, itself accords high professional recognition to the contributions of Theatre X. The OBIE and other awards received throughout its history attest to its stature as one of the important chapters in the history of twentieth-century experimental theatre. Recognition accorded to company members also includes John Schneider's nomination for the Pulitzer Prize for the writing of *Sweet Dreams* and a NEA Playwright Fellowship Award in 1983. Company members John Kishline and Wesley Savick received nominations for Best New Play of 1988 from the American Theatre Critics Association for their play, *I Can't Stop Loving You*. *The Desire of the Moth for the Star* by Deborah Kishline, Flora Coker, and Wesley Savick also received a nomination for best play in 1990. Each of these awards serves as a measure of the success of Theatre X.

Evidence of the interest in Theatre X's contributions to the life of experimental theatre is also apparent in the noteworthy list of its major financial supporters. Among these were the National Endowment for the Arts, the National Endowment for the Humanities, the Dutch Ministry of Culture, the Japan-United States Friendship Commission, and major private foundations including the Rockefeller Foundation, the Jerome Foundation, and Philip Morris Incorporated. Additional support for Theatre X was provided by the Wisconsin Art Board, the United Performing Arts Fund of Milwaukee, the Milwaukee Foundation, and various other corporate foundations including the Kohler Foundation, as well as private individuals.[4]

In short, the accomplishments of Theatre X speak clearly to the truth that its aims as a noteworthy contributor to experimental theatre have been realized in good measure and often under difficult conditions with respect to funding and site facilities. As the poet Henry David Thoreau once reminded, "To affect the quality of the day, that is the highest of the arts." And this indeed Theatre X has accomplished, if not in every attempt, still on many a day. Still, when the activity of a live theatre company comes to an end, the question remains: how then must we regard its existence? The activities that comprise the artistic identity of Theatre X are for the most part memories, memories in the minds of the former company members and the audiences that enjoyed the performances over time. Or perhaps the company's identity resides in the newspaper reviews, scripts, and any visual documentation that might remain. Surely archives exist that would preserve important documents, but without organization and placement within an institutional setting the likelihood of their survival remains uncertain. In lieu of a formal archive, I have gathered below the following comments from company members, their collaborators, and supporters.

REFLECTIONS ON THEATRE X

Editor's Note

The material archives and historical traces of ensemble theatre in the United States, apart from the better-known collectives based on the East and West Coast (such as the Living Theatre, the Open Theatre, the Performance Group, San Francisco Mime Troupe, and El Teatro Campesino), are rapidly disappearing. Most companies as well as many participating artists, while they lacked the means to establish their own archive, retained a good deal of company memoranda, marketing materials, scripts, and photographs (and sometimes film) related to rehearsals, productions, and tours. Theatre X is paradigmatic in this regard, and so to close this initial case study several important contributors to the company's long and successful tenure were asked to share their reflections on the ensemble to provide a sample of the rich materials available for further research. (Comments have been lightly edited for clarity.)

Conrad Bishop (Founding Co-manager)

Theatre X grew out of a workshop exploring diverse modes of improvisation at the University of Wisconsin Milwaukee. The first show, *X Communication*, was a collection of short sketches in many styles: whatever we could toss together in five weeks. Accidental in a way, the collective couldn't decide on a single story or play but it gave us a structure we could change, expand, condense, for the next five years. Eventually, since it was our one money-maker on tour, it wore out. But for us it did several things: Though a lot was developed through improvisation, stuff was eventually scripted. I did most of the scripting, and eventually started to think of myself as a playwright. Others did writing as well, and when we left, John Schneider found his voice. That necessity was extremely productive. It offered a huge range of styles and structures, which I think benefited us all in creating longer works—a fluidity in finding the right style for a story.

Among the strong motives driving us to push Theatre X as a performing ensemble, rather than simply a workshop, were (a) seeing the world and playing for audiences outside the academic setting; (b) finding a way we could work as artistic peers, not as students/faculty; (c) being part of a theatre with a soul, as opposed to simply directing one show in a four-show season; (d) our first experience with puppetry in *The People as the People* and *Alice in Wonderland*; (e) keeping at least some work in long-term touring repertory, finding how it can grow. Secondarily, I suppose, was being engaged in immediate response to the political climate of the time, including the anti-war protests—but always, I think, with stories and images you couldn't immediately pigeon-hole. All those elements were the gateway to what we've done in the past forty-five years.

Our formal connection with Theatre X ended in 1974 when we hived off to form The Independent Eye, though we returned several times to stage *Hedda Gabler* and our play *Full Hookup*, to see their staging of our play *Dreamily*, and to do guest performances of *Action News* and *Mating Cries*. But we saw a lot of the work of Theatre X and feel enormously gratified in having a hand in planting the seed.

Flora Coker (Founding Member, 1970–2004)

I have a lot of memories and my mind reels. "x", the algebraic unknown ... I took that literally as something to be defined by me and others in the group and I was hooked. I arrived in Milwaukee from Virginia in a stylish long black Carnaby Street cloth coat and patent leather boots. It was February 2, and I had never felt such cold.

A production of Bertolt Brecht's *The Measures Taken* at the University of Wisconsin-Madison during the student strike against the US invasion into Cambodia and following the Kent State massacre. I was a member of the chorus and the glorious music was by Hans Eisler. Long drives across

Wisconsin in a van, sleeping on a built-in platform with props and costumes and baggage stored underneath, touring colleges with plays and workshops. We were in Ashland at the top of Wisconsin on Lake Superior in January, as cold and beautiful a place as I have ever been.

Spending a boiling hot August in Denver, living off the small box office proceeds from our best touring production *The Unnamed*, a play based on a story by H.P. Lovecraft that required only four actors, three shrouds, one simple wooden frame, chalk, a flashlight, matches and total darkness. I answered an early morning telephone call and heard a melodious foreign voice ask if Theatre X would consider performing in Amsterdam. "Oh, um, um, gosh, gosh," say I, "how could we possibly do that?" "Well," says he, "I saw your play last night and I would like to bring you all to my theatre in Amsterdam as guests of the Dutch government." The beautiful voice belonged to the late, great Ritsaert ten Cate of the famous Mickery Theatre, home for experimental theatre from around the world. He was Santa Claus.

I understood, FINALLY, like a lightning flash, that what I was about to say in the scene I was performing on stage was really, really funny ... the writing ... so I should just say it out loud and clearly, which I did and I brought down the house. You should know that till then I had presented myself as a dramatic actress. To try for a laugh scared me too badly.

Everybody wants to know about Willem [Dafoe]. I have many happy memories of him. Among them: as we huddled backstage before going on for a play he'd say, "I'll be scared for you if you'll be scared for me." With such pleasure. Also, in the dark and dingy basement of our warehouse theatre, Willem and I, for days, boiled the flesh and hair off a cow's skull and some other bones to be used for props in a play.

It felt awful to thrust small boxes of glass from shattered car windshields into the hands of audience members in a play about torture at the Mickery. On the other hand, never was there more fun than the comedy about a difficult and fracturing family on the Mickery stage, with live ducks, and live carp and live trees lining a large pool. It was very funny and called "smartass" by the *Village Voice*.

I could of course go on and on: we used different processes over the years to create many original plays ... from simple ideas (i.e., fear of the unknown), books (Kubler-Ross's *On Death and Dying*), scenarios developed around a theme or presented by our resident playwright, John Schneider, and developed by us the actors. I think I could say that I was often more interested in the process of making the play than I was in performing it. That was not always true.

Theatre X

I could list play after play: *I Used to Like This Place Before They Started Making All Those Renovations*, *Happy Days* (I love Samuel Beckett to death), the Milwaukee history plays, *CHOMSKY 9/11* (which nearly killed me), *TOBACCO ROAD* (played on a mound of dirt—huge fun), three plays by Ibsen, one more wonderful than the next. And, really, on and on.

Many came and went in Theatre X. We had a long-lived strong core of actors and we had a company playwright almost the entire time. If I think back to what kept me going ... Year after year, we planned something I did not want to miss.

Victor de Lorenzo (Founding Member)[5]

My experience with Theatre X began in the Summer of 1976 after I had successfully secured a position with the company after auditioning to fill a spot left vacant by the soon to be departing Willem Dafoe. I had been studying theatre, music and literature at the University of Wisconsin at Milwaukee when I saw a notice posted on the Theatre Department bulletin board that Theatre X would be holding auditions for two acting positions with the company.

I decided to try out. I had never done an audition before, so I was more than amazed and excited to find out that I had passed the audition and would soon be employed as a full-time actor in the world of experimental theatre! Little did I know at the time how much this job would go on to influence and shape my future creative life. Theatre X not only taught me how to think in a dramatic context, but it gave me the thirst and drive to find the truth in everything I've done on and off the stage ever since. I particularly loved the development and live performances of the play, *A Fierce Longing* (a study of the life and work of Japanese novelist Yukio Mishima) that won the company an OBIE award in 1978! Theatre X was an incredible way of life and I'm proud to have been a part of its glorious history.

Deborah Clifton (Core Ensemble Member, 1976–2004)

Theatre X was my first professional audition and then my first professional job after graduating from Carroll University. I had it in my mind to seek out a company just like Theatre X but in NYC. Imagine my surprise when I found it in my backyard.

The first two shows I worked on with Theatre X were stepping into *The Unnamed* and then the development of *A Fierce Longing*. Remarkably, I had read the entirety of both authors' works before joining Theatre X: H. P.

Lovecraft in high school, and all of Mishima's work after I left a failed marriage to a Japanese man. So it seemed the universe was in sync with my new career.

Being in Theatre X was profound. I loved the creation of new work, the extensive research, playing with styles and, of course, audience responses. We were so lucky to have had long development periods. And living in Milwaukee at that time was affordable. I rarely had to pick up other jobs. But we held to a grueling schedule and attacked at every project with ambition. Our association with Ritsaert ten Cate was the apex of this approach to theatre. Daunting projects, artistry, ambition, and Dutch funding made for a great and fertile time.

While we were in Seattle, performing *The Unnamed*, I ran across a book at a bookstore, *Memoirs of a Medieval Woman*, the story of Margery Kempe. I brought it back to Wes Savick and Flora Coker, and we made a play, *Desire of the Moth for the Star*. We each took a chapter of her life. Mine was the first act. It was the comedic version of Margery Kemp's visions done in a vaudevillian style. We had the good fortune of a visiting Dutch guy, who was young, beautiful and had great comedic timing, to play Jesus. The numerous curtains for this production were designed and painted by visual artist Robert Kushner, paid for by the Milwaukee Art Museum's Fine Arts Society. It was a luscious mise-en-scene.

The touring was great fun and a way to connect with other artists of our ilk. Our association with Phillip Arnault and the Baltimore Theatre Project was a big part of our lives. Phillip remains a true friend and when he heard our board was trying to dismantle us, he sent in a ringer, asking Sommerset Waters to join the board. That held the board at bay for a while.

John Kishline (Core Ensemble Member, 1972–2004)

Our conception of Theatre X as an ensemble of six artists seeking their own way for the last thirty years, as opposed to an institutional corporation, is the conception that most of Milwaukee holds true. The ending was too sad. The board did not know what they had in us and thought they could create a better company. Their insistence that we needed hierarchy in structure was a death knell. We had operated as a collective, with all its blemishes but it worked.

What I cannot forget:
Offending the Audience
The Unnamed

Razor Blades
A Fierce Longing
Renovations
My Werewolf
Sweet Dreams
Rembrandt and Hitler or Me
The History of Sexuality
I Can't Stop Loving You
Success
Pilgrims of the Night
The Desire of the Moth for the Star
Good
Chomsky 9/11

Jan Fabre (Theatre X Guest Visual and Theatre Artist, Director of the Troubleyn Company)

Milwaukee, May 10, 1981

Arrived, haven't even opened my suitcase.
    Worked for the rest of the day at Theatre X.
    Setting up—technical things—lighting.
    At 11 pm started the dress rehearsal for the American premiere of *Theater geschreven met een "K" is een Kater*.
    I took part in it myself.
    The other actors didn't spare me.
    I'm hurting all over; I'll be covered in bruises tomorrow.
    Will Beckers, director of the Nieuw Vlaams Teater, played his part as the writer with just the right phlegmatism.

Milwaukee, May 11, 1981

We all went for it in the extreme.
    There was the right concentration and a sharp action-reaction impulse in the performance.
    There was intensity in the physical transfer of energy.
    Which is why we immediately received energetic applause at the end.
    So I can't complain.
    The American premiere was OK.

Milwaukee, May 12, 1981

Spent the whole day under negative tension.

    First the rumour went round that the performance would be banned.

    Then that there would be a protest against it.

    Then came the message that we could perform if we left out certain scenes and actions. (Censorship; you can guess I wouldn't allow that!)

    We went ahead with the performance.

    But it was not alive. It died before we even started.

    The performance was a corpse that tried to seize hold of life.

    At the end of the performance, even before the applause had died down, we were rounded up and arrested.

    We already have to appear in court tomorrow.

    We shan't go.

    A lawyer arranged by Curtis L. Carter will appear in court for us.

Milwaukee, May 13, 1981

Curtis L. Carter is sticking his neck out, defending me in public in interviews for newspapers and on TV.

    In an article in *The Milwaukee Journal* (the biggest paper in Wisconsin State) Curtis ended with: "I'm amazed that this incident could happen in America. It's not too late for Milwaukee to offer our apologies."

Milwaukee, May 15, 1981

To avoid the symptoms of fatigue one could sleep or rest.

    I write or draw.

    (To get all the press fuss about *Theater geschreven met een "K" is een Kater* out of my mind.)

Milwaukee, June 17, 1983

Learnt a lot about turtles today.

    How stupid can people be? At the last moment I had accepted turtles instead of tortoises because tortoises were apparently impossible to find and on top of that more expensive than gold.

    The performance had been going on for four hours.

    The action began, the gambling contest with the tortoises with burning candles on their backs.

    Normally this scene lasts 15 to 20 minutes.

    This time it was over after 2 minutes.

Those stupid turtles started squeaking and crying because their shell was too thin for the burning candles.

And apparently turtles do not suffer from vertigo (logically, as I realised later).

So they didn't stop at the edge of the stage but fell two metres to the floor with a cracking blow.

The audience went very quiet.

I tensed up and didn't know where to hide.

And after 20 seconds another cracking blow and 10 seconds later again, crash.

There was complete tumult; the audience started shouting and screaming.

I thought they would stop the show.

The audience became the personification of the hypocritical, devastating conflict between man and animal.

Marc, The Moon, saw a brilliant solution: he metamorphosed and himself became a turtle.

He too splattered to the edge of the stage and fell to the floor with the same sort of blow, picked up the three turtles, blew out the candles, started kissing them all over and went backstage with them.

Calm returned to the audience and their gaze was once again focused on the poetry of the performance.

A triumph of improvisation and living proof of how well I have trained my actors.

My actors are an embodiment of animal chaos and tamed intelligent energy.

The evening was back on the right course.

And now I'm ready to demolish the night.

Ritsaert ten Cate (Director of the Mickery Theatre, Amsterdam)[6]

Could Theatre X come to perform in the Mickery (Amsterdam)? They could and did (1975–85). They dealt with forbidden emotions and terrors with things many people never seem to face. ... Discussions developed between me and Theatre X company members: long and excruciating, fruitful and inspiring. And work followed: a trilogy performed in Amsterdam as well as in Milwaukee. Personal, close to the skin, vulnerable, searching .... Mickery and Theatre X were still moving in a mutually shared direction. John Schneider wrote the scripts, the company developed material and performed. But we wanted still more, Mickery and Theatre X were moving in a mutually shared direction.

American Theatre Ensembles Volume 1: Post-1970

John Schneider (Core Ensemble Member and Company Playwright, 1971–2004, and Author of "The Theatre X Book"*)*

I'm proud of everything we did. We showed that original experimental personal and engaged theatre could succeed in Milwaukee, could make work that mattered to people, that was of high quality and that could provide a living for artists. We planted many seeds here in terms of careers, spaces and the kinds of matters theatre could address and the many ways they could be addressed. We brought national and international attention to Milwaukee as a city that supported artistic experiment. It's the work we did that was and that remains important. Somehow that work meant something important to so very many people. So very many people played a role in it, were indispensable to its realization in so many ways—so very many more than are referred to in this piece.

CHAPTER 4
MABOU MINES
Jessica Silsby Brater

Mabou Mines was founded in 1970 in Nova Scotia, near the mining town that is its namesake. Cofounders JoAnne Akalaitis, Lee Breuer, Philip Glass, Ruth Maleczech, and David Warrilow gathered there at a home owned by Akalaitis and Glass to develop their inaugural piece, The Red Horse Animation. Though this was the company's first official production, the five founders had already collaborated for several years in Europe. When they established Mabou Mines, they conceived a structure of co-artistic directorship that would animate their ethos of collectivity. This model has persisted throughout the company's existence and has applied to its creative as well as administrative division of labor and power.

It has also made the company's aesthetic complicated to articulate; rather than a uniform style, the artistic directors' visions have tended to coalesce around a shared set of interests. The most conspicuous of these are an emphasis on multidisciplinary creation; a pioneering use of multimedia in performance and a practice of multimedia storytelling; the radical adaptation of classic texts; the creation of new works; an incorporation of intercultural stories and techniques; an interest in heightened language and speech; a commitment to a slow and intensively collaborative development process, a high degree of artistic autonomy for collaborators, and rigorous expectations for audiences. As the company describes itself, "Mabou Mines develops original works and re-imagined adaptations of classics through multi-disciplinary, technologically inventive collaborations. Each work is created in an extended development process" (Mabou Mines, "Company").

These common prerogatives were what brought the cofounders together in the first place. Profoundly influenced by their training in and exposure to European theatre in the 1960s, Akalaitis, Breuer, Glass, Maleczech, and Warrilow were part of a wave of avant-garde artists in the United States to import these techniques and use them to reinvent American theatre. For Mabou Mines, this revolution, once agreed upon in Canada, began in New York's East Village, which has remained the company's home.

What exactly does "avant-garde" mean to Mabou Mines artists? For Maleczech, the phrase always retained its militaristic roots. Mabou Mines has habitually been on the cusp of theatrical innovation. Maleczech often described the company's artists as "cannon-fodder." Though the terms are often used interchangeably by artists and scholars, Maleczech favored avant-garde over "experimental" because, she said, the latter indicates "you don't know what you are doing."[1] The danger associated with front line combat is appropriate for a company that has repeatedly risked financial stability and commercial success in favor of sweeping artistic freedom. For Breuer, the company's avant-garde status is tied to downtown theatre's seminal role in introducing New York audiences to groundbreaking theatrical techniques. "The city lives on tourism," he explains, and "theatre is a gate to tourism and downtown is the key. It's kind of like the laboratory for uptown. Whenever they can come down and steal anything that was invented downtown, they'll take it uptown."[2]

The Red Horse Animation, though produced by Ellen Stewart, founder of the decidedly downtown La MaMa ETC, in fact took place uptown at the Guggenheim Museum in November 1971. The selection of this nontraditional performance site was an announcement of the company's intention to break the mold. The production was later presented at the Paula Cooper Gallery in New York and at a number of other galleries around the country. Beyond its unconventional approach to theatre space, *Red Horse* was, according to Breuer, "not a play." Instead, it was a "stage piece" that "tries to exist in its own terms": "Stage time. Stage space. Dramatic structure" (Mabou Mines Digital Archive, "The Red Horse Animation"). Such a progressive concept required equally inventive performances. Rather than traditional characters, the cast played abstract qualities of the horse: Akalaitis its outline, Maleczech its heartline, and Warrilow its storyline. Together, these "combine to form and animate the red horse" (Ibid.).

Though written and directed by Breuer, the performers were integral to the ideas of the production, signaling the company's collective philosophy. For example, Akalaitis, Maleczech explained, played the outline because she

> is a structuralist. She structures everything. She doesn't ever want anything on the stage that isn't a structure. It can be an emotional structure, it can be a physical structure, it can be a movement structure, it can be a language structure, but it's got to be structured. … it's very appropriate that was her part.

Mabou Mines

In what was to become one of the hallmarks of Mabou Mines's approach, performers were central to conception, development, and interpretation. Philip Glass's specially designed flooring, which amplified the sound of the performers' bodies as they made impact with the deck, pointed to what would become the company's signature approach to multimedia storytelling.

Stewart presented *Red Horse* at La MaMa several months after its premiere, bringing the Mabou Mines artists' work to the neighborhood in which they lived. The East Village would also become their long-term artistic home. In the mid-1970s, the company moved into 122 Community Center on First Avenue and 9th Street, where they have remained, though their productions have been regularly produced throughout New York City and across the globe. This chapter traces Mabou Mines's influences and history through several key productions that reveal vital aesthetic tropes.

Inspirations and Reverberations

What happened before the cofounders arrived in the East Village? Akalaitis first met Maleczech and Breuer in San Francisco in the 1960s. Akalaitis was a graduate student in philosophy at Stanford when Maleczech and Breuer arrived in the Bay Area after meeting as undergraduates at UCLA. In San Francisco the young artists encountered beat poets and bohemian musicians such as Alan Ginsburg and Bob Dylan in cafes and immersed themselves in the city's burgeoning unconventional theatre scene. There they also met the performer Bill Raymond, who was a co-artistic director of the company from 1974 until the mid-1990s.

A central institution for the group was the San Francisco Actor's Workshop, founded by director and scholar Herb Blau with actor and director Jules Irving. Blau's project to establish an alternative to commercial theatre forecasted the explosion of American avant-garde companies in the 1960s and 1970s (see Blau 1964). The Actor's Workshop "was the first place where I ever read Genet or Beckett or Ionesco or Dürrenmatt," Maleczech said. In fact, it was the first theatre to produce Samuel Beckett's works in the United States; Beckett was to leave a profound imprint on Mabou Mines's early history. Genet's work was to become especially important for Akalaitis, who directed a number of his plays, including the notoriously difficult-to-stage *The Screens* in an epic production featuring Maleczech at Chicago's Guthrie Theatre (1989). Breuer served as Blau's assistant director on three productions as well as directing works on his own, including Beckett's

Comédie. Maleczech performed at the Actor's Workshop occasionally and took on a variety of jobs, serving as a dresser on Blau's production of *King Lear* starring Michael O'Sullivan, which inspired her own interpretation of the role in Mabou Mines's radical adaptation, *Lear* (1990).

Ronnie Davis's intensely physical approach was equally seminal, though quite different ideologically and technically. Davis founded the R.G. Davis Mime Troupe, which later became the San Francisco Mime Troupe. Maleczech recalled,

> We trained for hours and hours every day, and we did standard Commedia dell'Arte, from people like Goldoni. We did a little bit of pantomime, because it was good for physical training, although we didn't ever use pantomime. We used American mime, which is when the body becomes the object, rather than pantomime, which is pretending that you have the object.

Breuer and Raymond worked with the Troupe as well. In describing the difference in styles the artists experienced at the Actor's Workshop and with the Mime Troupe, Maleczech remembered:

> Herb [Blau] did not link acting to psychology, but to what you were using the play to say. And that's very important to me. He was the first person I ever encountered who did that. Ronnie [Davis] was interested in fulfilling his idea of what the play meant politically, always. Not that Herb wasn't, but Herb also saw the theatre as a way of connecting to the audiences' intellectual life, or teaching the audience that it could have an intellectual life. Ronnie was very skilled at using theatrical representations to elucidate his political agenda. Maybe because Herb's agenda was very complicated, it included more than just politics. He had a philosophical agenda. It was very interesting to see a play being used to do something other than it was written to do.

True to Davis's political aims, Breuer recalls that Davis introduced him to the work of Bertolt Brecht, whose approach became a central influence on Mabou Mines in general and on Breuer in particular. Blau's technique of using the play "to do something other than it was written to do" also became a crucial Mabou Mines strategy, while Davis's physical approach laid groundwork for the training Maleczech and Akalaitis would do with Jerzy Grotowski.

The Tape Music Center was a third site of inspiration, where Akalaitis, Raymond, and Maleczech worked with dancer Anna Halprin and composers Pauline Oliveros, Mortin Subotnik, and Ramon Sender. "They were looking for actors to be part of their music," Maleczech explained, "maybe to talk while the music was being played or maybe to walk through a series of objects while the music was being played, various things like that. Very discreet, very minimal." Oliveros would compose and perform music for Mabou Mines on productions including *Lear*. The Tape Music Center also set an important precedent for *Red Horse*'s decidedly non-Aristotelian form of storytelling and its use of gallery spaces rather than traditional theatres in New York and beyond.

Raymond moved to Topanga Canyon in 1964, where he remained for a decade. Akalaitis moved to New York in the same year, where she met Glass; later in 1964, the couple moved to Paris when Glass received a Fulbright to study there. Maleczech and Breuer followed Akalaitis to New York and then traveled in Europe, meeting the recently married Akalaitis and Glass in Greece. Breuer and Maleczech joined them on their return to Paris, where they encountered a lively scene of American ex-patriots, including Frederick Neumann, who became a co-artistic director in 1971 and remained with the company until his death in 2012. Neumann had been living in Europe since 1947 and met his wife, Mabou Mines associate artist Honora Fergusson, in Paris before Akalaitis, Glass, Breuer, and Maleczech arrived there. They also met the English-born Warrilow, who had been in Paris since 1957. As the group—Warrilow and Neumann included—developed plans to stage Brecht's *Mother Courage* at the American Theatre of Paris, Brecht translator Ralph Manheim sent Maleczech, Breuer, and Warrilow to Berlin to meet members of the Berliner Ensemble and to observe rehearsals.

At the Berliner Ensemble, the trio met Helene Weigel while smuggling Beatles records to the company. Weigel invited them to observe rehearsals for a reconstruction of Brecht's staging of *Man Is Man* and a new production of *Coriolanus*. In rehearsal, they watched as a small cohort of directors spoke simultaneously with individual actors about the same scene. This collective approach set a precedent for Mabou Mines's structure of co-artistic directorship. The young artists were also deeply impressed by the Berliner Ensemble's acting style. The performances they saw, Maleczech explained,

> were always revealing of the person. Not even the actor, but the *person* who was on the stage. The opinions, or the feelings or the history of the person playing the part, who the role is then a part of. So it was

twice removed from the role. It's very hard to do it. I think Brecht tried often to give them the signals, the signs, the gestures, that would do it for him—say for *him* how Ekkehard Schall should play that moment in *Arturo Ui* or how Helene Weigel should play saying goodbye to Coriolan or how Aufidius and his wife should say goodbye in *Coriolanus* … I think he directed the alienation. I'm not sure that the actors had all that much to do with it.

Though Mabou Mines has produced only one play by Brecht, *In the Jungle of the Cities* (directed by Ann Bogart in 1991), this strategy of acknowledging the performer as an active agent in the storytelling process has had powerful reverberations throughout Mabou Mines's history both in rehearsal and on stage. As former company member and frequent collaborator Greg Mehrten explains,

> Mabou Mines's style of acting, is not the kind of acting where the actor disappears … It's more that the actors try to find something within themselves that they can grasp onto to portray the character. It's not really showing that thing but it's using it; it's using yourself. (Mehrten 2011)

While Maleczech suggests that Brecht's directing was responsible for the acting style the Berliner Ensemble is known for, here Mehrten places responsibility on the performer. Breuer notes that

> most actors I work with for the first time who are not used to my way are shocked by how much input I do want from them. Most directors don't want to hear a thing. You got people with great ideas, how can you possibly not want to hear them? What I want is permission to say, do that, but not that.

This is in keeping with Mabou Mines's emphasis on autonomy for collaborators, especially performers.

Brecht was influential on approaches to directing in the company as well. Breuer describes himself as a "dialectical director," explaining that "you're supposed to think and feel two different things and then you're supposed to sit back and analyze the difference between your feeling and your thinking and that is the synthesis." Mabou Mines has regularly set challenging expectations not only for collaborators but also for audiences, expecting spectators to meet them halfway in the process of making meaning.

In 1966, Warrilow traveled to Poland to observe the legendary Polish director and acting teacher Jerzy Grotowski in action. In 1969, Akalaitis and Maleczech traveled from Paris to train with Grotowski in Avignon. Maleczech described physical training that

> went on for hours and hours and hours. Endless hours. It was really, really tiring. Exhausting. And then around the end of the fourth day we started doing other kinds of things, taking the plastiques and integrating them into some way of talking or some way of waiting or some way of listening. Other things started to be incorporated into what had been purely physical, learned stuff. After the sixth day there was no more gymnastics. It was just performing. And he would give a scene, you had to learn some speech and come out and give it and he would criticize you and he would do things to you to make you do it better—in his terms, better, but you weren't quite sure what his terms were, so it was a very mysterious sort of process to go through.

Akalaitis and Maleczech returned to Paris and taught what they learned to Breuer, Glass, and Warrilow. Maleczech also traveled with Breuer to Poland to see one of Grotowski's productions.

Though Grotowski's techniques certainly shaped the company's approach to acting, the cofounders were not especially influenced by the style of his productions. Grotowski "said that he didn't think that people should take his aesthetic, that the ideas behind it were for everyone to use but that it shouldn't come out looking like him," Maleczech explained. The Mabou Mines artists were, however, impressed by Grotowski's way of working. "The model of Mabou Mines," Breuer says, "was created by Grotowski's troupe. A small bunch of actors squirreled away in a basement somewhere could change the vision of theatre—inspired by Grotowski to change the face of theatre." This is exactly what the cofounders would set out to do in Nova Scotia.

During this period, the group began work on a production of Beckett's *Play*. According to Beckett scholar Ruby Cohn, the Mabou Mines collaborators brought together these disparate influences as they developed *Play*. "They evolved an approach to acting," Cohn writes, "that Breuer called Mr. Outside (Brecht) combined with Mr. Inside (Grotowski)." Cohn suggests that the project was initiated as an exploration in acting that ultimately provided the artists a vehicle with which to "work their way through and beyond realism" (Cohn 1999, 219). Mabou Mines's *Play* was first produced at the American Cultural Center in Paris in 1967.

As 1970 approached, Breuer, Maleczech, Akalaitis, Glass, and Warrilow explored the feasibility of making work in several cities, seeking a home base for a theatre company. Breuer and Maleczech remained in Paris, while Warrilow went to London. Akalaitis and Glass went to New York. As Stephen Bottoms details in *Playing Underground*, theaters and collectives such as Caffe Cino, La MaMa, and Theatre Genesis had already broken ground on new kinds of processes and performances in downtown New York in the 1960s; it was therefore a fertile landscape for the Mabou Mines cofounders' innovative theatrical goals (Bottoms 2004). Judith Malina, Julian Beck, and the Living Theatre provided another important precedent. In fact, Akalaitis and Breuer had seen the Living Theatre's production of *The Brig* (1963) and met Judith Malina in New York and the company cites "the politics of the exiled Living Theatre" among its influences (Mabou Mines, "Company"). It was clear that New York was the obvious choice for Mabou Mines's home base.

Early Becketts

After presenting *Red Horse* in New York, Mabou Mines turned its attention to Beckett's *Come and Go* in a production featuring Maleczech, Akalaitis, and former Mabou Mines company member Ellen McElduff. *Come and Go* was directed by Breuer and originally presented under the Brooklyn Bridge in May 1971. A month later, the company remounted *Play* at La MaMa. The performers wore a paste containing pancake batter and oatmeal on their faces, which Cohn remembered "flaked off in the rapidity of their delivery" (Cohn 1999, 220).

Play and *Come and Go* were later billed together with Warrilow's performance of Beckett's *The Lost Ones*, also directed by Breuer and first produced in 1975. With Beckett's permission, Warrilow and Breuer transposed this short story for the stage. As a student at Reading University, Warrilow had studied French language and literature, making him a sensitive reader of Beckett's texts. John Calder describes *The Lost Ones* as

> a metaphorical fable about the futility of most human activity, where Warrilow recited the text while moving tiny figures around on the ground, and up and down ladders inside a vertical cylinder, opened on one side to the audience's view. (Calder 1995)

When *The Lost Ones* was remounted in 1976 at the Public Theatre, Warrilow was awarded an OBIE. *New York Times* critic Mel Gussow, who wrote faithfully about Mabou Mines's encounters with Beckett's work, described the performance as "stunning" (Gussow 1976). Though he resigned from Mabou Mines in 1979, Warrilow continued to perform *The Lost Ones* until his death in 1995.

Warrilow's dramaturgy and performance were central to *The Lost Ones*, highlighting Mabou Mines's emphasis on agency and autonomy for collaborators, especially actors. "I felt quite independent as a performer," Maleczech says. The company "didn't want people to feel that they were stuck in whatever their initial artistic role was whether it was as a director or as a performer." According to Maleczech, the company wanted to "formalize the fact" that collaborators could serve as the lead artist in any collaborative role, an ideal that the collective structure of the company has supported.

Warrilow's astonishing performance, alongside the work of Breuer, Akalaitis, Maleczech, and MacElduff, drew notice from Public Theatre/New York Shakespeare Festival founder and artistic director Joseph Papp, who attended "Mabou Mines Performs Samuel Beckett" at Theatre for the New City, based then at the Jane West Hotel. Papp offered the company a residency at the Public Theatre, which lasted until the mid-1980s. As Maleczech remembers, "he came and he said afterwards, 'why don't you come over to my place.' And that was the first inkling that maybe we could do this kind of work in a theatre."[3] Mabou Mines also took possession of space in 122 Community Center in the mid-1970s.

Though a number of critically acclaimed Mabou Mines productions were presented at the Public over the course of the company's residency there, Papp indicated the unconventionality of Mabou Mines's work by referring to the artists as his "black sheep" (Gussow 1997).[4] That did not stop him from choosing Akalaitis as heir to his artistic directorship. Akalaitis resigned from Mabou Mines and served a short and controversial term at the helm of the Public Theatre from 1991–3. She remains the only woman to have held the post. Her 1984 American Repertory Theatre production of Beckett's *Endgame* had been equally provocative, drawing the playwright's ire over reports describing her set, music, and casting choices.

Endgame was not the first play of Beckett that Akalaitis directed. Her 1976 staging of his radio play *Cascando* with Mabou Mines was favorably reviewed by Gussow, who describes the "environment" Akalaitis creates: "As we enter the theatre, the back room of Richard Foreman's space on lower Broadway, seven actors are sitting silently around a long table. Taking a cue from Beckett's theme, each is obsessively and endlessly involved in specific artistic talk" (Gussow 1976). These actors included Warrilow, McElduff, and

Raymond, who had joined the company in New York in 1974. Maleczech provided a radio voice. Akalaitis's inventive transposition of Beckett's auditory world to a visual one garnered an OBIE for direction.

For his part, Neumann's interpretations of Beckett's texts at Mabou Mines led to a series of fruitful exchanges between the two that lasted until Beckett's death in 1989. Neumann returned to the United States in 1971 to join the company and first met Beckett in 1976. In 1979, Neumann performed in and directed a stage version of the novel *Mercier and Camier* with music by Glass and performances by Raymond and Terry O'Reilly. O'Reilly had seen the company perform in Memphis in 1971; two years later he followed Mabou Mines to New York, becoming a co-artistic director in 1974. O'Reilly also performed in and served as assistant director for Neumann's staging of the novella *Company*, co-directed with Fergusson in 1983, again with music by Glass. Both productions were first presented at the Public Theatre.

With Beckett's permission, Ruby Cohn shared the prose piece *Worstword Ho* with Neumann. The resulting 1986 production, presented at City Stage Company, was met with critical praise from Gussow, who lauded Neumann's "faithful" adaptation from page to stage, noting that the performer

> found his setting from within the text, placing his narrator (played by himself) knee deep in an open grave, a visualization of the author's "black hole agape in all."
>
> Mr. Neumann, who looks like a Shakespearean gravedigger, probes the text, telling us in sepulchral tones about birth and death and what passes in between. Next to the grave, which lies on a steeply inclined plane, is a skeleton imbedded in the earth. The skeleton appears to be in a racing position, as if it were the relic of a man running for his life, such as one might find in the ruins at Pompeii. (Gussow 1986)

Neumann, who staged his own solo piece, delivered the same kind of virtuoso performance Warrilow presented in *The Lost Ones*, one that Mabou Mines has regularly returned to with Maleczech's OBIE-winning performance in *Lear*, co-artistic director Karen Kandel's Drama League Award-winning one in *Peter and Wendy* (1996), and artistic associate Maude Mitchell's OBIE-winning work in *Dollhouse* (2003). The company's commitment to investing performers with creative power has fostered a hospitable environment for singular performances.

Less famous, perhaps, but equally innovative among the company's encounters with Beckett's texts was Maleczech's staging of the short story *Imagination Dead Imagine*. Presented in 1984 at the Wooster Group's Performing Garage, Maleczech and collaborator Linda Hartinian worked with the Holographic Museum to create what was at the time (at 4 feet, 3 inches long) the largest hologram ever to be used on stage. Hartinian had worked with Raymond in Topanga Canyon on a 1970 production of Beckett's *Play*. In seeking Beckett's permission, Maleczech described her concept "as a holographic visualization with the complete text on tape. This would be an installation in a gallery or museum and would not involve any live performer" (Beckett 1981). Maleczech's idea builds upon her early work at the Tape Music Center and on her experience with *Red Horse*. A hologram of a young woman's body rotates slowly above a bier sculpted with the outline of everyday objects, designed by L. B. Dallas. The recorded voice of an elderly woman reads Beckett's text aloud. John Lennon's "Imagine" drifts in and out with the lights. The image in the hologram was Maleczech and Breuer's daughter Clove Galilee; the voice Ruth Nelson's. Maleczech's groundbreaking incorporation of holography is another example of Mabou Mines's pioneering use of multimedia in performance.[5]

Despite the imagination Breuer, Warrilow, Neumann, Akalaitis, and Maleczech brought to Beckett's words onstage, by the end of the 1980s the company had virtually ceased to produce new productions of his work, though Mabou Mines remounted a La Jolla Playhouse production of *Happy Days* featuring Maleczech and directed by Robert Woodruff in 1998. In Lois Oppenheim's *Directing Beckett*, Breuer suggests that what he perceived to be Beckett's increasingly "rigid" perspective on how artists could stage his work influenced the decision to move in other directions (Oppenheim 1994, 23).

New Works and Adventurous Adaptations

While Mabou Mines's productions of Beckett's texts brought significant critical attention to the company, the development and presentation of new works were equally important in building an artistic identity. Breuer and Akalaitis are the best-known directors in the company's history, but every co-artistic director has, in turn, been at the helm of creating new work. Projects initiated by each of the co-artistic directors are presented in a queue, and several productions may be in development simultaneously.

Accordingly, even as the company was delving deeply into approaches to staging Beckett's texts, Breuer was continuing to flex his muscles as a writer. The resulting body of work—his "Animations"—also includes *The B. Beaver Animation* (1974), *The Shaggy Dog Animation* (1978), *An Epidog* (1996), *Ecco Porco* (2002), *Summa Dramatica* (2009), and *Porco Morto* (2009). Breuer has consistently directed these pieces himself and they form an important body of new work that has spanned Breuer's career and the company's history. *B. Beaver* and *The Shaggy Dog* are early examples of Mabou Mines's use of puppetry in performance. In *B. Beaver*, performers manipulated the beaver's robe by operating it with sticks while lying on their backs.[6] Mabou Mines's interest in puppetry is another example of its commitment to multimedia storytelling.

The central character in *The Shaggy Dog* is a female dog named Rose who appeared as a Bunraku-style puppet manipulated by four performers. Rose was created by visual artist and designer Julie Archer, who first collaborated with the company on *Dressed Like an Egg* (1977) and served as co-artistic director from 2005–13. Rose's voice was collectively created by a chorus, Maleczech, Akalaitis, Hartinian, Neumann, O'Reilly, and the seven-year-old Galilee. *Shaggy Dog* was published in 1979 with *Red Horse* and *B. Beaver* in *A Trilogy for Mabou Mines*. In her introduction, Bonnie Marranca notes Breuer's emphasis on choral performance, a trope that has run throughout his career (Marranca 1979, 6–27). In *Summa Dramatica*, Maleczech originated the role of Sri Moo Parahamsa (played by Karen Kandel after Maleczech's death in 2013), an acting guru who happens to be a cow. In a kind of physical chorus that echoes the group puppetry work in *B. Beaver*, a second performer (Galilee; later Jessica Weinstein) plays Sri Moo's bottom half. Breuer combined his animations into the epic *La Divina Caricatura*, which was presented at La MaMa in 2013.

Although she performed in Mabou Mines's early Beckett pieces and in several of Breuer's Animations, by 1980 Akalaitis had turned her attention from performing to directing. Following *Cascando*, Akalaitis directed *Dressed Like an Egg*, based on writings by the French poet Colette. That production, featuring Maleczech, McElduff, Raymond, Warrilow, and Akalaitis herself, won an OBIE for distinguished production. Akalaitis expanded her interest in devising with *Dead End Kids*, which she was prompted to develop in "response to the tremendous political movement in the country" mobilized in protest of the controversial use of nuclear power (Akalaitis 2011). Echoing the polyphony of grassroots political movements, *Dead End Kids* was developed collaboratively by an interdisciplinary company of artists based on a collective research process. The production incorporated an eclectic mix of excerpts from writers as diverse as Paracelsus, Marie Curie, Goethe, and General L. R. Groves.[7] As Mehrten remembers,

> Originally it started out as a workshop where a lot of people who weren't in Mabou Mines were invited to think in collaborative ways—musicians and filmmakers, all kinds of people—because it wasn't meant to be like a normal play. It had all these vignettes from different periods in history all around the subject of nuclear power. (Mehrten 2011)

Mehrten's description is indicative of a growing interest in collective creation in the final quarter of the twentieth century in the United States—a movement that has continued into the twenty-first century. Mabou Mines helped to establish this trend.

In addition to multidisciplinary artists, the production featured performances by co-artistic directors Maleczech, Neumann, O'Reilly, and Raymond and former company members Mehrten and McElduff. There is no video of the stage production, originally produced at the Public Theatre before touring nationally, but the company returned to the project to adapt it for film in 1984. That version begins with a scientist eagerly explicating the atom. Shortly thereafter, Neumann appears, ensconced in an armchair and smoking a cigarette, to guide the audience through a history of attempts at alchemical transformation. Other vignettes feature a television show about alchemy, school children learning about atomic warfare from a picture book, and a stand-up comedian (David Brisban) making sexually exploitative jokes.

After an early introduction, Marie Curie, played by Maleczech, appears repeatedly on the periphery of subsequent scenes, providing a moral touchstone for the audience as she witnesses the increasingly dangerous unanticipated fruits of her discovery. For Akalaitis, Curie formed the center of the piece as a rare historical example of a woman in science. Curie, Akalaitis says, was "a woman who was a pre-eminent scientist and basically killed herself doing her work, who was incredibly important in a world where women are not important" (Akalaitis 2011). In a holistic approach to female leadership, the production frames Curie as a mother as well as a scientist.

Akalaitis harnessed the collective energy of the *Dead End Kids* company in service of unabashedly political aims, presenting antinuclear as well as feminist perspectives, managing to link these seemingly disparate issues. By the conclusion of the performance, scholar Elinor Fuchs had noticed "the most unsettling version of the connection Akalaitis had been making all along between the war state and the sexist state, male nuclear fantasies and the exploitation of women" (Fuchs 1996, 111). The mash-up of Curie's presence as a pioneering woman in science, references to the Manhattan Project, and Brisban's misogynistic stand-up "comedian" underlines Akalaitis's view of the patriarchal forces at work in both international and American scientific and military worlds.

Hajj, presented in 1983 also at the Public Theatre, was less overtly political than *Dead End Kids* but equally theatrically inventive. Rather than the history of science, *Hajj* draws instead on family history. The piece began as a poem Breuer wrote about a friend who died before he paid back $40 he owed her. Breuer adapted the text into a solo piece for Maleczech when her father, Alexander Reinprecht, took his own life before she could pay back several hundred dollars he had lent her to support her first directing project for Mabou Mines, *Vanishing Pictures* (1980). In his program note, Breuer described *Hajj* as a "performance poem," which is "a simultaneous pilgrimage into the future and the past … concerned with the relationship between emotional and fiscal debt" (Mabou Mines Archive, Production Files). The title finds its origins in Muslim religious pilgrimage; footage of the hajj plays at one point during the performance.

Intertwined financial and emotional distress reverberates not only with Breuer and Maleczech's biographies but also with company history. "When we were rehearsing *Hajj* the first time and we were having real money troubles," Breuer says, "I couldn't put 10 minutes together to rehearse because [Ruth] had to make phone calls." In publications and interviews throughout his career such as "The Funding Game" for *Other Stages* (1982) and "The Two-Handed Gun: Reflections on Power, Culture, Lambs Hyenas and Government Support for the Arts" for the *Village Voice* (1991), Breuer has decried the severe economic limitations on American artists. "We should be paid a research and development fee by Broadway" for the pioneering work of downtown artists that often makes its way into commercial theatre, Breuer argues, "but we're not and that's the whole point. If we were in the car industry and we were inventing a bumper, we'd be paid a research and development fee. But we're not. So that's a little bit of the problem."

The predatory arrangement Breuer describes finds echoes onstage in *Hajj*. Currency is emotional as well as biological. "Love is money, Alex," Maleczech says early in the performance (Breuer 1987, 24). And later, "I rip you off," she says as she unhusks a latex mask of her father's face from her own (122). While Maleczech's performance cannot rid her of fiscal or emotional debt, she has the power to summon a version of her father to the stage. "Here in the dark box of my throat I bring you back to life," she says, "You can't leave me; that plan has a flaw / We'll never sort each other's atoms out" (122). Maleczech resurrects a patriarch to confront a father-daughter relationship of epic proportions, introducing questions of gender and power into *Hajj*'s intersection of economy and psychology.

Hajj also capitalizes on the company's multimedia storytelling. Maleczech and Breuer's collaborators were Archer and Craig Jones. Archer designed a vanity and three-sided mirror where Maleczech begins the performance, making herself up. Jones created projections that appear in the mirrors, including a film based on a cross-country road trip Maleczech took with her father as a child. Jones uses live feed to project Maleczech's face into the mirrors as she sits at the vanity. Mabou Mines received a grant from Sony, which gave the company access in rehearsal to the cameras and equipment needed to execute what was at the time a groundbreaking incorporation of technology in performance.

Strikingly, the four collaborators worked without a director—an anomaly in Mabou Mines's history. "There couldn't be a singular decider of things," Maleczech explains, "because it was so complex. ... Eventually," she says, "we all bent our efforts to realize the writing." Archer explains, "We all worked on it, and, with the exception of the writing, we all weighed in on all aspects of it. We moved forward collaboratively. We worked by sort of piling on and pulling off and piling on and pulling off" (Archer 2011). The group's collective work earned OBIEs for Maleczech and Archer. In another of Mabou Mines's virtuoso performances, Maleczech brings personal history to the stage but moves her own experience beyond autobiography, placing elements of family history into a social context, just as Mehrten describes.

Mabou Mines's earliest significant reconsideration of a classic text was Breuer's *The Gospel at Colonus*, a bold interpretation of Sophocles's *Oedipus at Colonus* first presented in 1983 at BAM's Next Wave Festival. Breuer was struck by the intercultural link Zora Neale Hurston drew between Greek tragedy and the Pentecostal church. "As was the classic Greek performance, the Pentecostal service is a communal catharsis which forges religious, cultural, and political bonds," he writes (Breuer 1989, ix). Further inspiration came from the gospel group the Five Blind Boys of Alabama. Musician and composer Bob Telson, who first collaborated with Breuer on *Death in Venice* (1980), worked with the Five Blind Boys and took Breuer to a concert. There, Breuer began to form an idea that Oedipus could be played collectively by the Five Blind Boys. The resulting production featured lyrics by Breuer with Telson, music by Telson, design by Alison Yerxa, and was produced by Liza Lorwin, who previously served as the producer for Mabou Mines's residency program, ReCherChez.[8] Following three years in development and a premiere at BAM, it was presented on Broadway (1988) as well as internationally. In 1996, *The Gospel of Colonus* was presented at Carnegie Hall, marking its thousandth performance. It was remounted at the Public Theatre/New York Shakespeare Festival's Delacorte Theatre in Central Park in 2018, in celebration of the thirty-fifth anniversary of its premiere and Breuer's fifty years of contributions to the theatre.

Classical theatre scholar Helene Foley suggests that *The Gospel at Colonus* is "aimed at a modern form of tragic catharsis" and is

> the only adaptation of Greek tragedy ... that attempted to make the choral engagement in the story grow logically out of a contemporary ritual setting. It deploys a reimagined version of the full mixture of speech, act-dividing song, and shared lyrics between actor and chorus contained in the original. (Foley 2014, 108–9)

Enhancing the communal storytelling through song that Foley describes, the Messenger (originally played by Morgan Freeman) and Five Blind Boys each play Oedipus in turn. A featured white grand piano further underscores the centrality of music. As Foley describes, the piano functions as "Oedipus's sanctuary and descends and rises with his death and resurrection" (Foley 2014, 109). Following his demise, the piano (as deus ex machina) sinks into the floor, carrying the deceased Oedipus down with it.

As the company's residency at the Public Theater came to an end in the mid-1980s, 122 Community Center increasingly became the center of Mabou Mines's artistic activities. The office there had already been the locus of the company's administrative work. Among the founding co-artistic directors, Maleczech took on significant organizational labor. Mehrten assisted in the office, recalling that Maleczech

> had been a legal secretary so she knew how to work in the office, and I did too, and some of the other people didn't. And so it just evolved that we would work in the office. It's like the Soviet system, each according to his needs and to each to his abilities. Wherever your strengths were they tried to utilize those.

Under Maleczech's leadership, the company has also regularly relied on managing directors and company managers who have included Tony

Vasconcellos, Joe Stackell, and, after Maleczech's death, Yasmeen Jawhar. In addition to the office, Mabou Mines has also relied on their 122 Community Center rehearsal space. As Smith Fischer explains,

> [T]he performance and rehearsal space called ToRoNaDa—"no bull"—is named for four individuals whose legacies have continued, despite their deaths, to sustain the company: former managing director Tony Vasconcellos; Ron Vawter, a founding member of the Wooster Group and Mehrten's partner; Nancy Graves, who helped the company during its first years in New York; and David Warrilow, who died of AIDS in 1995. (Smith Fischer 2012, 244)

Though the ToRoNaDa served as a performance space—*Happy Days* and *Summa Dramatica* were both performed there, for example—it did not have the capacity for the company's more technologically ambitious and larger-scale productions, such as *Lear*.

In *Lear*, which opened in 1990 at the Triplex Theatre in New York, Mabou Mines once again took aim at the conventional canon. Maleczech, inspired by the 1961 Actors Workshop production, was driven to play the title role. "I just wanted to say the words, and of course I realized very quickly that there wasn't a way for me to say those words—there wasn't a provision for any woman, not only me, but any woman to say those words," Maleczech said. Though there is a history of actresses in Shakespearean breeches roles—Sarah Bernhardt famously played Hamlet—there was no such tradition for *King Lear* until Maleczech set the precedent, paving the way for Glenda Jackson's 2016 turn in the role at London's Old Vic, reprised on Broadway in 2019.

Determined to avoid an anomalous Queen Lear, Breuer developed a concept that would contextualize Maleczech in the role. With dramaturg Alisa Solomon, Breuer envisaged a matriarchy set in a fictional American South, cross-casting roles and changing gender pronouns but keeping the rest of the text intact. Raymond played Goneril; McElduff was Elva (Edgar). Karen Kandel, who became a co-artistic director in 2015, made her company debut as Edna, a female Edmund. Mehrten played the Fool as a drag queen in a fitting transliteration of a type that regularly traverses the borders and boundaries of Shakespeare's texts. Allison Yerxa's design, which includes a sprawling front porch replete with rocking chairs, supports the imaginary Southern American matriarchy imagined by Breuer. Actors often travel the stage in golf carts dressed as cars. The heath recalls rolling Southern hills. Lear's retinue is comprised of bird dogs.

Breuer and Maleczech's interventions prompt the audience to reconsider theatrical as well as societal conventions. "Lear is queen and mother figure of an extended family and she has neglected the nuclear aspects of being a mother tremendously in order to be a powerhouse in the extended family," Breuer says. "This is a person who is more a king than a father. Or more a queen than a mother" (Breuer 2002, disk 2, hour 3). The posture Breuer identifies is likely to have been one familiar to Mabou Mines's audiences. "Look at every powerful woman CEO in New York because you're looking at Lear," he says. While Shakespeare's story of a generational struggle is still present in *Lear*, Mabou Mines's production also serves as a cautionary tale about the potential consequences for women with too much power, typical of the company's feminist interrogation of classic texts.

Jill Godmilow's documentary, *Lear '87 Archive*, reveals a process typical of Mabou Mines as well, with actors chiming in to make thematic contributions that shaped the direction of the production. Kandel, working with the company for the first time, was surprised to encounter a rehearsal room in which "lots of people said things like, I don't think that's right, I disagree" (Kandel 2012). During these first experiences with the company, says Kandel, she "became acutely aware of what it means to be a full creative participant" (Mabou Mines, "Karen Kandel"). Because the *Lear* company was so large, the production spent three years in development as performers took on other paid gigs and the company fundraised to pay them all. This is characteristic of Mabou Mines's regular financial obstacles. Eventually, in a vexed dynamic that Smith Fischer describes, the company accepted corporate sponsorship from AT&T (Smith Fischer 1993).

Though the production earned OBIEs for Maleczech, Kandel, and Isabell Monk (Gloucester), it also marked what Fogarty describes as "a bad time in the company." Akalaitis resigned from Mabou Mines, and Mehrten, McElduff, and Bill Raymond followed after *Lear*. Fogarty initially came on staff to assist in the office, and as with Maleczech, with her administrative responsibilities came creative power. She became a co-artistic director in 1999. Despite the turmoil of this changing of the guard, the shift in co-artistic directorship paved the way for fresh artistic voices, creating a dynamic that blended vintage Mabou Mines approaches with new perspectives.

Peter and Wendy is one such work. A 1996 commission by the Spoleto Festival USA, the piece is based on J. M. Barrie's novel. Though it was directed by Breuer, the text was adapted and produced by Lorwin, designed by Archer, and featured a virtuoso performance by Kandel. All four worked closely on concept and development. Lorwin and Archer were inspired by their children to create the piece. Kandel provides voices for all of the characters, who are embodied by puppets inspired by Bunraku. The production garnered another OBIE for Kandel, "a graceful performer of 1,000 voices," including "a gruff Scottish burr for Mr. Darling, a musical lilt for Smee, a scamp's pout for Peter. She even manages to give each Lost Boy a personality," according to *New York Times* critic Peter Marks (1997). One of the company's most popular productions, *Peter and Wendy* has been remounted several times at New York's New Victory Theatre and traveled to the Edinburgh Festival in 2009.

Bunraku puppetry, though deeply influential on Breuer in particular, has not provided the only global influence on the company. *Sueños* (1989), directed by Maleczech, was adapted from writings by Sor Juana Inés de la Cruz, Eduardo Galeano, and Homero Aridjis. In 1999, Mabou Mines presented *Belén: A Book of Hours* at the XV Festival del Centro Storico at El Claustro de Sor Juana in Mexico City; the bilingual production subsequently toured in the United States and Mexico. Conceived and directed by Maleczech, *Belén* drew on the history of the Catholic Church's infamous Mexican prison for prostitutes and pregnant, unmarried women. The piece was collaboratively created with international artists—designer Archer, American poet Catherine Sasanov, Mexican performer Jesusa Rodriguez, and Argentinian composer and musician Liliana Felipe. O'Reilly's work has also been characterized by internationalism; he directed Stan Lai's English translation of his play *Secret Love in Peach Blossom Land* and, with Simon Wong, wrote a children's puppet play inspired by Chinese and American folk tales. He also received a 2014–15 Fulbright scholarship to study aboriginal ritual and theatre at the Taipei National University of the Arts.

Maleczech took on another international woman in history with Lucia Joyce in *Lucia's Chapters of Coming Forth by Day*, written and directed by Sharon Fogarty (played by Maria Tucci following Maleczech's death). *Lucia's Chapters* was Fogarty's first project as co-artistic director; in it she builds on the company's emphasis on interrogating dominant historical narratives from a feminist perspective. Lucia Joyce, the daughter of James and Nora Joyce, was emotionally intense and sexually adventurous. She spoke several languages fluently and was a promising dancer. Some scholars credit Lucia Joyce as the originator of the portmanteau language her father's writing is known for. She was diagnosed with schizophrenia by Carl Jung and institutionalized for the remainder of her life while still in her twenties. Inspired in part by Carol Loeb Shloss's book, *Dancing in the Wake*, which considers Lucia Joyce as an artist in her own right and reassesses her mental illness as a misogynistic misdiagnosis, Fogarty set out to create a performance that would present Lucia Joyce in a complex and powerful light.

Initially, Fogarty thought she would devise the performance rather than write the script herself:

> I had seen Mabou Mines in action with *Lear* and with *Epidog* and a few other things, but it didn't seem like anybody was the author per se. I mean, Lee was the author of *An Epidog*, but it certainly felt like other people had some authorship and certainly with *Lear*, everybody in the room was rewriting this thing. So, I didn't feel too worried about the writer part. (Fogarty 2011)

After extensive research, she says, "I had all this material and here's the composition part and I don't know what the hell to do. I was trying to channel JoAnne Akalaitis." With dramaturg Jocelyn Clark, Fogarty developed a script, originally titled *Cara Lucia*, which featured three versions of Lucia: young, old, and a riff on Anna Livia Plurabelle of *Finnegans Wake*. *Cara Lucia* was performed at HERE Arts Center in 2003. Galilee played the young Lucia to her mother's older version and Rosemary Fine played the "Fictional Lucia." Fogarty subsequently revised the script, condensing all three Lucias into one performed by Maleczech. She also added James Joyce, played (often in shadow) by Paul Kandel. "I really felt like Joyce was there, however the hell I tried to keep him out," Fogarty says (2011). The new production, *Lucia's Chapters of Coming Forth by Day*, was first presented at Colby College in Maine in 2007.

The production opens with a sequence of Archer's projections inspired, as was *Finnegans Wake*, by Egyptian hieroglyphics of the afterlife. When the lights come up on Maleczech's Lucia, she is seated in a chair with her own book, which she uses to guide the audience through memories of her past. "My name is Lucia Joyce," she says in her first line, "My father is James Joyce, the famous Irish writer. I am seventy-five years old, I like to smoke, and it costs a lot" (Fogarty 2007, 2). This opening salvo frequently resulted in laughs. Although Archer's projections introduce a mysterious and dreamlike element, Fogarty and Maleczech make dynamic use of comedy to instill their Lucia with power. "Mabou Mines uses comedy to cut through sentimentality," Galilee explains (Galilee 2012). In Mabou Mines productions, comedy frequently functions as a dialectical strategy, scrambling emotional signals and forcing the audience to grapple with conflicting thoughts and feelings. In this case, comedy is juxtaposed with the ominous atmosphere created in part by James Joyce's shadowy presence.

In a reference to Nuvoletta in *Finnegans Wake*, he emerges from behind a scrim at the conclusion of the performance to escort his daughter into the next world.

Another technique characteristic of Mabou Mines is what Fogarty describes as Maleczech's use of a slight British "old lady" accent. Maleczech likewise employed an accent in her representation of Marie Curie. Akalaitis remembers it as "a kind of comedic Polish accent. It was very, very funny and I have no idea how she did it, but she did it. I think it is because Mabou Mines is very interested in accents and different ways of speaking" (Akalaitis 2011). Co-artistic directors have often deployed "different ways of speaking" to put the world of the play into a social context for the audience. This strategy also functions to elevate language and, often, as in the chorus used to voice Rose the Dog, to depart from realism.

It is also the case with associate artist Maude Mitchell's collaboration with Breuer on Mabou Mines's *Dollhouse*, which makes use of over-the-top Norwegian accents. In a version that stages the play's subtext for contemporary audiences, Little People play Ibsen's small-minded men, Mark Povinelli as Torvald, Kristopher Medina as Nils Krogstad, and Ricardo Gil as Dr. Ranke. Nora Helmer (Mitchell) and Kristine Linde (Mabou Mines artistic associate Honora Fergusson; after her death Janet Girardeau) tower over them, squashing their bodies into tiny furniture on a set several sizes too small, an analogy for Nora's stifling social context. "This is such a physically extreme production," Mitchell says, "I say it's like doing an extreme sport. I have to physically diminish myself and make myself smaller. I'm on my knees, or picking up the children, picking up Torvald" (Metz 2005). The idea to play with scale in *Dollhouse*, Breuer explains,

> first came in 1968 when I saw a Brecht-adapted production of *Coriolanus*. It's the first time I saw a tragedy turned into a comedy, and they also did it with scale. Because the two stars of the Berliner Ensemble represented the patriarchy and they were about five feet tall, and the armies were about 6'5". And it worked for sending up the aristocracy, so I thought the same idea would work for setting up the patriarchy. (Del Signore 2009)

Mitchell and Breuer question the relationship between gender and scale. In what Povinelli describes as a "challenge to the audience," here Mabou Mines deploys a dialectical strategy, which asks spectators to reconsider societal assumptions (Metz 2005).

As subsets of the dialectical technique typical of Mabou Mines's social critiques, the company also employs humor and different ways of speaking—the accents—to provoke critical cultural analysis. For Breuer, the company's intervention "turns the play into a wonderfully ironic comedy" in which audiences "don't know whether to laugh or cry. We engage in this melodramatic style of acting, in the style of silent movies, and when you put all this together—the over-the-top comedy, the visual punning—it becomes a tragic sort of comedy." Some of the humor is found in Mitchell and Povinell's manipulation of the physical contrast between them. The resulting comedy is entertaining but simultaneously disquieting. The juxtaposition of comedy and searing social critique was highly successful for audiences; among other awards, Breuer and Mitchell received OBIEs for direction and performance, respectively, and the production toured around the world for seven years after its 2003 premiere at St. Ann's Warehouse in Brooklyn. The production was also adapted to film in 2008.

Playing It Forward

In 2012 and 2013 the company experienced another upheaval of the kind Fogarty describes in the early 1990s. Neumann and Fergusson died in 2012 and Maleczech in 2013, leaving Breuer as the last remaining cofounder. These losses coincided with a major positive development for the company: for the first time in its history, Mabou Mines would have a dedicated performance space. 122 Community Center, the company's longtime home, is a former school building owned by the City of New York and shared with several other arts institutions, including Performance Space New York (formerly PS122). In 2013, the city began renovations and in 2017 the building reopened with refurbished office space, storage, dressing rooms, two rehearsal rooms, and a new theatre for Mabou Mines. Acknowledging the importance of its history, the company painted the ceiling of the new theatre the distinctive royal blue color Archer had chosen for the walls of the ToRoNaDa.

Mabou Mines Theatre opened with *Glass Guignol: The Brother Sister Play*, in which Breuer and Mitchell orchestrate a mash-up of Tennessee Williams and Mary Shelley, inspired by Dadaist ready-made art. A puppet of Shelley intermittently texts a puppet of Lord Byron, giving Mabou Mines's multimedia storytelling a decidedly twenty-first-century perspective. So does Fogarty's *Faust 2.0*, a 2019 adaptation of Goethe's *Faust II*, in which deities and devils appear on a swath of screens surrounding the playing space, recalling a Zoom conference. Fogarty's attraction to Goethe's play first came from Doctor Marianus's worshipful commendation of the "eternal feminine" at the play's conclusion, bringing the company's feminist revisions of the canon into a contemporaneous "the future is female" philosophy.

While the company has always been conscious of honoring its history, co-artistic directors have also kept eyes on the future by investing in the work of emerging artists. This began as early as the late 1970s with the residency and mentorship program ReCherChez, founded by Breuer, Maleczech, and Raymond and produced by Lorwin. Though ReCherChez lasted only five years, it established the foundation for SUITE/Space, which began in the ToRoNaDa studio and has moved into Mabou Mines Theatre. With the support of public and private funders, the residency program provides space, mentorship, development support, and performance opportunities for emerging artists who "share Mabou Mines' commitment to breaking new ground in form and content" (Mabou Mines, "Suite/Space"). The luxury of a dedicated theatre also allows the company to program runs of productions by former resident artists in its own space, as it did with Mallory Catlett's *This Was the End* in 2018.

The loss of Neumann and Maleczech and the introduction of a state-of-the-art performance space alter the company's future calculus in unforeseeable ways. Associate artists Galilee and David Neumann, both children of Mabou Mines artists, have sought answers about the future of the company on stage in productions that honor the legacy of their parents. Galilee, working with her wife and artistic partner Jenny Rogers, completed a work begun by Maleczech before her death. *Imagining the Imaginary Invalid*, a meditation on Molière and medicine, was presented at La MaMa in 2016. David Neumann's *I Understand Everything Better* juxtaposes Neumann's experience of Fred Neumann's illness and death with the impending arrival of a hurricane, using some of the intercultural dance techniques that influenced his father. Kandel's first work as co-artistic director, *The Vicksburg Project*, still in development as of this writing, is "a song cycle following women's lives in Mississippi from the Civil War to today" (Mabou Mines, "Karen Kandel"). Though there are echoes in the description of Maleczech's *Song for New York: What Women Do While Men Sit Knitting* (2007), a site-specific performance on the Hudson River for which Kandel wrote a poem and performed, her new work is certain to introduce a unique perspective in the company's trajectory. Mabou Mines moves into the future with a firm grip on its historical priorities and an openness to new possibilities.

If its past is any indicator, the company will continue to position itself at the forefront of theatrical innovation, seeking new ways to tell stories, challenge artists, and surprise audiences. In a fitting acknowledgment of the significance of Mabou Mines's contribution to American theatre, Breuer—the last remaining founding co-artistic director—received TCG's 2019 lifetime achievement award.

CHAPTER 5
GOAT ISLAND
Nicholas Lowe and Sarah Skaggs

As an extended orientation to the work of Goat Island, this chapter offers an initial narrative outline of the grounds and the overall tone of the company's approaches. This narrative will be followed by a description of their performances and a reflection on the closing of the company and the context of its legacy. It is important to recognize how the working environment in Chicago, but also the wider arts landscape outside the United States, played so significantly into the making of the company and their ability to sustain a long working process for each piece. The specific location at the Wellington Avenue Church Gymnasium in Chicago was Goat Island's studio and performance space from 1987 to 2009, the entire life of the company. In twenty-two years the company made nine performances, an average of about two and a half years in the making of each, which in part illustrates a key aspect of their preferred approach to working.

The temperament of the company can also be understood as a long-standing exploration of collaboration. Based upon an ethical commitment to each other and each project, collaboration infused every part of the company's activities, as a creative response to politics and structures. Part of this commitment initially was financial; sharing the rental costs of the gymnasium gave the company a solid home base and starting point. This collective operating support structure postponed the need for more in-depth fundraising through grant writing and individual donor support and to some degree aided the development and confirmation of robust creative habits.

In the processes of making each of the distinctly named performances, there was an extended iterative working approach where each piece would go through a sequence of phases. Work on a performance typically began with a period of research based upon a prompt or directive. As work progressed, an emergent quality developed, where any unresolved aspects were carried forward for further investigation into the next piece. Following the information-gathering and research period, the company would work from an initial sharing of their individually found creative responses, into a period of collective content building. How a performance came together was usually based upon a series of pragmatic experiments that would look at material for its resonances regardless of its original location, the original theme, or prompt. At a particular and undetermined moment in the process, the company would turn to a period of editing. It is here that the role of Lin Hixson as the company's nonperforming director was significant. Sometimes describing her role as being that of an outside eye, Hixson developed an approach through working with Goat Island that involved her being a facilitator and coordinator helping to present the ideas that were generated by the others. Significant was their habit of sharing research as a part of their working process, but also of sharing details of their research with audiences through work-in-progress presentations, teaching, and the publication of reflective writings.

The company established its reputation early in the UK, which modified their reception to some degree in the United States. It has been anecdotally noted often that the company was "better known" in Europe than in the United States. This could be because once Goat Island established a network of presenters, performances were toured to more cities in Europe and the UK. While every piece was performed in Chicago and the United States, each work was presented sometimes nearly three times more often in the UK and Europe. While the work was in development in Chicago, work-in-progress performances were usually held at the Wellington Avenue Gymnasium. Once established, the company would generally present a work-in-progress early in the process, and then working through numerous invited residencies in the UK, a performance would be polished and premiered prior to a European touring schedule. At its most extended, as much as three and a half years might pass from the first rehearsal before returning to Chicago in its final form. Additionally, it was common for a performance to be programmed into a festival long after work on a subsequent new piece had already begun. For example, the initial production and development for Goat Island's third performance, *Can't Take Johnny to the Funeral*, began in spring 1990, went through its work-in-progress presentations, into its premiere performances first in the UK and then much later in the United States. The company carried this piece through an extensive touring schedule culminating in its final performance in June 1994 at the Philadelphia Museum of Art. This was a year after *It's Shifting, Hank*, the subsequent work, had premiered in the UK. Disappearing from view at home for such long periods of time often surrounded a Chicago premiere in an atmosphere of great anticipation, like a homecoming.

The initial performances were met with very mixed reviews in the United States and it is significant that their successes were more immediately recognized and loudly declared in the UK. Certainly this was the case in 1990 when Goat Island made its European debut at the Third Eye Center Festival in Glasgow with their second performance, *We Got A Date*. Subsequently Goat Island became an enthusiastically welcomed presence in the UK, contributing regularly to the already thriving performance art network there. From this network, the company would later spring forward into many extended European tours and attendant workshops. Perhaps a benign dismissal of Goat Island's work in the United States had as much to do with the unashamedly hermetic qualities the company embraced. The performances adopted structures as an iterative explication of process and content in their form. While sometimes not clearly legible in the performances, an examination of the scores and scripts reveals structure to be an insistent aspect of Goat Island work from the start.

For many, the iterative qualities were a meditative and intensely intuitive quality in the work. Gestures and sequences were introduced and revisited within the world of the performance and over time made a collective language between audience and performer. This approach also led to an occasional reporting of the work as jumbled and confusing, repetitive or even boring. Live material was built from both found and devised sources that were edited into layers. The embodiment of new material produced a reinterpretation of everyday gestures and utterances that emphasized a sense of presence, like watching thoughts or ideas unfolding. There were self-evident poetic structures at play that might reveal a kinship with a William Boroughs style of cutup or perhaps a knowing deference to cyclical and rhythmic qualities found in Gertrude Stein's writing. The performances were understood as setting a different ground on which to explore the relationships between performer and audience and meaning. Goat Island performances offered an experience based upon a more subtly explored approach to dramaturgy and choreography.

The performances were potentially rich poetic encounters that challenged the idea of specialist knowledge. Company director Lin Hixson has suggested that there was no need for a specialized knowledge to understand Goat Island performances.

> I think of the work very much like my own life. When I get up in the morning and take a shower I'm listening to the radio, I'm putting those two things together. I might be listening to a story on Rwanda,

and I'm taking a shower. I go and have my breakfast and there's a child shouting in the ally. You know I actually think it's very close to how one lives their life in the sense that we are always processing different information and putting it together. So a Goat Island piece, I think relates more directly to that kind of life experience than something that is wrapped up in a package and everything is resolved. Because my own personal experience is that things don't resolve that way— and I am constantly living with ambiguity, where I'm putting things together. (Hixson 1997)

Pertinent to an understanding of all of Goat Island's performances is the attention that was paid to the performance space itself as a site. As the company moved forward through their nine performances, the space of a new piece would be one of the first structures to be established. A line of Gaffers tape was placed on the floor to evoke and complicate the space as a deliberate architectural referencing device. For Goat Island, the performance space was a frame for the work that would literally and metaphorically set the ground for an audience as they entered the room. An initial and deliberate physical question is posed for the audience: "where am I" and "[w]here are they going to be"? The staging of Goat Island works frequently placed the audience in a face-to-face relationship with each other, and it would often complicate the sight lines inside the work too as a conscious departure from the one-point perspectival view of a proscenium theatre. The Gaffers-tape boundaries declared the performance area as a site for shared activity rather than as a stage for viewing. Between Brecht's democratic theatre as social space, and Grotowski's dissolution of the fourth wall, or Peter Brooks itinerant "empty space," Goat Island performances built their content through acknowledging the realities of the means of production in counterpoint to their content. An emphasis on the materiality of the site in performance created a level playing field into which the physicality of all the elements was delivered. A language of equivalences, not least of which included the performers' bodies.

The frame required an almost cinematic precision through which to pay meticulous attention to every detail. The performers themselves would demonstrate a remarkable degree of embodiment working within the self-defined constraints. Goat Island often gave the appearance of performing on pure reflex, each performer working with their own muscle memory to produce what appeared to be an instinctive flexing unit. The unyielding architecture in the edges of the space, in proximity to the perception of the performers as a unit, produced an emphatic sense of the body as prone to failure. Being a member of the audience meant witnessing a demonstration of human frailty as a yielding architecture against the unyielding material boundaries.

Extending from the experience of witnessing the bodies and the space as converse architectural elements was a hermetic temporal framework. As a humble invitation to engage, the duration of the work placed an equal amount of responsibility upon the audiences as it did on performers. Performance running times sometimes stretching to more than ninety minutes without an interval were intense distillations of an extended working process. A Goat Island performance would appear as if it was unfolding in its own time, offered as a shared process of encounter with content that might be understood or not. If not, this was the failure of the performers not the audience. From a genuine place of generosity and offered through the invitation to engage with equal generosity, in the company's own words, it was incumbent upon the viewer to put the work together for themselves. Just as the company had made it their work, to "discover a performance by making it" (Bottoms and Goulish 2007, xv). The work has been recounted as having ritual-like qualities leaving the viewer with a sense of something having been witnessed, an experience where meaning might continue to unfold long after a performance had concluded, and in this sense too there was a hermetic, "you had to be there" quality.

Further to the physical and temporal elements that contributed to the hermetic qualities of Goat Island the appearance of the performers was also significant. For each performance the group appeared in a specifically coordinated set of costumes. In the first five performances these were combinations of clothes as altered readymade. *Soldier, Child, Tortured Man* featured sports attire, for example. And there was the visually memorable plaid lumberjack shirts and khaki pants that were worn in *It's Shifting, Hank*, creating a kind of casual uniform. In the making of their sixth performance, *The Sea & Poison*, Cynthia Ashby was engaged as a collaborator and designer of the costumes. This working relationship consolidated a uniformity in appearance of each performance and continued through four performances up to the close of the company with *The Lastmaker*.

The involvement of a number of artist collaborators contributed much to the technical aspects of the company. The individual developments specific to each performance with its own shaped footprint brought collaborative conversations with lighting designers, sound artists, film and video makers, graphic artists, and digital artists. The particular technical needs of a production emerged as a part of the working processes like the physical shape of the performance itself, responsive to the shaped performance space. The physical size of each footprint was informed materially by the expectations associated with touring. Particularly in the UK, the stage space was relative to a number of regular venues that comprised the robust live art networks there.[1] The performances grew technically more specific to the point of utility, incorporating subtle lighting design, microphones and sound amplification equipment, mechanical devices, and found and altered objects that were ceremoniously delivered into the performance space to be activated by the performers. The culmination of these details produced economies on a number of scales but, significantly, they enabled the company to tour each performance without a tour bus. Each performance was typically made to fit into five or six custom-made flight cases. Members of the company carried all the props and costumes along with their luggage.

Alongside their performances the company made a number of publications, films, and audio works. Initially as an extended form of program notes the publications became a way of sharing information about the making of each performance. Graphic artist Chantal Zakari joined the group as an additional collaborator during the production of *It's Shifting, Hank*, the group's fourth performance. Taking the form of a series of visually rich printed items, programs, and detail-oriented books, Zakari's contributions produced a distinctive and lasting visual identity for Goat Island. The publications and presentations grew responsively with the processes of performance-making, as did the significant film and video collaborations that were produced with the British filmmaker Lucy Cash. The company turned to a series of collaborators beyond the performing members of the group who are acknowledged readily for their input on productions, from the designers and technical artists to company managers, documenters, and audiovisual artists across many disciplines.

Another key aspect of their work was the commitments made by company members to teaching and pedagogy. The initial collaboration that founded Goat Island grew from a workshop Lin Hixson led at the School of the Art Institute of Chicago (SAIC). The ongoing proximity of company members to teaching went on to help establish *The Goat Island Summer School* that was sponsored by SAIC as a recurring artist-in-residence program from the mid-1990s onward. The Summer School became recognized as its own institution operating under the Goat Island name from 1996 to 2007. Goat Island also became frequent and active participants in international performance studies gatherings and conferences, as presenters and publishers of their own body of performance research presented alongside a significant body of writing about Goat Island by an associated group of performance scholars.[2] The suggestion that Goat Island invented a method has often been refuted, and it is understandable that the formation of a summer school might have given this impression. A close examination of the two Schoolbook publications yields a sharing of pedagogical ideas that can be taken as workshop guidebooks. It might be more accurate to articulate the idea of method or pedagogy through an ethical lens and a way of thinking about working. Sara Jane Bailes describes Goat Island's approach as "a collective that values the individual" (Bailes 2011, 111). It has been noted anecdotally both by students in the classrooms of Goat Island, as much by company members themselves, that the workshops like the performances bought them closer to an understanding of themselves rather than an understanding of Goat Island. While at the time of this printing there is not a published dramaturgy, it is fortunate that their output included an extensive documentary habit and gave rise to a significantly well-kept archive, which contains among other things the scripts and writing drafts in relation to the developments in each performance, alongside many well-articulated handwritten and type-scripted accounts and reflections in the notebooks, letters, faxes, and marginalia.[3] Company members frequently spoke and wrote very eloquently about their work, and so in these materials a sense of the poetic is preserved.

Nine Performances, One Company, Twenty-three Years

For the purposes of this chapter, Goat Island's production will be broken out into three phases. In the first phase, the first four performances, the company established a series of creative habits that yielded formal experiments in content development, and iterative compositional and structural articulations. Important in understanding the initial performance is the structural formation that was established and would subsequently inform later performances. In various forms, this would be explored through choreography and content in the performances: *Soldier, Child, Tortured Man (1987)*; *We Got A Date (1992)*; *Can't Take Johnny to the Funeral (1991)*; and *It's Shifting, Hank (1993)*. The second phase includes the fifth to seventh performances. The performance *How Dear To Me the Hour When Daylight Dies* (1996) marks a moment of evolution and transition, sometimes called the "second" first performance. Continuing through *The Sea & Poison* (1998) and *It's an Earthquake in My Heart* (2001) a distinct poetic emerges in the synthetic interplay between objects, texts, and space. The third phase includes the last two performances, which succeeded in challenging assumptions both for the company and audiences that might be characterized by their playfulness, their structural facility, and innovation. *When will the September roses bloom? Last night was only a comedy (a double performance)* (2004) and *The Lastmaker* (2007) are the culminating performances for Goat Island that point to a completeness and maturity in the company's practices and pedagogy.

Genesis and a Beginning, the First Four Performances

Work on the performance that would be the first of Goat Island began before the company was formally established. Following Lin Hixson's move to Chicago from Los Angeles, the group's first collaboration was a performance called *Goodbye, Mrs. Solski* (February 1986). Involving a number of performers including the three members of The Scan (Goulish, the two McCain brothers), the work demonstrated Hixson's experience of having created site-specific theatre in Los Angeles. The production was developed through a workshop led by Hixson at the School of the Art Institute of Chicago where participants were included as collaborators. Hixson was already known for her "quintessentially postmodern mixing techniques" that reputedly built theatricality by "scavenging signs and texts from everyday life, news media and entertainment" (Frye Burnham 1988, 37). The production of *Goodbye, Mrs. Solski* in Chicago introduced Hixson's own new wave sensibility to Chicago, anticipating much that would become recognizable in the work of Goat Island.

Initially, as with all Goat Island performances, work began with a prompt that was offered to the performers by Hixson as the company director. Using an approach designed to situate the discovery and ownership of the work between the performer and the director as a series of exchanges, content was discovered and produced as a collective. Hixson had come to Chicago with a strong reputation for collective working habits. Her work shows influence from a range of experimental theatre approaches, particularly those that emphasize democratization and the reflection of social contexts that exhibit political awareness. Lin Hixson has acknowledged her work as being in dialogue with many influential theatre and dance-makers. She begins, significantly, with Grotowski, whose *Poor Theatre* proposes that every object on stage has multiple iterative uses or lives. The quotidian nature of movement and found gesture for Goat Island has been influenced also by the dance creations of Yvonne Rainer and Pina Bausch. In inventing and developing dramaturgy, scripts, and performance texts the structure of Goat Island performances resonates with the work of the Wooster Group and in the use of found texts, interpretation, and reinterpretation with performances by Mabou Mines.

Making conscious investigations of theatricality, Hixson's work often explores the site of performance, the location of audience in relation to the performer, and the performers' body as object and as a subject that is active or subservient to gesture and utterance.

The role of Hixson in this experimental work set a very different tone as compared to a director's traditional role. For Hixson the aim was to discover the performance as a collective, and in this mode she took up her position with the company as co-facilitator and outside eye. This entailed facilitating the focus of research and then watching the response material alongside the performers and eventually working with them to build and edit content toward a performance. The extended making process typically revolved around three rehearsal meetings per week. Rehearsals early on in the development process consisted of the performing members showing each other their research, which after a few meetings would grow from an exchange of ideas into some initial sequencing experiments that might be proposed by Hixson, a piece of material brought in by another company member, or might develop through general conversation between all members.

The assignment for *Soldier, Child, Tortured Man* was offered from Hixson to The Scan, as an invitation to make an installation in which to perform.

> Choose a specific incident from the past. Find an historical event that occurred at approximately the same time. Create an environment and/or performance expressing the feeling of a memory in relation to an historical event. (Hixson 1990, 13)

A dedicated rehearsal space would come a little later on. So at this time, each member of The Scan made their responses at home (the McCain Brothers were roommates and Goulish had an apartment in the same building). A 1988 article describes their performance-making process through three phases, the first being one of "gathering material and formulating it"; the second phase is characterized by "development as a separation or stepping back from raw material to become writers organizing personal and 'found' material'"; third and finally, an editing and review process is opened up to an audience for feedback through a work-in-progress presentation. As Peneff describes it, "the work underwent a complete edit of text and movement, during which it was both refined and cut down to its essentials" (Peneff 1988, 9–10). This process of initial individual research, then collective editing into construction and refinement, is important to understanding the production of all nine Goat Island performances. While each began as an individual response, it was understood that as things developed the material would change into a collective artistic production. The primary mode of communicating in *Soldier, Child, Tortured Man* is through movement, setting the tone for the work that would follow.

The content of *Soldier, Child, Tortured Man* begins to unfold through a demonstration-like regimented drill sequence. This establishes the tone and pace for the work where the performers move responsively to a series of tightly barked verbal commands, issued by Tim McCain, much in the manner of a drill sergeant. The verbal commands appear to direct the subsequent movement—for example "Seven Packed Like Sardines" or "Shake, Rattle, and Roll"—but the peculiarity of both the language and movement evokes a micro-narrative or critique that is approached obliquely through reintroducing information over time and within the relations made between segments. In the movement, an initial sequence would be performed through three iterations, followed by the addition of a new sequence each time, with completion being deferred until the final iteration. The accumulation of performed sequences was clearly informed by a logic, but one that is not clear to the audience, which compounds the sense of duration and fatigue.

Immediately the piece takes on an atmosphere of training and display and situates itself somewhere between a parade ground and a sports arena. The dimension and proportion of the space are strongly evocative of a boxing ring, adding to the sense of the space as a place for physical demonstration. The presence of traditional theatricality is almost totally absent, and the strong lighting feels like a sports event, again bringing to mind a boxing ring. There are no ropes and the performers are working at floor level, the same level on which the chairs for the audience are located. Sitting on all four sides, the audience is unavoidably dazzled by the intensity of the lights. In every sense, the viewer is implicated in the work and as the performers move through the intense choreography, they begin to sweat and the physicality continues unrelentingly for the duration of the piece. At just under an hour the pitch is maintained throughout with three short spoken interludes delivered by each of the performers. In a culminating narrative, the performers become actors who perform a scene from the 1948 play, *Mr. Roberts*.[4] The work presents familiar semiotics in movement and text but presented with a poetic structure that feels self-aware and critical of the excessive and nonsensical regimentation.

The movement activity itself is very tightly choreographed, with the performers frequently working right up to the white Gaffers-tape line and situated in very close proximity to the audience throughout. Physical control of the performers' bodies is demonstrated in all nine of Goat Island's performances; the skill in timing and internalized muscle memory is an evident part of the experience of a Goat Island performance. The physical effects of the performance on the three performing bodies and on the audience were a palpable part of experiencing the work; the performers sweat and breathe heavily for forty-five of the fifty minutes' duration. The performers' prolonged and rapid activity produces natural bodily excesses, saliva, sweat, and body odor, which the audience is unavoidably affected by.

Goat Island performances frequently include political details, not least in this initial piece that was made while members of the group were volunteering with the Chicago chapter of the Committee in Solidarity with the People of El Salvador (CISPES). The physical, drill-like activity became synonymous with the dehumanizing effects of training that American military service personnel were enduring in order to facilitate them in being able to commit acts of atrocity in El Salvador. The company felt that the endurance being performed and witnessed in this performance was representative of the complicity of ordinary citizens in acts of violence being committed in the name of their country and supported by a rhetoric of "rehumanization."

The work was met by mixed responses in the press, who were mostly critical of the relentlessness of the performance itself. Reviewers appeared to be seeking a more didactic guide to the symbolic qualities in the performance and almost failed to see the physical bodies and their excesses as the material. The mixed responses from the media indicate to some degree how challenging this work must have been both to perform and to watch and, importantly for Goat Island, these comments confirmed their commitment and approach to working with subject matter. Whether or not the original material from research was evident in the finished work became immaterial; the source, the content, or the material had allowed something new to be produced.

Between 1987 and 1989, Hixson, Goulish, and the two McCain brothers made a series of important decisions that would establish the company artistically and as an official entity, including eventually filing for not-for-profit 501(c)(3) status. Supporting the individuals in the group meant not losing sight of their ethical responsibility to each other and to the performances. In subsequent years the company would articulate their ethical intentions, most notably perhaps, in the preface of the book *Small Acts of Repair*, where they state "how we communicate is as important as what we say" (Bottoms and Goulish 2007, xiii). In the summer of 1987 the company would select its name, and in a narrative that has been reproduced often, the company was formalized on Thanksgiving Day later the same year. For Goat Island that formation meant a commitment to supporting the creativity of its members alongside a commitment to the security of the company in financial terms too. Each member of the group agreed to make equal and regular financial contributions to a company bank account. These contributions would facilitate the costs of renting a space in which to work. Through their campaign group volunteer involvement, the group had been working within the Wellington Avenue Church of Christ in Chicago, centered in the church gym on West Wellington Avenue. The financial commitment facilitated their occupation of the gym as a shared rental space, and the Wellington Avenue Church gymnasium would be Goat Island's studio and home until the company dissolved in 2009.

At the advent of their second performance We *Got A Date*, the dynamic of the company took on a significant change when in the summer of 1988 Joan Dickinson becomes the fourth performing member. Dickinson and Hixson met as friends when Hixson was first in Chicago; Dickinson has characterized her beginnings with Goat Island as a gradual involvement. She says, work began "as a soft start to our collaboration on what came to be called *We Got A Date*, with my first contribution being the laying down and picking up of copies made from the instructions for tampon insertion found in a tampon box" (Dickinson 2019). This description illustrates how movement sequences were founded in observations of quotidian physical activity for Goat Island. In the process of building a performance through to a finished edit, some ideas would stand out and become sequenced, as it were, abstracted out while holding onto an image of their origins. In this case Dickinson is describing one of Goat Island's first signature choreographic sequences. "The up and down—depositing and gathering-movement eventually translated into the opening 'hopping' sequence of *We Got A Date*" (Dickinson 2019).[5] This signature quality to a movement sequence would become refined and explored in later performances, positioning Goat Island in relation to dance discourse and scholarship. The presence of a fourth performer changed the dynamic of these movement sequences significantly. Their combined physical qualities bought Goat Island toward a number of performance characteristics that contributed subsequently to the works' acknowledged originality. Each of the performers' physical attributes more strongly resembles laboring and working bodies rather than those of trained dancers.[6] The physical manipulation of Goulish in *Soldier, Child, Tortured Man* is a particular and rather breathtaking feature of that performance, as is a relative development of a physical handling in *We Got A Date*, and the subsequent third performance *Can't Take Johnny to the Funeral*. The two small bodies, Dickinson and Goulish, are tossed around and thrown to each other in jive dance routine-like moves. The duet and quartet configurations stand out in this sequence of performances as a recognizable feature of Goat Island's choreography.

We Got A Date signaled the beginning of the company in a mode that it would continue to develop and move forward. This performance toured the UK to great success. The company also ran workshops as part of touring this piece. A lead article in the *Times Educational Supplement* offers an insightful and nuanced reading of the work, whereas reviewers in the United States were mostly baffled by it (Cohen 1990, 1). Audiences in the UK were characterized as being ready to engage in such politicized approaches, as indeed were the students in their workshops. In the same article, Hixson is quoted reflecting on how advanced the students in Leicester, UK, were when it comes to reading both politics and theatre. The performance art networks in the UK would prove key to supporting Goat Island work throughout the company's existence (Cohen 1990, 1).

At the end of 1989, while touring *We Got A Date*, Karen Christopher began rehearsing with the group as work on a new piece began. The collaborators had become interested in the way society destroys its children by making them the inheritors of real and imagined violence. To begin the movement work, Hixson continued with a method that had worked in the past. For *We Got A Date* Hixson isolated the hand gestures of men in authority from press conference images to build the choreographic parade pattern (Hughes 1990, 15). Goulish described the origins of the visual motifs that materialize as movement in *Can't Take Johnny to the Funeral*: "We used sports photographs to generate movement for the first time in 1990. While on tour in Glasgow, Scotland, Lin found an old book in a thrift store, *Rugby Football for Schools*," a small "book full of photographs demonstrating drills, catches, tackles, kicks, foot positions, and team formations." While still in the store, Lin showed me the book and said, "I'm going to photocopy these pictures and make dances for our next piece" (Bottoms and Goulish 2007, 149). Multiple images would be cut from photocopies and arranged in a linear fashion on a blank page.

The performers were then given the task of making movement from the still images. Over time, other such athletic instructional images were introduced, and the opening sequence of *Can't Take Johnny to the Funeral* was developed. By the time the work premiered, Joan Dickinson had transitioned away from performing with Goat Island to follow other professional interests, and Karen Christopher remained as the company's sole female performer. This maintained the relationship of four bodies in the work, two larger, two smaller.

The fourth performance, *It's Shifting, Hank*, began with the poetic prompt, "Why were you in pain in such a beautiful place?" The work dramatized narratives of the pain and the effects of institutional power on childhood by exploring breath and breathing as a metaphor. Hixson again explored the territory of a choreographic technique that used still images. In 1990 the group received an invitation to develop a new work while in residence at the Ferens Art Gallery in Hull, UK. Beginning in the spring and continuing into the early summer of 1993, the company worked in a space with regular "open-studio" hours. Periodically, they offered workshops and presentations based on the research materials that were on view in the gallery. The residency culminated in June 1993 with the premiere. *It's Shifting, Hank* is the culminating refinement of the first phase of the Goat Island history. This performance, the first to exceed an hour in length, also marks the understanding of the signature elements of a Goat Island aesthetic.

Hixson seems to have honed her role as director, as she later describes in *Small Acts of Repair*: "One of my tasks as the director of Goat Island when making a performance is to foreground the not seen, and background the seen. To do this requires: (1) the formation of attention; (2) slowing the traffic of the mind; (3) and enclosed encounter area; (4) spaces between" (Bottoms and Goulish 2007, 30). By 1994 Goat Island had cultivated a collective process philosophy, "submerged (mind and body) within a world of flow and perpetual becoming" (Bottoms and Goulish 2007, 56). Alongside these strides in the development of the artistic practice, they had built strong relationships with programmers and producers in the UK. So in 1994, Goat Island were invited to participate in a UK-based national survey of work from Chicago. *Chicago, Oh Chicago* was a series of performances, video, and music from "the Windy City." The UK tour provided an opportunity to explore new grounds for developing work, and in July 1994 the group traveled together to Croagh Patrick in Western Ireland to participate in the pilgrimage that takes place annually there.

Goat Island

The "Second" First Performance

Details from the pilgrimage were shared by the company in a newsletter produced the following spring, and on the second page the company relays some tragic news. Upon arrival at their bed and breakfast in the town of Kesh, "the woman of the house gave us the message she had received from America. Richard W. McCain had died the previous day" (Goat Island 1995, 2). Tim and Greg McCain's father had seen every Goat Island performance to date. As a beginning to their next performance, the company undertook the four-hour climb that the pilgrimage requires. A sense of this endurance coupled with the bleak atmosphere of the place and its history, infused with the loss of a close relative and friend, also appears to have prefigured the subsequent two years as a series of transitions took place. With rehearsal space in Belfast provided by the New Museum Art Center, work began almost immediately after the pilgrimage was completed. The newsletter announces a work-in-progress performance, which took place the following May 1995. Quite unexpectedly and unrelated to the work and its development in the summer of 1995, Greg and Tim McCain decided they would leave the company. Following a small break in production, two new members were found. Bryan Saner was invited to join and then shortly after Antonio Poppe. Both were familiar with the work of Goat Island and known by company members for their performance work in Chicago and elsewhere. The addition of these two new members changed the dynamic of the company considerably. In tandem with this change Matthew Goulish's independent writing practice was growing in visibility. As a result of these changes, a new and more contemplative and literary quality can be seen in the performances from this point forward.

In relation to the group dynamic and at this stage in the company's career, it is important to understand the facility of company members in the devised nature of their work. Building upon the emergent qualities of the previous four performances, when writing reflectively in 2003, the company would reiterate their process in the maxim, "We discover a performance by making it" (Bottoms and Goulish 2007, xv). As an explication encompassing a wide array of detail, this idea would sustain the company through the subsequent work and one more quite sudden personnel change. The company returned to Chicago and while still working out the new company dynamic, Antonio Poppe left Goat Island to continue his work as an individual artist. With US and Canadian performances scheduled for *How Dear To Me the Hour When Daylight Dies*, Mark Jeffery, an emerging English performance artist, was invited to join on very short notice. Jeffery arrived in Chicago in the early fall of 1996 where he learned the piece in five weeks and went on to perform it as his company debut at the Chicago premiere.

How Dear To Me the Hour When Daylight Dies was co-commissioned by Arnolfini Live in Bristol and the Centre for Contemporary Arts in Glasgow. The piece reflects a refined approach to working with found texts and recitation. Again, building from the modes of discovery that are at play in the previous works, text was assembled and collaged from film scenes, intercut with accomplished character-based narrative presentations.[7] Each member of the group would take up research toward a kind of embodiment and personification that defies conventions of character acting. Karen Christopher explains how the reproduction of a persona "is not an attempt to produce an illusion, but rather to suggest an avenue of thought" (Bottoms and Goulish 2007, 94). The changes in personnel had brought the company toward a new set of ensemble choreographic possibilities. With Bryan Saner at 6 feet 2 inches, standing out as taller than the other three, the performance took off in a different mode, producing one of Goat Island's most singular choreographic motifs known as the "Puppet Jump." This comprises a movement sequence where the performers bend their bodies forward at the hip and swing their limbs down in front. Eventually launching themselves into the air, then turning and rotating in such a way that seems arbitrary or accidental, they eventually achieve a unison when the level of precision becomes clear. It was introduced by Matthew Goulish as homage to choreography that was featured in *Two Cigarettes in the Dark* (1985) by Pina Bausch and Dominique Mercy.

The next performance, *The Sea & Poison*, received its name from the book *The Sea and Poison* by Shusaki Endo. Although an initial prompt for this piece asked three questions—"What is impossible? Who is unwanted? What have you lost?"—research by company members began to coalesce around ideas of the social body alongside the individual body as a site of poisoning. *The Sea & Poison* features two types of movement. There are demonstration-like sequences that focus on object activations where the narrative content takes on a pragmatic tone. The piece opens with a vignette-like discussion about the ethics of care and neglect of a family member but is then followed by an energetic movement sequence, which the company named the "impossible dance." The four performers work in unison through an extended rhythmic sequence of rapid jumping and falling. Goat Island ephemera describe the sequence in following terms:

We have also set out to construct "impossible dances" from a series of unperformable individual movements linked together by endlessly complex patterns and formulas, which challenge the limits of human ability, and as dance hover somewhere between musical composition and the clumsy marathon dance competitions of American depression years. (As of September 5, 2019, goatislandperformance.org)

The "impossible dance" is considered to be another of Goat Island's most iconic performance innovations, continuing their investigation into choreographic directives that began in the early performances and shifted with the change in the composition of the company. This work marks the introduction of the collaboration with fashion designer Cynthia Ashby. The visually striking reversible jackets, earth brown on one side and chemical yellow on the other, responded to and informed the movement and transitions in the work. Additionally, the performers engage several objects, each referring to the natural world, but artificial—rubber frogs and fish, plastic "ice-cubes," AstroTurf, even potting soil made of nonorganic synthetic material. In *The Sea & Poison* the performers are like post-apocalyptic gardeners, and it is often unclear if they are ameliorating or exacerbating environmental tragedy.

The seventh performance, *It's an Earthquake in My Heart*, grew from the initial rehearsal directive: "Create a chase/pathway with your body" and "Create a circulatory chase." Gathered source materials speak to considerations of transportation circuits, traffic patterns, neighborhood maps, migratory patterns, and the development of the first artificial heart pump. With the addition of a subsequent prompt, the new piece took on a new direction. Hixson asked company members to "[r]e-create dance movements from Pina Bausch's *Cafe Muller* by way of a three-minute dance video" (Bottoms and Goulish 2007, 161). Each member was given a specific three-minute sequence to learn and then to teach to the other company members. A compelling movement quartet developed through a combination of ideas from each prompt. The company arrived at a rich series of articulations about human fragility and the inevitable failure of the body. In observing their initial interpretations of *Café Muller*, Hixson has commented on how the performers were "reaching for a gesture outside of themselves while performing the gesture with themselves—a process of self-quoting and citation from another source, simultaneously. I liked the idea that we would never get these movements right, that we were staging failure. With the inability to succeed, we were given a stuttering. We were given fragility. We were given unstable possibilities" (Bottoms and Goulish 2007, 156). At its premiere in Vienna in the summer of 2001, audiences appeared to misunderstand the quotation of ideas from Pina Bausch and the intentional sense of play and homage that the company delivered. Upon returning to Chicago, material was reworked. In contrast to earlier Chicago reviews, a *Chicago Sun-Times* "Dance Notes" offers a sensitive read:

> With the audience seated around the performance space to create an exceptional sense of intimacy, the performers will use both the spoken word and the 15-year-old troupe's trademark high-powered movement as they travel through a series of connected scenes—glimpses from a childhood, a revelatory hallucination, an instructional radio show, a dialogue with a dying man, a call from a phone booth and a church ceremony. (Weiss 2002, 54)

Lasting and Repair

The experience of watching Goat Island's eighth performance, *When will the September roses bloom? Last night was only a comedy (a double performance)*, took place over two consecutive nights. Conceived, as the title suggests, in two parts, a note in the program for a Chicago work-in-progress presentation describes the two-night structure: "[W]e intend the piece to have a three-part structure. The first and last parts remain constant. The middle part has two parts that change places on consecutive performances. First night: a/b1/b2/c Second night: a/b2/b1/c. Today we will show a/b2 and the beginning of b1, or the first 66% of a second night performance" (Goat Island 2003). This performance demonstrates Goat Island as having gained a significant stature and creative capacity. The elegance in the structure points to a mode that Goat Island used all along, but its legibility and more complex relation to time set it apart somewhat from the previous seven performances.

In the fall of 2000, as the company was touring *It's an Earthquake in My Heart* in Europe, Litó Walkey was invited to join as the fifth performing member. She had first interned with the company earlier in 2000. Walkey was the only member of the company not based full time in Chicago and one outcome of this situation was a new working mode, which the group called "The Year Long Writing Project." Devised as a way to maintain a connected creative process among company members separated by geography, it involved each member developing writing based on agreed structures such as the days of the week, the length of daylight in their different locations, and an awareness of diurnal and nocturnal writing. The project resulted in ancillary presentations like the audio project *What Would Your Shadow Do?* (Goat Island, Falsewalls, [fw06] 2004).

Assembled at Hixson's home in Chicago in early 2002, the group gathered for a first working meeting to welcome Walkey as a fifth performing member. The beginning of what would become the new performance was read by Hixson in the form of a letter to the company: it contained the question, "How do you repair?" Coming out of a narrative about restoration and less than six months after the devastation of the terrorist attacks on September 11, 2001, the task in hand was framed by Hixson as one of scale. Following an encounter in Wales with a 1970s home repair manual, Hixson articulated an equation between the "small acts of repair" being described in the instruction book and the existential enormity of the violence witnessed in global terrorism (Bottoms and Goulish 2007, 23). Finding solutions that can work in such a "damaged world" and understanding our "aptitude at repairing it" became the goal of the piece (Bottoms and Goulish 2007, xv). There is a reason to connect and collaborate inside the idea of repair being expressed: "Calming the hands in a troubled worlds. Restoring damage to renewed use. Wiping a stain with a cloth" (Bottoms and Goulish 2007, 23). These are intensely relatable human responses that might also form the basis for all the previous performances of Goat Island.

This performance revisits a number of previously explored concerns, notably the props used in *September roses* that included a series of objects made from recycled corrugated cardboard boxes, which echoes the environmental politics infused throughout *The Sea & Poison*. Mark Jeffery has reflected on the reuse of the material for its echoes across the years of Goat Island: he suggests "that in all of our pieces materiality has its own language" (Bottoms and Goulish 2007, 41). Stephen Bottoms contributes to this narrative of reuse as repair, too, when he thinks through the use of material in Goat Island's work. He writes that "assembling appropriated fragments is to treat them less as fragments (deconstructed originals) than as constituent components in a new structure, a new ecology of interconnected points" (Bottoms and Goulish 2007, 63). *When will the September roses bloom? Last night was only a comedy (a double performance)* presents Goat Island in a more than usually reflective mood. There was a level of seriousness and observation in this performance and a distinct fluidity in the form that shows the company in its prime.

At the first work-in-progress presentation of Goat Island's ninth performance, the audience received a copy of the following statement: *The Lastmaker*, "our ninth performance, will be the last Goat Island piece. After we have completed creating and performing it, the company will end. This decision comes from the challenge that all artists face: how to continue to grow, to venture into the unknown. We intend this end to present itself as a beginning" (Bottoms and Goulish 2007, 223). The performance employed the fully formed and integrated studio practice, and the ethos of the collective, to explore how to make a work that could say goodbye. In framing the closure and the unknown as the creative constraint, *The Lastmaker* offered the group a process-based way to reflect on the impending change. Goat Island's performances have been described as presenting alternative ways of making, working, and operating in the world. In the paired acts of making *The Lastmaker* and then disbanding as a collective, the artists first explored in the performance the metaphorical implications and then modeled them by moving forward with new projects. The working process became a place where the literal considerations for coping with endings and transcendence could be explored by the company and audiences.

Work began on the ninth performance based upon research into an Islamic architectural dome in Zagreb, Croatia, and elicited by Hixson's prompt: "Construct a dance in the shape of the Dzamia dome." The Company had been in residence in Zagreb, and while presenting their eighth performance, *September roses*, new material had begun to emerge. A subsequent constraint was added: "Construct a public display or a demonstration of a concept or thought from the material you presented in Zagreb that is 3–5 minutes in length." Upon returning to Chicago the focus changed again, based upon a personal decision by Hixson that this would be the last performance she would direct with the company. The news that she would leave was delivered to the company members in the form of a letter that included the following question: "What if making a last performance becomes one of our directives for making a new one?" Company members embraced this idea and the following performance directive was formed: "Construct a last performance in the form of a human foot that weighs two tons and remains in good condition."

Lasting and lastness emerge as conditions for found texts to be incorporated into the work. Mark Jeffery opens as a fusion of St. Francis of Assisi and the British stand-up comic Tommy Cooper, and as a companion, woven throughout the performance, Karen Christopher embodies Lenny Bruce in his final stand-up comedy performance. An electronic pulse metronome sets

Goat Island

time for choreography performed in unison. Informed by the Dzamia dome, the Hagia Sophia is presented as literal and metaphorical architecture. The building's history first as a church, then a mosque, and now as a museum reminds the viewer that endings can be recontextualized over time. The building as an object is the palimpsest of this history, layering the iterations of the building over one other. The context of the making opened space for Goat Island as a collective to present a self-aware and bittersweet reflection on their practice. To complete the image of comedy and pathos, *Puff the Magic Dragon*, recorded by the band Broken Social Scene, scores the final sequence.

The following text from goatislandperformance.org (a site still live today) states: "The *Lastmaker* recapitulates the concerns of 20 years of Goat Island, in what we hope will be a fitting conclusion to our contribution—a journey, within a restrained structure, from the intellectual to the emotional, with lasting resonance." The final presentation of *The Lastmaker* was in February 2009 at the University of North Carolina at Chapel Hill.

The Legacy and the Archive

The Lastmaker as a performance echoes a broader philosophical orientation and served as collective ritual for artist and audience to cope with the sadness and hopefulness that this sort of transcendence evokes in us, of working all along with the knowledge that it is impossible to anticipate saying goodbye. Sara Jane Bailes describes this as a "poetics of failure" where the attempt at the impossible helps bring it into being, describing "the category of the impossible as an expansion of the possible: that is to say, the realm of the possible is enlarged by inclusion of the notion of the impossible" (Bailes 2011, 116). Rooted in this poetic, *The Lastmaker* investigates lasting and lastness as a position for an imagined future or alternative. In some ways abstracted and counter-sensical, these nevertheless offer what Bailes calls a "wish-image," imagined realities that we can render into reality through the performance. Articles written about *The Lastmaker* report the sense of loss felt by a future without new work by Goat Island. But when asked about the ending, Hixson is quick to remark on the unknown future this change can represent for everyone. So just as Goat Island demonstrated alternative ways of making and operating, in ending or disbanding, they not only offer ending as an alternative trajectory for an organization, they also offer a way of saying goodbye, grieving collectively and as individuals. The completion of the practice of live events opened a space for new potentialities in the material the company produced in the form of publications. And in the second decade since the company ended, the Goat Island Archive has been established at the School of the Art Institute of Chicago, reinvigorating scholarship and presenting opportunities for the work to serve as inspiration or score for those who discover the company after the work has ended.

> We try to respect each other with a sense of dignity, without judgment or prejudice, with the understanding that each contribution has its place. More than once I have come to rehearsals feeling inadequate with my contribution in an uncertain, tentative, un-creative state and we have used the small fragment of a poorly articulated idea to its highest potential. With this vision it is possible for all things to have a new life, including human beings. I have said in all honesty that this process has saved my life.
>
> (Goat Island 2000, 52)

CHAPTER 6
LOOKINGGLASS THEATRE COMPANY
Jane Barnette

General Introduction

In 2018, the Lookingglass Theatre Company celebrated its thirtieth anniversary as an ensemble based in Chicago, Illinois.[1] I still remember how energized and inspired I was after seeing *The Arabian Nights* in 1992, their first collaboration with director/adapter Mary Zimmerman. Our country had recently declared war on Iraq, at the outset of what would come to be called the Gulf Wars, and the final image of the ensemble's adaptation seamlessly morphed from an ancient storytelling world into one that mirrored the horrors of the nightly news. Repeating the line "And the nights over Bagdhad were whiter than the days" while they looked up to the ceiling, two cast members mimicked the sound of an air-raid siren and the entire ensemble onstage began to make the sound of wind and roll their bodies upstage, settling, finally, in silence against the stage wall. At that moment what had seemed a far-away collection of stories was all too recognizable, and the arresting image of these actors in a fetal position at the far upstage wall stuck with me for decades thereafter.

In the 1990s and the first few years of the twenty-first century, Lookingglass performances were somewhat difficult to catch, since the company performed at different venues, many of which had limited seating and short runs, in part because of the expense of renting space in Chicago. But in 2003 the ensemble opened its doors to a permanent space on Michigan Avenue, and by 2011, when they were awarded the Tony Award for best regional theatre, they had gained nationwide recognition and virtually universal praise from arts critics. As part of their celebration for their thirtieth anniversary, Lookingglass released a series of short YouTube videos, one of which contained the video of their acceptance speech for the Tony, delivered eloquently by founding ensemble member Andy White. At the heart of what they have always wanted to achieve, White noted, was to form an ensemble based on the principles of "take risks, support each other, and tell the story." That same philosophy guides the ensemble today, with twenty-nine artists (actors as well as designers) who make up their ensemble membership, with several others listed as associate artists. In what follows, I trace the development of this exceptional company from its inception to 2017, with an emphasis on their uniquely improvisational and collaborative approach to literary adaptation.

A History of Development and Methods

The ensemble that would form the basis for Lookingglass Theatre got its start from the extracurricular interests of a handful of intrepid Northwestern University (NU) students in 1986.[2] Led by David Schwimmer, who would later become a household name for his role as Ross on the NBC sitcom *Friends*, this small group of acting students decided to explore their physicality and the challenges of Jerzy Grotowski's Poor Theatre methodology by performing *Alice in Wonderland* (an adaptation of Lewis Carroll's writings by André Gregory and the Manhattan Project) in the arts dormitory on campus. The reception was so positive that they did the fundraising necessary to support a trip to Scotland, where they remounted the performance as part of the Edinburgh Fringe Festival in 1987. As founding ensemble member David Catlin recounts, after a night at the pubs there, they decided to start an ensemble that they would come to call the Looking Glass Theatre Project, before a publicity typo led them to change their title from "project" to "company."[3]

Central to their early influences was the emphasis that Northwestern University acting teacher David Downs placed on storytelling—Downs, in turn, had learned this approach from Alvina Krause, the founder of what would become the theatre program there. Krause herself never took an acting class when she attended NU but instead studied oral interpretation. The oral interpretation method of adapting literature for performance stems from yet another Northwestern professor, Robert Breen—at its core, Breen's chamber theatre technique amplifies the language and narrative voice of the written page through the embodiment of the stage.[4] This genealogy of performance training—from Breen to Krause to Downs—continues to proliferate today, as Catlin himself now teaches theatre courses and directs productions at NU. In addition to their university acting training based in canonical drama and theatrical style, the founders of Lookingglass also took classes in performance studies with Frank Galati, Paul Edwards, and Dwight Conquergood that encouraged them to look to other sources as scripts for performance, including fiction, nonfiction, and archives.[5]

This influence of theatrical adaptation continues to sustain the substance and style of Lookingglass Theatre's seasons, although they also perform new work and (less frequently) previously produced plays. Today, Lookingglass is known as an ensemble that specializes in the adaptation of sprawling epic stories, with a style that simultaneously embraces the language of the source/s while reimagining these tales in physically spectacular ways.

The ensemble's early fascination with the physicality of poor theatre has been both heightened and transformed by their association with circus arts. Serendipitously, at the same time that the ensemble was forming in the late 1980s, Catlin and other founding members had an opportunity to see touring productions by Pilobolus and Cirque du Soleil. The Lookingglass founders relished the awe they felt as spectators of these two athletic styles of performance, observing that "audiences found themselves breathless, at the edge of their seats watching the impossible, experiencing the defiance of danger and gravity" (Catlin 2009, 107). They wanted to harness a similar energy for their spectators—to captivate them with arresting images and the muscular grace necessary for feats of flight and balance. Training for this kind of activity required the development of skills that go beyond the usual movement for the stage or dance courses that actors might take: to balance on a tightrope or trapeze, performers needed to learn a combination of circus arts and gymnastics. The movement training typical for acting students—including more specialized dance training, if they pursued it—was simply not enough. Recognizing this need, the Actor's Gymnasium opened in Evanston in 1995, led by Tony Hernandez and Lookingglass founding ensemble member Larry DiStasi, solidifying an informal partnership between the two companies that frequently results in coproduced shows.

As students in Evanston, founding ensemble members had the advantage of attending and working with theatres in Chicago, a city that is known for ensemble theatre as well as being the "risk capital of the world" for theatre-making (Jackson 2017, 101). With mentorship from members of Steppenwolf and the Remains Theatre, among several other Chicago-based ensemble theatre companies, the Lookingglass founders had several possible examples of group dynamics to emulate. By the mid-1980s, American theatre critics were fond of describing a "Chicago style" of theatre that typically signaled a "raw, sometimes violent, mode of play" and that the *Chicago Tribune*'s head theatre critic Richard Christiansen would designate "rock 'n' roll acting" (quoted in Jackson 2017, 76). However, as Julie Jackson persuasively argues in "Not Just Rock 'n' Roll: Chicago Theatre, 1984–1990" (2017), this concept of Chicago theatre-making as unpolished and crude misses the crucial influences of what we might call *purposeful play* in the city. In the years that Lookingglass founders were attending Chicago theatre, it was "intelligent, intensely focused, and highly crafted" (79). Contrary to a roughly hewn style, performance in the second city featured "ensemble, risk, and improvisation" (S. Patinkin, qtd. in Jackson 80). Indeed, by Jackson's count there were "more than two hundred artist-operated ensemble companies that operated in the city between 1980 and 1990," and "in no other urban center of the twentieth century did ensemble theatre dominate the environment as it did in Chicago" (102).

Many of these Chicago ensembles, including Steppenwolf, operated their companies based on collective decision-making, empowering actors and designers to contribute equally to season planning and casting. As theatre majors, they read about Mabou Mines and the Wooster Group and hoped to emulate this long-standing "mutual trust and understanding, an ensemble ethic" (Zimmerman 1994, 47). But Lookingglass drew their primary inspiration for how to structure their company from Theatre de la Jeune Lune in Minneapolis, according to Joel Hobson, who worked as the technical director and production manager for the Lookingglass from 2008 to 2016. Although now defunct, Theatre de la Jeune Lune (founded in 1978) was known for their whimsical approach to classic plays, inspired by the members' training at the LeCoq school in Paris. Made up of two Americans and two Frenchmen, Jeune Lune spent their first two decades in an experiment of egalitarian work distribution: all four founders shared the title of artistic director as well as various administrative, design, and technical responsibilities. The eight Lookingglass founders shared this vision of cooperative administration, giving every ensemble member an equal vote for all significant decisions and distributing tasks like marketing, fundraising, and prop building evenly among all members.

It was this utopian vision of collaboration that impressed a graduate student in Northwestern's performance studies program in 1989, when she had an opportunity to work with the nascent Lookingglass group. Mary Zimmerman had recently produced her adaptation of *The Odyssey* at the university, and the members who had seen this show "felt that there was a natural kinship between the kind of visually-oriented, highly choreographic developmental work [she] was doing, and the physical, group-oriented style of the company" (1994, 58). They invited her to remount *The Odyssey* with their members as the cast, and she agreed to do so, although this first alliance between Zimmerman and the Lookingglass was less than ideal. As she recounts in her dissertation, "The company and

I began our first collaboration at profoundly different levels of knowledge about the piece, a situation which I now believe is extremely detrimental to ensemble production .... The entire production labored in the shadow of its ancestor" (59). Crucially, this perceived failure had the benefit of solidifying Zimmerman's commitment to building a script *with* the ensemble, a practice she maintains to an extreme that requires reciprocal trust between playwright/adapter and performers: for her, new adaptations begin in rehearsal with no script whatsoever. This allows Zimmerman to mine the cast for individualized contributions to the text, based on their peculiarities and quirks. But the actors must be confident enough with the process that they might allow these discoveries to surface without the self-consciousness that all too often inhibits creative expression. "Often, if everyone is relaxed enough, significant parts of the performance are created in the 'margins' of the official space of rehearsal, in the liminal space that actors occupy when they are on break" (Zimmerman 1994, 18).

In order to reach that level of confidence and trust in the process, Lookingglass actors embrace the playful flow made possible by improvisational games.[6] Like many of their peers, at the heart of their rehearsal techniques are the exercises created by Viola Spolin that helped create the Second City sketch-based tradition as well as the more provocative chance-based work of the NeoFuturists, both based in Chicago. Notably, both of these improvisation-based ensembles create performances that are "directed outward, toward the audience in cabaret style," a trademark of the so-called Chicago style of theatricality (Jackson 2017, 82). As others have noted, the basic rules of improvisation work equally well for fully scripted plays as they do for extemporaneous scenes. Because of the enduring influence left by Spolin and her son Paul Sills, "the nimbleness and invention with which Chicago actors could 'say yes, and …' created the strong impression of spontaneity, immediacy, and invention associated with the Chicago style" (Jackson 2017, 83). At its core, successful improvisation requires equal risk-taking from all players. From blindfolded trust walks to mirror movement without obvious leadership, improvisational games help build an ensemble based in "trust, group awareness, and group decision" (Catlin 2009, 95). They also rely on a level of danger or risk that heightens performers' concentration in ways that become amplified when combined with acrobatic arts.

The ensemble's commitment to breathtaking spectacle only solidified as they continued to work with performers who had circus experience and training. Remaining true to their ideals of democratic, egalitarian leadership, they continue to make director-like decisions based on feedback from anyone sharing the rehearsal space, shaping the aesthetic quality of their productions by trusting the wisdom of the actors as well as the staff. For Lookingglass, as is true for many other Chicago-based theatre groups, rehearsals are open to technical staff and designers at virtually any phase. Because they resist the typical hierarchy or organizational flowchart of theatre-making, where the artistic director is at the helm of the company and directors lead shows based on their "production concept," it is not uncommon for aesthetic decisions to grow out of suggestions made by an assistant designer or an intern. Their modus operandi is to put the best creative minds in the room, establish trust and a group dynamic, so that anyone marginally or centrally involved in making the show can intervene.

For the first decade of their existence, the location of these collaborative rehearsals and productions varied, and the company embraced their nomadic status by considering the space for each production virtually a character in that show and taking inspiration for the design from the limits and opportunities of these settings. But in 2003, the Lookingglass ensemble moved into the Water Tower Water Works building on the Miracle Mile in Chicago, adjacent to the busiest pedestrian crossing in the Midwest. The theatre they built within this historic building reflects their earlier strategy of choosing spaces that could inform the design and aesthetic of each production, insofar as it is a genuinely flexible theatre that can transform into virtually any audience configuration. Marking their commitment to continue to integrate circus arts into performances, the ceiling for this theatre allows for intricate and abundant rigging (for bodies as well as lighting), so that actors can take flight and climb upward if the show warrants this choice. The result is a use of vertical space that is atypical for most theatres and mirrors the verticality spectators expect to see at circuses.

From a dramaturgical perspective, the fact that the Lookingglass Theatre space is located within the Chicago Water Tower Complex is also significant. In a place once occupied by a steam generation plant, the Chicago Avenue Pumping Station was one of very few structures to survive the 1871 Chicago Fire. Even after the Lookingglass Theatre converted the part of the building that had been used for storage and repair in 2003, the other half of the building continues to function as intended, pumping water for Chicago's North Side residents. The Lookingglass Theatre Company's permanent home was built to exist acoustically apart from the massive plumbing within— "new concrete floors were poured over rubber isolation pads, a massive new ceiling was constructed suspended on spring isolation hangers, and walls were built spanning from the isolated floor to the isolated ceiling without ever connecting rigidly to the existing pumping station walls" (Miller and Talaske 2013). Thus, spectators who recognize the industrial housing of the Lookingglass facility do so only visually and briefly, before entering the "room within a room" that is their theatre space.

The fact that the company can now rely on staging productions in their fully equipped and adaptable space has likely influenced their season selection process, as well as their creative potential. An ensemble that prides itself on igniting audience imagination, Lookingglass stages adaptations of novels, myths, and folk tales that create edge-of-your-seat experiences—the kind of stories that revel in adventure, dangerous journeys, and fantasy. Other companies and groups have taken inspiration from their style and methodology, but perhaps the most distinctive aspect of Lookingglass's legacy is the fact that colleges and universities, as well as regional theatres, have the opportunity to take on the challenge of mounting plays that were created with the ensemble, through the publication of Zimmerman's plays and the licensing of other adapter's work. For Zimmerman, the practice of publishing adapted work began with her doctoral dissertation in 1994, the appendix of which was the script for *Arabian Nights* as created with Lookingglass in 1992 (and performed at New York's Manhattan Theatre Club in 1994).[7] In 2005, she would publish this adaptation with Northwestern University Press, soon after publishing *Metamorphoses*, a Lookingglass adaptation for which she received the Tony award (for directing) in 2002, with the same press.[8]

To stage *Metamorphoses* without a swimming pool, without the element of water present onstage, is highly unlikely—not because it is required by licensing, but because the characters interact with water *as if it is a character itself* (and, arguably, for Ovid's tales, it is). The plot requires water. Yet this was initially a design choice made by ensemble member Dan Ostling, in consultation with Zimmerman and the rest of the company. Indeed, many of the lines in this published script reflect the quirks and cadence of specific ensemble members who developed these characters. While this observation may appear to suggest that Zimmerman's authorship is in question, such a concern does not stem from the company itself—insiders report that the ensemble fully embraces her authorial control of adaptations developed with Lookingglass. Instead, it points to the distinctive way that their style extends beyond an ensemble's typical reach—in addition to tours that introduce the company to new audiences, by purchasing the royalties to Zimmerman's plays, other theatres "try on" scripts that are so deeply interwoven with the Lookingglass way of theatre-making that several of the ensemble's aesthetic choices become unavoidable for new productions.

In addition to published scripts, Lookingglass has allowed other theatres to stage adaptations they created. In 2017, David Catlin gave permission to Baltimore Center Stage to stage a hip-hop reworking of *Lookingglass Alice*, the wildly popular circus-infused adaptation of Lewis Carroll's Alice stories he created with the company that premiered in 2005. The production team, led by director Jeremy B. Cohen with dramaturgy by Rebecca Adelsheim, "significantly reworked" the script, leading to a version that "is less athletic than the original, but certainly propulsive (a bit of aerial stuff remains)," according to *Baltimore Sun* critic Tim Smith. By shifting the focus from "inquisitive Victorian girlhood" to "Alice's quest to find her inner queen," this reimagined adaptation makes visible contemporary African-American political and cultural challenges in the topsy-turvy climate of a country led by white men whose grasp of truth is as slippery as the rabbit hole Alice descends.

But the Lookingglass legacy extends beyond the company's scripts, published or unpublished. Since 1990, the company has included a wing of educational programming and teaching artists, where local young adults and children can take classes with members of the ensemble or associate artists. Within what they cleverly call their Curiosity department, the ensemble currently creates both educational programming and community engagement efforts. Under the education wing, Lookingglass hosts camps, classes, school programs, and an audition-based young ensemble. Their engagement offerings include civic practice partnerships, community partner subscriptions, production coalitions, and their "reflect series"—dramaturgical conversations that typically occur after Sunday matinee performances and offer the public free access to Chicago-area professionals who are experts connected in some thematic way to their current production.

Lookingglass classes feature some of the same theatre games, collaborative storytelling methods, and movement techniques that the ensemble uses in their own workshop process of developing original work. These teaching artists serve around 3,500 students each year, and some of the students enrolled in the classes, camps, school programs, or especially the young ensemble have also been asked to audition for shows that feature young actors. In *Hephaestus*, the "theatrical circus" piece with a narrative told by a young girl wishing to escape her parents' bickering, both of the girls who played the role in the 2010 remount (in rotation) were recruited from classes they took with Lookingglass. In addition, for young aspiring performers close enough to Evanston, the Actor's Gymnasium also offers classes in the circus arts, and some of these gymnasts have also had an opportunity to be cast in productions that can showcase their physical virtuosity.

Lookingglass Theatre Company

Within the Chicago community, Lookingglass has been especially resourceful in their approaches to engagement. Recognizing the transferable skills that the theatre boasts for corporate training and community service needs (in problem-solving, listening, and empathetic leadership, for example), their civic practice partnerships connect artists from the ensemble with "organizations to help address a need, challenge, or goals identified by the organization or community" ("Community Engagement"). As participants in ReCharge: Arts for Brain Health, for example, Lookingglass joined with Chicago hospitals and other arts organizations to create activities for people with neuro-cognitive challenges as well as those who care for them. In addition, as "part of [their] commitment to lowering barriers and increasing accessibility to the experience of theatre," the company provides admission to 100 community partner subscribers for each of their mainstage shows without charge to the individuals or the organization to which they belong. Several of the groups participating in this effort cater to specific identities and economic classes, such as Latinos Progresando, which provides legal assistance for families in the process of immigration, and Chicago Help Initiative, a group dedicated to serving and feeding the homeless, jobless, and otherwise underprivileged citizens living in the near North Side of the city.

In their commitment to merge applied theatre techniques with dramaturgical curiosity, then, the Lookingglass Theatre Company has earned the respect of the broader Chicago community, by finding ways to both welcome the public into their home and to make themselves available to groups and corporations who may not yet know how powerful performance can be. Meanwhile, they continue to train and recruit possible new members through their education division. Because several of the artistic associates and ensemble members also teach at local universities, their educational reach also extends beyond their own classes and workshops, as undergraduate and graduate students study with Lookingglass-affiliated professors and gain insight into their techniques for design and performance.

Key Productions and Projects

Lookingglass is likely best known for *Metamorphoses* for several reasons: first, it was her first production to transfer to Broadway, and it was for this production that Zimmerman received the 2002 Tony award in directing; in addition, as noted above, several schools and theatre companies have produced *Metamorphoses* since that time. Having a pool of water onstage is also hard to forget. When considering the company's overall oeuvre, however, other works stand out as signature Lookingglass shows, both in terms of their creative process and the aesthetic product. Key among these is the adaptation that first forged the bond between Zimmerman and the ensemble: *The Arabian Nights*.

There were several dramaturgical interventions that Zimmerman, in collaboration with the ensemble, made to the sprawling epic *1001 Nights*—chief among them were the choices of which tales to include and therefore whose stories to tell. That said, the work we call *1001 Nights* is a collection of stories that were orally shared for a millennium before Sir Richard Burton collected them in 1884 as *The Thousand Nights and One Night*. In other words, what the English-speaking world would likely consider to be the "original" text for these Arabic stories is itself an edited collection that entailed both cultural adaptation and translation, along with the accumulation of centuries of potentially different tellings of these tales. In short, there is no singular authentic version of *1001 Nights*.

For their production, the Lookingglass ensemble used the Edward Powys Mathers version of this work, an English-language text published in 1923, translated from a French version compiled by J. C. Mardrus (at the turn of the twentieth century). At the core of their adaptation decisions was the principle Zimmerman would solidify while creating *The Arabian Nights*: that she begins the rehearsal process without a play in hand; rather, she creates the script organically, based on the discoveries made by the ensemble during their time together. In the original production, the pivotal role of Scheherezade (Sultan Shahryar's wife who captivates her husband by telling such riveting stories that he will forget to kill her) was played by Jenny Bacon, an actor whose presence onstage has been described as "commandingly centered." Inspired by Bacon's grounded strength as well as the basic conceit of the tales, Zimmerman shaped *The Arabian Nights* into a play that featured compelling and complicated female characters and highlighted the imaginative power of storytelling. "My heart was attracted to certain stories for a vast, intricate combination of personal and artistic reasons (if such a distinction can be made) including sympathetic identification with the heroines, affection for particular female ensemble members and the desire to show them off, and immediate visual apprehension of certain moments of text" (Zimmerman 1994, 108). The resulting text was a two-and-a-half-hour potpourri of comic and lyrical tales that highlight clever women and the ensemble's virtuosic skills to morph in and out of the characters brought to life by Scheherezade's vivid descriptions.

Staging these stories proved instructive for the ensemble. Because the first iterations of the production occurred during Lookingglass's nomadic phase, before they moved into the Water Works building, the scenic design had to adapt to the different demands of the spaces they inhabited. *The Arabian Nights* was first produced at Chicago Filmmakers (1992), with an invited extension run at the Remains Theatre later that fall. In 1997, the company remounted the production at the Steppenwolf Studio Theatre.[9] Fortuitously, this challenge could easily be resolved by the flexible and relatively portable use of Persian rugs—however, this approach also meant that the ensemble would aesthetically rely upon a stereotype firmly rooted in Orientalism. This challenge—of how a Midwestern white woman would/should adapt and direct a work so firmly grounded in Middle Eastern culture and aesthetics—was at the forefront of Zimmerman's mind when she first proposed the project to the nascent ensemble. "The very obvious problem in approaching a text such as this is how we Westerners might represent this 'foreign' or 'exotic' culture without a complete appropriation and corruption of the meaning of that culture," she admits in her proposal. Her initial idea, in fact, was to use the adaptation to deconstruct Orientalism—to perform the *1001 Nights* tales "framed by a continuous secondary story—that of a Western tourist couple in their initial encounter with, seduction by and final rape of this foreign culture" (1994, 62). As she recounts in her doctoral dissertation about this process, however, "I speak in this proposal as arrogantly as King Shahryar …. I do not seem to imagine the possibility that the text might have a will of its own, and that it will transform me" (1994, 63). As she delved back into the stories in preparation for rehearsal, the words did in fact change her, and she found that instead of using an additional frame to critique cultural appropriation, she would use the framing device of the tales themselves—the transformation of Shahryar by Scheherezade from the darkness of mistrust, misogyny, and betrayal into the light of imagination and performance.

While in the 1990s and early 2000s Zimmerman's frequent explorations of Eastern culture (*Journey to the West*, *Silk*, and *Mirror of the Invisible World* at the Goodman, *Argonautika* and *The Odyssey* at Lookingglass) received critical praise and awards, by 2013 when she was on the cusp of opening her adaptation of *The Jungle Book* for the Goodman Theatre, Jamil Khoury (the founding artistic director of Silk Road Rising in Chicago) had had enough. In a scathing blog post for his theatre's website titled "The Trouble with Mary," Khoury argued that "[o]n Zimmerman's stage, Asian and Middle Eastern people were never quite people, we were colorful textiles and choreographed movements and sensualized [sic] fables." The instigating incident for Khoury's post was an interview published in *Chicago Magazine* that quoted Zimmerman as saying that "racism is in the eye of the beholder" as her answer to Catey Sullivan's queries about the critiques of *The Jungle Book* as presented on film by Disney and by original author Rudyard Kipling. Three days after posting the blog, Khoury made another post detailing a conversation he had with Zimmerman, where she assuaged his concerns "with the utmost of integrity, honesty, and sincerity." He followed this summary of their conversation with a transcript of their e-mail interview, allowing her to explain why she stages texts from other cultures.

> In all my work, I inflect what I adapt with my own values; in vast works such as the *Book of One Thousand Nights and One Night* there is homophobia, racism, anti-semitism and misogyny; but there is also profound, calm wisdom, beauty, poetry, song, tolerance, love and great humor—it is everything bad and good that human nature can contain. I lean into these latter qualities and do not include the former.

Her response and especially Khoury's depiction of their interaction appeared to settle the debate, and Zimmerman's production of *The Jungle Book* was well received locally.[10]

Outside of Chicago (and beyond the *Metamorphoses* pool), if audiences recognize the Lookingglass Theatre Company's aesthetic, it is likely due to one of their several productions that feature circus arts. *Lookingglass Alice* helped to solidify this association, in part because the name of the production included the name of the company, but also because this was one of their shows that toured to several regional theatres. Like the collaboration that started the ensemble, *Lookingglass Alice* is based on Lewis Carroll's *Alice* stories, as adapted by one of the founding ensemble members David Catlin. For this rendition created in 2005, Catlin upped the ante regarding the physical movement that had guided their earliest explorations of Alice's adventures. With the aid of stilts and trapeze work, the company was able to recreate the hallucinogenic visions Alice experiences, so that the Red Queen's extraordinary height makes Alice appear to have shrunk. Conceived for and staged in their new space in the Water Tower Water Works building, *Lookingglass Alice* also features an audience reveal partway through the production, with seating in an alley configuration that originally appears to be proscenium to spectators, until Alice steps through the looking glass and the audience discovers "the other side"—of seating as well as reality itself.

That same year, the company created a wildly successful circus show based loosely on the myth of Hephaestus, the god of metalworking and fire whom (according to Hesiod) Hera exiled by hurling the child down from Mount Olympus, in disgust at her child's imperfect appearance. Hephaestus's imperfection was a physical deformity, a lame foot, gained either at birth or as a consequence of the fall. *Hephaestus* was cocreated by the co-owner of Actor's Gymnasium, Tony Hernandez, and ensemble member Heidi Stillman, and what it lacked in dialogue it more than made up for in spectacle and danger. The framing device of this show mirrors that of *Arabian Nights* insofar as it relies on a female narrator—in this case, however, instead of a wife needing to divert a murderous husband, the narrator is a young girl who tells stories because she needs to escape her reality, especially the discord between her parents (heard offstage). Widely agreed to be more circus than theatre, *Hephaestus* helped to epitomize the ensemble's motto of "theatre without a net" with the finale, a high-wire pyramid that in the first two productions featured four performers but when the company moved the show to the Owen Bruner Theatre at the Goodman, the additional fly space allowed Hernandez to showcase a seven-person pyramid on the highwire, all without harnesses or a safety net.

The ensemble's skill with climbing and verticality was featured in the summer of 2015 when Lookingglass produced an adaptation of Herman Melville's *Moby-Dick* written and directed by David Catlin. In keeping with their remarkably flexible performance space, Catlin's vision for this adaptation was centered on the adventures of the high seas, with attention to the rigging and acrobatic feats that have become a specialty of Lookingglass performances. When I asked Catlin why he chose *Moby-Dick* to adapt, he related a story about reading it in a mad dash during the three days before final exams, how the story transported him to another world, and how this "feverish read" stuck with him, even as the novel sat on his shelf for two decades thereafter. Then, in 2010, he was invited to join a grant funded by the Boeing Corporation, initiated by one of the cofounders of Redmoon Theatre, Blair Thomas. This grant supported the simultaneous development of three distinct adaptations of *Moby-Dick*, created by Catlin, Thomas, and Shawn Pfautsch from House Theatre company (all Chicago-based theatremakers). The adapters met periodically at a local pie shop, where they would share their emerging ideas and collaborate on how to shape their different stagings of Melville's novel, suggesting passages and sections to each other and providing feedback on early drafts. This extraordinary opportunity culminated in a two-week residency at the University of Chicago, where the adapters worked with actors and a dramaturg (Derek Matson) who circulated among the three companies' work, continuing to provide feedback.

Catlin's *Moby Dick* highlights the power of water as well as the metaphor of rope (or rigging) as a connective tissue linking the men of the Pequod together. A central image that inspired Catlin, both in staging and scripting the adaptation, was that of the mother whale nursing her infant—the calm in the center of the churning of whales that readers encounter in the Grand Armada chapter, when the Pequod navigates the constricted straits of Sunda. "Starbuck saw long coils of the umbilical cord of Madame Leviathan, by which the young cub seemed still tethered to its dam." This moment proves transcendent for Ishmael, who remarks of it "there I still bathe me in eternal mildness of joy" (Melville 1851, 365). Thus, for Catlin, the hemp rope also served to reference the umbilical cord from this passage, as well as serving to showcase the acrobatic talents of the Lookingglass actors.

One of the obvious challenges of adapting a tome like Melville's *Moby Dick* is the title character: how do you stage the whale? For Catlin, the answer was to transfer the idea of a whale onto the human female body. He claims that he "knew from the beginning" that he would have women play the whale/s in his adaptation. Without question, it would be a "dude-heavy show," as Catlin put it, and thus from the start he wondered about those years on the ship, what it meant for the brief stints at home with their wives or (when applicable) female partners (Catlin 2015). In addition, Catlin recognized that we use feminine pronouns for ships ("Thar she blows!") and the ocean can be seen as a feminine force, even as amniotic fluid of the earth. The following passage (from "Loomings," the first chapter) in particular inspired how Catlin envisioned the three female roles in his adaptation: "Though I cannot tell why it was exactly that those stage managers, the Fates, put me down for this shabby part of a whaling voyage" (Melville 1851, 7). Willfully conflating the Greek understanding of the Fates with the Furies, while also calling upon the multiple allusions to *Macbeth* (and, in this case, the Three Weird Sisters) throughout the novel, Catlin created a haunting/avenging role for three women (the Fates), who also portray the whale.[11]

The female actors' costumes provide the means for much of the whale symbolism—they begin in traditional Victorian garb, with voluminous layers. The sound of their parasols opening and closing, for example, represents the opening and closing of the whale-spout. When "Stubb Kills a Whale" (Melville's Chapter 61) in Catlin's adaptation, one of the Fates is hoisted up onto the Pequod, wearing a black dress, her limp body slumped on the stage. Crewmen attach her feet to a rigging pulley, and she is raised upside down, her hooped skirt falling over her face and torso. The men unwrap the whale carcass as they might peel an orange, pulling the ribbon of clothing while the lifeless body spins above them. Finally, the dark skirt has been fully stripped away, leaving her under-hoops dangling over her head and her pelvis and thighs fully exposed to their white leotard base. As this shell of the mammal is lowered to the ground, the actor's costume has gone from a proper traveling dress to her white whale-boned corset and the skeleton hoops of her skirt: from a Victorian perspective, she is naked. In her role as the whale, she has been gutted.

This scene is particularly disturbing for the ways it signifies sinister male group activities—because all of the crew members are focused on one body, gleefully removing that body's clothes and exposing its underwear, it is difficult not to associate the butchery as sexual assault. Unsettling as it is, the resonance between the two events is not entirely misplaced—for animal and environmental activists, the brutal attempts of (hu)mankind to assert power over Mother Earth can be understood as a kind of rape. But the Fates in the Lookingglass *Moby Dick* are not powerless victims—quite the contrary, they control mortality itself, ushering the dead through a warmly lit door upstage left. When they embody the White Whale, they do so in tandem, with grotesque makeup exaggerating their mouths and eyes as they open both unnaturally wide. In the final moments of the play, one of the Fates stands center, her voluminous skirt extending around her to the limits of visible stage. As each crew member loses his life, he meets his Fate literally, walking up to her as she greets him with a kiss, before ducking under her enormous, billowing skirt representing the vast mystery of the ocean itself.

Critical Reception

Lookingglass Theatre Company matters to Chicagoans—one might even say they are as vital to them as water itself. Theatre critics embrace the Lookingglass ensemble as "an important cultural institution" within Chicago, a belief that was only solidified when they took root within the Water Tower Water Works building. In 2011, the ensemble was awarded a Regional Theatre Tony Award, leading Mayor Rahm Emanuel to proclaim the company as a "standard of artistic excellence in the city" ("Lookingglass" 2011). From their earliest productions of *The Odyssey* and *The Jungle* (Chicago Filmmakers, 1990), Lookingglass has enjoyed what Zimmerman has called a "curious, retroactive transformation" wherein critics have insisted that *The Odyssey* (for example) was a "cult hit" that played to full houses, when in fact "the two-part, four-hour and fifteen-minute show" performed for "a house of eight" spectators (Zimmerman 1994, 55). At the time, however, critics like Sid Smith (*Chicago Tribune*) were forthright about the paltry attendance, if not altogether bemused by the ensemble. In a 1990 review titled "Young Troupe Gives 'Odyssey' a Goofy, Impressive Staging," Smith notes that "the masses may not exactly be clamoring for this," although he gives credit to the "enveloping charm" of the production even if "the brief film segments, shown on a large rumpled sheet, are fraught with collegiate artiness." By their next show (*The Jungle*), critics began to see even more potential for Lookingglass, charitably suggesting that with "a few weeks to straighten up and tighten up … the flames of their talent could be fired into a real theatrical barnburner" (Christiansen 1990b). This prediction proved true when adapter/director David Schwimmer's *The Jungle* was awarded six Jeff awards and Zimmerman's *The Odyssey of Homer, Part I* received four. The Jeff awards, Chicago's annual custom of recognizing non-Equity theatre, are presented by the Joseph Jefferson Committee. Multiple recipients can win in the same category of award, unlike other award ceremonies. In 1990, *The Jungle* and *The Odyssey* both won for best ensemble, best director, and best original music (by Eric Huffman), and *The Odyssey* also won for best choreography. *The Jungle* was also awarded a Jeff for best production, lighting design (John Musial), and best new work or adaptation.

Arguably, this warm reception built upon the groundwork other ensembles laid before them, especially those companies (like the Remains, AboutFace, RedMoon, among others) that also embraced bold theatricality and literary adaptation. In 1990, Richard Christiansen, the lead theatre critic for the *Chicago Tribune* during the formative years for Lookingglass, recognized David Schwimmer and the ensemble he helped found alongside two other up-and-coming young leaders as representing a sea change in the Chicago style of theatre-making.[12] Christiansen set the scene for the revolution, noting that all of these men recently graduated from NU, where "they shared, and in some instances rebelled against, the same classes, teachers (including David Downs and Frank Galati) … [and] made their first independent ventures into producing and directing off-campus events." While they might have different styles and processes of creating performance, all three embraced literary adaptation and expressed a desire to make theatre that, in Schwimmer's words, "is visual, which to me is physical" (Christiansen 1990a).

In the early peripatetic years of Lookingglass, their need for space often yielded fortuitous collaborations, such as their productions of *The Master and Margarita* (1993) and *S/M: A Dream Biography* (1996), both produced in association with Steppenwolf theatre company and mounted within Steppenwolf's smaller studio space. While *S/M*, Zimmerman's ambitious exploration into the lives of the Marquis de Sade as well as Baron Leopold von Sacher-Masoch, may have left some critics wanting, it nevertheless had the advantage of appearing within the same season as Steppenwolf's main-stage production of Stephen Jeffreys's *The Libertine*, starring John Malkovich and Martha Plimpton. Both plays "served up two contemporary interpretations of notorious sexual renegades," encouraging audiences to connect the ensembles both in terms of their spatial proximity and subject matter (Montgomery 1996, 374). By the mid-1990s, Zimmerman's reputation had solidified as a gifted adapter/author, although critics agreed that *S/M* was uneven in its treatment of Sade and Sacher-Masoch, with the former receiving far more attention within the dream-like show. The bare-bones nature of the space and especially the audience configuration also pulled focus from the biographies onstage, or perhaps was designed to reflect their sexual tastes, leading Christiansen to proclaim that *S/M* was "presented in an environment that seems to have been designed by sadists for enjoyment by masochists" (Christiansen 1996).

Pithy summaries aside, what seemed clear by 1997, when the ensemble decided to remount *The Arabian Nights* (first produced in 1992) was the fact that the Lookingglass ensemble was becoming synonymous with Mary Zimmerman, alongside other company members who were finding success in television. The wildly successful sitcom *Friends* premiered on NBC in the fall of 1994, launching David Schwimmer's career in popular culture, and solidifying his identity as Ross, the nerdy on- and off-again boyfriend to Jennifer Aniston's Rachel on the show, which would run for ten seasons. On the same network (and sandwiched between *Friends* and *Seinfeld* on NBC's "Must-see TV" roster for Thursday nights) for two years was a lesser-known sitcom, *The Single Guy*, that starred another Lookingglass ensemble member, Joey Slotnik. While this television role would not make Slotnik a household name, later appearances on drama series *Boston Public* (Fox, 2000–4; Slotnik aired from 2000 to 2001) and *Nip/Tuck* (FX, 2003–10; Slotnik aired from 2003 to 2006) increased his recognition in popular culture, as did his roles in film.[13] While Slotnik and especially founding member Schwimmer continued to acknowledge their roots with Lookingglass, and would return to Chicago several times to make live theatre, their larger fame and popular appeal arguably detracted from the general public's ability to recognize the ensemble-driven nature of the company. More to the point, within theatre circles, especially after she received the MacArthur "genius" grant in 2000, audiences were more likely to recognize Zimmerman's name as a director and perhaps an adapter, but less often as a member of the ensemble herself. Part of this misattribution might also have stemmed from her role as an artistic associate at the Goodman (since 1995), one of the most established professional theatres in Chicago.

However, the Lookingglass crew had several aces up their sleeves: their experiments with circus-infused theatre, puppets, and culinary performance would expand their appeal beyond audiences who gravitated toward theatre and attract spectators who sought different kinds of entertainment. One review of the 2010 remount of *Hephaestus* gives a glimpse into this kind of spectator: it begins with "As a big fan of Blue Man Group and Cirque du Soleil, I was intrigued the moment I heard about 'Hephaestus: A Greek Mythology Circus Tale.'" The closing sentence of this review appeals once again to a broader audience base: "The show ... also will be great for fans of 'Stomp'" (Virtusio 2010, FW19). By comparing a Lookingglass production to shows and companies with popular appeal and widespread publicity, this critic reassures readers that they will enjoy the experience of seeing it, even if they don't immediately recognize the name of the event or company. As a result, many audience members have come to associate the ensemble with a theatrical circus aesthetic, rather than the more image-based literary adaptation of Mary Zimmerman.

Other innovative approaches to making theatre have also carved out a new niche of spectators for Lookingglass, such as their sold-out runs for *Cascabel* (2012 and 2014), a culinary theatre experience that featured circus feats as well as the celebrity chef Rick Bayless, the Chicago-based star of PBS's cooking show, *Mexico: One Plate at a Time*. With this production, "Lookingglass sought not only to capitalize on the popularity of celebrity chefs, but potentially to imagine a new form of theatre that engages with a multitude of sensual pleasures" (Abrams 2013, 285). Tied loosely together by a love story, *Cascabel* features flamenco dancer Chiara Mangiameli, cast as an owner of a boardinghouse, who mourns the loss of her partner who has deserted her so that he can perfect his mole sauce. "In a 'twist' that was predictable from the beginning," academic critic Joshua Abrams quips, "Bayless's character was Raul [Chiara's long-lost love]—'his love had no place to go, so it went into the food'—who reopened her taste buds to passion, which she revealed in a stunning flamenco solo, pulling Bayless into a clinch to tango" (287). While from a discerning critical perspective, this narrative remains problematic for its stereotypes of Latin American culture (all the more obvious to those who note Bayless's graduate education in anthropology and linguistics, as Abrams does in his review), local critics and audiences nevertheless ate this offering up with nary a hiccup—both mountings of *Cascabel* played to sold-out houses.[14] This favoritism is all the more remarkable given the ticket prices of over $200 per seat, which included a multicourse dinner (and, in 2014, beverages as well), but it also signals the readiness of Chicago audiences to welcome new experiences and the expansion of the Lookingglass aesthetic to include the tastes and smells of cuisine in their recipe for adventurous and visceral live performance.

This attention to risky, collaborative, innovative theatre-making is precisely why Lookingglass continues to make an impact on American theatre today, over three decades after they formed their ensemble. Their earliest instincts, to "save American theatre" by doing "the most exciting, physical, visceral, amazing multidisciplinary work that [they] could come up with," have continued to guide their season selection, their design choices, and their rehearsal and creative processes. To hear members or even artistic associates with the company describe their relationship to each other, one immediately recognizes the frequency with which they call each other "family." When they rehearse, plan, and perform together, they do so by building on a "secret history" forged by decades of familiarity and the rituals of social drama they have shared, including marriages and children as well as their successes and failures (Zimmerman 1994, 218). The respect they have for each other is matched by the audience's palpable awe and their continued curiosity for more: more danger, more delight, and especially more stories to tell.

SIGNIFICANT PRODUCTIONS 1997–2017

The Arabian Nights (1997), Steppenwolf Studio Theatre
Adapted from *1001 Nights* by Mary Zimmerman (1992); design by Dan Ostling (set) and Mara Blumenfeld (costumes); directed by Zimmerman
Reimagined and remounted in 2009 at Water Tower Water Works, in association with Berkeley Repertory and Kansas City Repertory theatres, where it also toured.

Metamorphoses (1998), Ivanhoe Theatre
Adapted and directed by ensemble member Mary Zimmerman; design by ensemble member Dan Ostling (set); from Ovid's poem
Remounted in 2012 at Water Tower Water Works, with productions in 2001 at Second Stage and 2002 at Circle in the Square (New York City) and 2013 at the Arena Stage (Washington, DC).

Eleven Rooms of Proust (2000), Ravenswood Warehouse
Conceived and directed by ensemble member Mary Zimmerman; design by ensemble member Daniel Ostling (set) and Mara Blumenfeld (costumes); inspired by *Remembrance of Things Past* and *Swann's Way* by Marcel Proust
In association with the Goodman Theatre and About Face Theatre.

Metamorphosis (2000), Ruth Page Center for the Arts
Adapted from Franz Kafka by Steven Berkoff; design by ensemble member Mara Blumenfeld (costumes); directed by ensemble member David Catlin
Remounted in 2012 in Water Tower Water Works.

Hard Times (2001), Ruth Page Center for the Arts
Adapted and directed by ensemble member Heidi Stillman; design by ensemble members Daniel Ostling (set), Mara Blumenfeld (costumes); with design by artistic associate Brian Sidney Bembridge (lights); based on novel by Charles Dickens
Remounted in 2002 and 2017.

They All Fall Down: The Richard Nickel Story (2001), Ruth Page Center for the Arts
Adapted by ensemble member Laura Eason and Jessica Thebus; directed by Jessica Thebus; from book by Richard Cahan.

Race: How Blacks and Whites Think and Feel about the American Obsession (2003), Water Tower Water Works
Adapted by ensemble members Joy Gregory and David Schwimmer; directed by David Schwimmer; design by ensemble member Daniel Ostling (sets); based on book by Studs Terkel.

1984 (2004), Water Tower Water Works
Adapted and directed by ensemble member Andrew White; design by ensemble members Mara Blumenfeld (costumes) and Daniel Ostling

(sets); with designs by artistic associates Christine A. Binder (lights) and Scott Silberstein (video); based on book by George Orwell.

Lookingglass Alice (2005), Water Tower Water Works
Adapted and directed by ensemble member David Catlin; design by ensemble members Mara Blumenfeld (costumes) and Daniel Ostling (sets); with design by artistic associate Christine A. Binder (lights); based on stories of Lewis Carroll
In association with The Actor's Gymnasium (Evanston, IL)
Remounted in 2007, 2008, 2014–15; toured in 2007 (New Victory Theatre in New York City) and 2010 nationally.

Hephaestus (2005), Water Tower Water Works
Coproduced with Silverguy Entertainment
Created and directed by artistic associate Tony Hernandez and ensemble member Heidi Stillman
Remounted in 2008 at Water Tower Water Works and in 2010 at Goodman Theatre in the Owen.

Argonautika (2006), Water Tower Water Works
Written and directed by ensemble member Mary Zimmerman; based on translations by Peter Green and David R. Slavitt.

The Brothers Karamazov (2008), Water Tower Water Works
Written and directed by ensemble member Heidi Stillman; design by ensemble members Mara Blumenfeld (costumes) and Daniel Ostling (sets); with design by artistic associate Rick Sims (sound); based on the novel by Fyodor Dostoevsky, translated by Richard Pevear and Larissa Volokhonsky.

Fedra: Queen of Haiti (2009), Water Tower Water Works
Written by ensemble member J. Nicole Brooks; directed by ensemble member Laura Eason; with designs by artistic associates Christine A. Binder (lights), Josh Horvath (sound) and Alison Siple (costume); based on the Phaedra plays by Euripides, Seneca, and Jean Racine.

Cascabel (2012), Water Tower Water Works
Coproduced with Frontera Grill and Silverguy Entertainment
Cocreated by chef Rick Bayless, artistic associate Tony Hernandez and ensemble member Heidi Stillman; codirected by Tony Hernandez and Heidi Stillman; design by ensemble member Mara Blumenfeld

(costumes); with design by artistic associates Brian Sidney Bembridge (sets and lights), Rick Sims (sound), and Andrew Pleuss (sound)
Remounted in 2014 at the Goodman Theatre in the Owen.

Still Alice (2013), Water Tower Water Works
Adapted and directed by ensemble member Christine Mary Dunford; with design by artistic associate Rick Sims (sound); based on the book by Lisa Genova.

Moby Dick (2015), Water Tower Water Works
Adapted and directed by ensemble member David Catlin; from book by Herman Melville
Remounted in 2017.

Blood Wedding (2016), Water Tower Water Works
Written by Federico Garcia Lorca and translated by Michael Dewell and Carmen Zapata; directed and scenic design by ensemble member Daniel Ostling; design by ensemble member Mara Blumenfeld (costumes); original music by artistic associate Rick Sims.

Thaddeus and Slocum: A Vaudeville Adventure (2016), Water Tower Water Works
Written by ensemble member Kevin Douglas; codirected by ensemble member J. Nicole Brooks and Krissy Vanderwarker; with design by artistic associate Christine A. Binder (lights).

Mr. and Mrs. Pennyworth (2016–17), Water Tower Water Works
Written and directed by ensemble member Doug Hara; design by ensemble member Mara Blumenfeld (costumes), with puppet designs by Blair Thomas and shadow animations by Manual Cinema (Drew Dir, Sarah Fornace, and Julia Miller).

CHAPTER 7
ELEVATOR REPAIR SERVICE
Roger Bechtel

Introduction

In a way, their name says it all: Elevator Repair Service (ERS). What could that possibly mean? What does it tell us about this company's work? The answer: nothing. The story goes that, as a preteen, founding artistic director John Collins and his cousin visited his aunt's office and took a computerized vocational aptitude test. Collins dutifully and seriously entered responses to a variety of questions: What are you interested in? Do you like working with people? With technology? After crunching this data, among the career options recommended by computer, one stuck out: "Elevator Repair Man" (Bailes 2002, 196). As Collins admits, the decision to label his theatre company Elevator Repair Service was, at the least, coy: "we chose that name in the spirit of a joke or prank, a contrarian and silly name. But if I could change anything, I'd give us a more neutral sounding name. But I don't really care so much about that anymore" (Horwitz 2004).

In fact, the name is an apt reflection of the company's early approach to making work. From their inaugural piece in 1991, Tristan Tzara's Dadaist *Mr. Antipyrine, Fire Extinguisher*, through their 2002 take on Henry James's *Turn of the Screw, Room Tone*, the aesthetic approach of the company had been marked by playfulness, mystery, and, yes, in-jokes. At the same time, while never eschewing text per se, the company had a penchant not only for "deconstructed" text and collage, but for placing dance front and center in their work. Structure for the pieces as a whole was primarily musical, rather than narrative, and dance became a natural and energetic manifestation of that dynamic. "Dance is coming into our work more and more," remarked company member Rinnie Groff at the time, "and that brings so much joyous energy to it," to which co-director Steve Bodow added, "Dance is also a good way of getting directly at that musicality we were talking about. It's a chance for us to focus exclusively on the musical composition of a non-musical element of the show" (Fusco 1999, 53).

While the company has never lost its playfulness and physical dynamism, its work underwent something of a sea change in 2004 with its adaptation of *The Great Gatsby*, titled *Gatz*. "Adaptation," while not inappropriate, is something of a misnomer insofar as it suggests the novel was turned into dramatic form for the stage. In actuality, the entire novel is read aloud, word for word, by the actor who assumes the role of Nick Carraway. The theatricality of the piece is provided by its pretext: an office worker, confronting a breakdown of his computer, discovers a copy of *Gatsby* in a Rolodex and, to relieve his boredom, begins reading it aloud. Soon the other workers are swept up in the story, have taken on roles, and are acting out scenes to the incessant narration of the entire novel, all 49,000 words of it. The transformation is undoubtedly playful, but also mysterious and even magical—not unlike ERS's previous work. At the same time, the text is the thing, marking a substantial break from their norm.

Following *Gatz*, the company decided to do something they had never done before: repeat themselves. Their next full-scale project was an adaptation of the first chapter of William Faulkner's *The Sound and the Fury*, followed by Hemingway's *The Sun Also Rises*, which they titled *The Select*. The company considers these pieces, along with *Gatz*, as comprising a trilogy of literary adaptations, and if they haven't returned to working with iconic novels in this way again, their textual turn has been ongoing. Their next project, *Arguendo*, also staged a text verbatim, but this time of the oral arguments of the US Supreme Court case *Barnes v. Glen Theatre*, in which a group of erotic dancers claimed a First Amendment right to dance nude. Text has remained central to their work post-*Arguendo*, but another shift has occurred: instead of adapting novels or political documents, their three most recent projects have been plays expressly written for the stage. The first, in 2015, was the original *Fondly, Collette Richard*, by Sibyl Kemp in collaboration with the company, followed by *Measure for Measure* in 2017, and another original work, Kate Scelsa's *Everyone's Fine with Virginia Woolf* in 2018.

Because Elevator Repair Service is very much alive and active today, it seems premature to impose historicizing categories on their work. At the same time, as a heuristic aid, it is useful to organize their work into a tripartite scheme here: the deconstructive, collage-based work that took them from *Mr. Antipyrine* in 1991 through *Room Tone* in 2004; the literary trilogy through *Arguendo* in 2013; and the trio of dramas that brings them to the present. Progressing through these three chronological phases, this chapter will examine their diverse body of work, charting the development of their aesthetic as well as their company identity. To cull one particular production from their oeuvre for closer scrutiny is difficult; their recent mounting of plays with bespoke stage sets contradicts their earlier disdain for the trappings of traditional theatre, just as their literary trilogy has little in common, at least on the surface, with their early deconstructions. Still, it is undeniable that *Gatz* has proven to be a turning point for the company, both as a company and aesthetically. And in fact, *Gatz* has never left their repertoire for long: they performed it every year from 2004 to 2012, and a remount ran in September 2018 at New York University's Arts Center in Abu Dhabi and will open at its home campus in Manhattan in January 2019. A closer look at *Gatz* and the problem of adaptation, then, will round out and conclude the chapter.

1991–2004: Dada, Deconstruction, and Collage

Given ERS's early unconcern with text per se, it is no surprise that their 1991 inaugural production was the Dadaist *Mr. Antipyrine, Fire Extinguisher*. As Collins, who has directed all their productions, would later point out, at the time they were less a company than a group of college friends from Yale relocated to New York continuing their undergraduate preoccupation. Influenced by the Wooster Group's ensemble process, however, the originating members—Collins, Groff, Bodow, Bradley Glenn, and James Hannaham—soon embraced their identity as a company and incorporated in 1993 (Horwitz 2004). *Mr. Antipyrine* was given a midnight premier at the now-defunct Theatre Con Nada, a storefront space on the lower east side that produced bare-bones shows for a split of the box office with the artists.

To say that ERS was influenced by the Wooster Group is something of an understatement. Collins began attending their productions while still at Yale, and as he notes:

> I probably unconsciously imitated them ... But what influenced me the most about the Wooster Group was not so much their work itself, or what I saw in it. It was more about the way they worked and the kind of freedom they had. They make their work without any idea about what theatre should be, without any preconceptions, except that it should be enjoyable to watch. (Fusco 1999, 55)

Watching the company's show reel for *Mr. Antipyrine*,[1] it also seems an understatement to say the Wooster Group was "unconsciously imitated"— in fact, it would be very easy to mistake *Mr. Antipyrine* for the work of the Wooster Group itself. Most immediately, the production *sounds* like a Wooster Group performance. The performers almost uniformly speak into microphones, often with special effects like reverb or faux-telephone tininess. A musical soundtrack accompanies much of the action, such as it is, which occasionally gives way to dance breaks choreographed in an ersatz, pedestrian, sometimes pop-culture-referenced Wooster Group style, set to campy, kitschy tunes. Sound is often used to create the sensation of stasis, which is usually abruptly interrupted by a contrapuntal sound effect that correlates with an equally jarring change in stage activity. Visually, the staging is landscape in style, every action working in conjunction with or counterpoint to some other action. The one noticeable difference is the complete absence of television screens—an omission likely due to Nada's round-robin performance scheduling, in which two or three companies might perform in a single evening, forcing setup and strike for each into an inconceivably short span of time.

If Collins's approach to staging is almost slavishly imitative of the Wooster Group in these early pieces, the reasons stretch beyond sheer youthful infatuation. His working entre to the New York theatre scene came right out of college at the invitation of David Herskovits, artistic director of Target Margin Theatre, to design sound for his production of *Titus Andronicus*. Herskovits had taught directing to Collins at Yale and was impressed with Collins's final project for the course, in which he had substituted audio recordings for live performances—an initially pragmatic choice rather than an aesthetic one prompted by a lack of rehearsal time (Weiner 1997, 48). Through *Titus Andronicus*, Collins was "discovered" by Richard Foreman, and designed the sound for his 1991 *The Mind King*, which led to an interview with the Wooster Group. Although nothing immediate came of the meeting, when the Group lost its sound designer in the middle of the run of *The Emperor Jones*, they called Collins, who became their full-time sound person (Weiner 1997, 48).

Sound has always played a significant role in the work of ERS, and because Collins worked for both companies at the same time, its aesthetic development is closely parallel with the Wooster Group.[2] Despite the overwhelming similarities between the Wooster Group and ERS at this time, a close inspection can nonetheless locate the seeds of difference that would come to distinguish ERS. Like the Wooster Group, with *Mr. Antipyrine* the company began with a text that it would deconstruct in performance—albeit one that is arguably self-deconstructing. And like the Wooster Group, the company interpolated this source text with other texts, in this case what seem to be job application questions (reminiscent of the job aptitude test taken by the preteen Collins?). Yet whereas the Wooster Group always seem to maintain a cool distance from the text, using it, as Heiner Müller might suggest, as a sculptural object, the cast of *Mr. Antipyrine* embraced the text with exuberance, using it to create absurd comic scenarios that generate more heat than irony. In fact, the production played as an absurdist farce in large part because of the unifying quality of the setting, which was, in an echo of the future, a corporate office. In this context, the nonsensical text of *Mr. Antipyrine* itself served an almost narrative function, serving as a stand-in for the nonsense-speak of the corporate workplace and thus taking on a structurally connotative meaning.

The distinctive humor of *Mr. Antipyrine*—including an actual fire extinguisher as a kind of holy grail of corporate ambition—is something that has typified ERS from this first production to the present. "What I like about performing with ERS," said Rinnie Groff in 1999, "is the feeling that whatever is happening to us on stage is so much more loaded and funny for us than it could possibly be to any other human being in the world, because we've been there through the whole process of watching it being created and working on it" (Fusco 1999, 53). If that sounds self-indulgent, Collins located their distinctive brand of humor in its indeterminacy: "When something feels funny in an easy way, it's a sure sign we're not doing enough. So we'll look for a way to undercut it or give the impression that there's more to it; that describes our sense of humor. We're always saying we want people to laugh, but don't want them to know *why* they're laughing" (Fusco 1999, 53). The company's concern with veiling humor in their early work found its corollary in their refusal to embrace or even monitor intellectual meaning. Their Ivy League education clearly provided them with a sophisticated understanding of things theatrical, like Brecht, as well as things political, like gender. Yet even when confronted with a questionable representation of women, as happened in the 1998 *Total Fictional Lie*, the company prioritized organic creation over message. "We try not to comment too much on anything," noted Groff. "But I think we are aware of gender issues. In the end, we try not to be made so heavy by those things" (Fusco 1999, 55). And, Collins added, "We don't want to make things in a calculated or intellectual way. We let the show physically evolve in front of us in rehearsal" (Fusco 1999, 55).

It is no surprise then that, for their second project, mounted in 1992, the group—now under the official moniker Elevator Repair Service—was inspired by the idea of a lost screenplay Salvador Dali had written for the Marx Brothers called "Giraffes on Horseback Salad." Without the actual script, the company was left to imagine what it might have contained and further to imagine the relationship between Dali and the Marx Brothers. The result, *Marx Brothers on Horseback Salad*, incorporated the familiar dance breaks and inventive use of sound, and even, *a la* the Wooster Group, the recycling of a particularly recognizable prop from *Mr. Antipyrine*, but unlike *Mr. Antipyrine*, while their influence is clear, there is no mistaking the work for the Wooster Group's. The piece was marked by whimsical humor and fantastic imagery, including a multiarmed Groucho sitting Shiva-style, a harp with barbed-wire strings and a statue-like Harpo in angelic repose on roller skates. A style had begun to emerge that would become unmistakably that of the newly christened Elevator Repair Service.

Style itself became the prompt for their next production, *Spine Check*, which used film-noir aesthetics and an original devised script—including, of course, "found" text such as a physics lecture—to tell the story of a stereotypical noir detective. This detective, however, is obsessed with climate change. Despite the subject matter, the action of the play is madcap, involving a femme fatale whose dead husband was a prehistoric hunter fortuitously preserved in the ice age and a gang of criminals attempting to deprive the public of the news of a new, imminent ice age. Brian Parks's review in *The Village Voice* was as much an introduction to the company as it was criticism and included bits of an interview with Collins. In it, Collins explained the company's evolving approach to making performance: "Trash-picking the culture," Parks wrote, "they'll find a language tape or a curious noise on a sound-effects record, then shape a scene or character around it" (Parks 1993, 88). In that process, Collins added, it's often what would usually be considered rehearsal detritus that becomes the crux of a scene: "'When I was an actor ... what I enjoyed most were all the strange things that happened during rehearsal that got tossed out because they didn't make sense. I think those things *do* make sense, have their own logic. Because they're real'" (Parks 1993, 88). In the end, Parks couldn't resist categorizing ERS for his readers: "Appropriation, collage, and a dada side of radical juxtaposition. Postmodernism, anyone? Well, yeah. There's life in 'ol Betsey yet" (Parks 1993, 88).

Parks's laudatory review must have provided a heady moment for the company, but the "postmodern" label—entirely appropriate—was a perfect predictor of later, less positive criticism. The term itself was regarded as having two possible theoretical valences. Some, like Jean-Francois Lyotard, believed that postmodern art of all kinds not only could embody political critique but, as a rejection of Enlightenment rationality and its socially instrumental usage as veiled form of oppression, was inherently critical.

Others, like Fredric Jameson, saw postmodernism as the reflection of an advanced mode of capitalist production that, in its particularly rapacious and accelerated capacity to commodify art, evacuated it of critical potential. In ERS, Parks clearly saw the former: "Their work is inherently a critique, a challenge to visual-aural-narrative assumptions" (Parks 1993, 88).

Parks's colleagues at *The Village Voice*, however, proved harder to win over. ERS's next production, *Language Instruction: Love Family v. Andy Kaufman*, was a mash-up of a mad team of Berlitz language instructors and famed comedian Andy Kaufman in his addled, language-challenged immigrant persona. A work-in-progress performance in 1993 generated this from *Voice* critic Roderick Mason Faber: "At times, it appears to be a nonlinear, abstracted skit from *Saturday Night Live*, at other times an inane parody of the Wooster Group" (Faber 1993, 105). When the show officially opened in 1994, *Voice* critic Francine Russo was quick to see in the piece postmodernism's trademark self-reflexivity: "Elevator Repair Service deconstructs the dead comedian's life and routines to poke into the nature of self-consciousness and performance" (Russo 1994, 97). Unlike Parks, however, she had less patience for the company's antic disposition: "As it clowns too long, *Instructions* trickles into watered-down repetitions of its basic silliness, but the agile cast oozes a surreal charm" (Russo 1994, 97).

McGurk, the company's next project, was inspired by the name of a legendary nineteenth-century saloon in the Bowery nicknamed, after its owner, McGurk's "Suicide Hall." The production received two runs in 1994, both "work-in-progress" showings, despite the fact that the *New York Times* briefly previewed the piece before an ostensible "official" opening (McNeil 1994, C2). This would, however, explain the absence of critical attention by the press; still, one review emerged in *Back Stage*. "McGurk," wrote Jonathan Abarbanel, "is one of the most baffling things I've seen onstage in a long time. Between glances at my watch to find out how much longer I had to sit through this messy performance piece, I kept wondering why ... [they] would present themselves in such an unbecoming way" (Abarbanel 1994, 30). McGurk was followed by *Shut up I Tell You (I Said Shut up I Tell You)*, a take on old radio plays, which was workshopped at Richard Foreman's Ontological-Hysterical theatre and then, following a second workshop, premiered at P.S. 122 in 1996. Again, press attention was scant. In a 149-word review in the *Voice*, Charles McNulty observed, "The humor, ranging from the screwy to the sophomoric, is most effective in pointing out the zany lengths to which artists will go to strike chords of imagination. A little less whimsy in the overall structure of the piece might have made things sturdier for the ensemble" (McNulty 1996, 84). However, if recent press had trended toward the negative—or nonexistent—they would get a lift from Steven Drukman, writing for *Artforum*. "In an admittedly spotty theatrical season, the work of Elevator Repair Service, in a work of sideshow-style shenanigans titled *Shut Up I Tell You* ... stands out not only for its humor and intelligence, but also for its defiant theatricality" (Drukman 1996, 104). Importantly and astutely, Drukman made a case that the company had transcended its forbears and stood *sui generis*:

> ERS is representative of a generation of performers that was weaned on Richard Foreman and the Wooster Group, sweetly merging the mind-bending perception of the former with the hi-tech hijinks of the latter. The troupe is a sort of recombinant DNA of discrete theatrical strands ... The overall effect is of an altered and wholly original spectatorial experience, something Foreman-esque in its aims. So while the pulse of the experimental theatre has felt faint in New York this winter, ERS has demonstrated that the scene still has an EKG. (Drukman 1996, 104)

A single review in a journal devoted almost exclusively to the visual arts likely had little effect on the wider reception of ERS and its work, but it does seem predictive that ERS was soon to occupy their own place, firmer and more established, in the New York theatrical firmament.

Next up, *Cab Legs*, the only project in their 1996–7 season, was a departure for the company in several ways. They began the project with the idea of staging the fire department. The cast, without the costumes that would give away the conceit, would dance manically as firefighters whenever an alarm sounded and, waiting for the alarm, would do as little as possible. Eventually, and for the first time, the company introduced the text of an extant drama into the piece: Tennessee Williams's *Summer and Smoke* (pun presumably intended) (Bailes 2002, 193–4). If the ERS performance style until this point had been almost uniformly large and loud, the textual interludes in *Cab Legs* were restrained and quiet, almost inaudible, in a deliberate attempt to strip away theatricality and arrive at something more "real" (Bailes 2002, 190–1). Eventually they went even further, using Tennessee Williams's text as a loose source for improvised dialogue. Finally, some scenes were played off-stage—*far* off-stage in other rooms of the theatre—paradoxically subverting the theatricality of the text and heightening the theatricality of the performance. Although neither the *New York Times* nor the *Voice* reviewed the performance, it was given in-depth treatment by Mark Zimmerman in

PAJ: A Journal of Performance and Art. Zimmerman bemoaned generally the subservience of language to performers' idiosyncratic physicality in "this age of post-everything" but found a kind of antidote in the performers' *sotto voce* delivery here: "Elevator Repair Service achieve moments that funnel meaning and story to an apex of expression not by tossing aside language and dialogue, but by enmeshing delicate glimmers of speech within a framework of often brutish motion" (Zimmerman 1998, 43). In the same vein, Zimmerman rightly addressed the "story" of the play—the surprise being that, aside from the fractured and facetious plotlines of some of their previous pieces, ERS had never before concerned itself with narrative. However attenuated it may have become through improvisation, and despite dance breaks inspired by Bollywood films, *Summer and Smoke* remained the core of *Cab Legs*. Zimmerman was rapturous in response: "its art is an art that seems to have devoured its references, eating its parents and birthing its own poetic and comedic child, always reminding us of things best kept hidden. And through it all we are laughing. It is funny because it is awkward. It is powerful because, at some level, we get it" (Zimmerman 1998, 44). Arguably, "getting it" had very much to do with the piece's narrative through-line—it was certainly a counterpoint to previous critical responses that professed bafflement or confusion.

Cab Legs, then, with its coherent story and subdued style, proved a radical departure for ERS aesthetically, but it also marked an institutional step forward for the company. During this time, the company first began applying for grants, and *Cab Legs* actually premiered not in New York, but at the Belluard-Bolwerk Festival in Fribourg, Switzerland, in July 1997, before moving on to the Sommerszene Festival in Salzburg and the Städtklang Festival in Münster that same summer. The following year, it toured again to Europe, performing at the Berlin Festival, the Künsten Festival des Arts in Brussels, and the Holland Festival in Amsterdam. International recognition clearly added to their growing New York cachet, but the extensive touring was also, importantly, a sign of growing financial wherewithal. The production values may have continued to appear shoestring, but ERS was, for an experimental theatre company, entering the big time.

Between touring and the American premier of *Cab Legs* in 1998, ERS began work on a new project. It is ironic—or entirely appropriate, depending on the perspective—that they would follow a foray into dramatic literature with a piece titled *Total Fictional Lie*. It is also ironic—or entirely appropriate—that they would take as their urtextual material dialogue from documentary films. For the first time, *Village Voice* chief critic, Michael

Feingold, weighed in and, while praising the "intelligence, integrity, and precision" of ERS, as well as its "imaginative skill," used his critical bully pulpit to ask more of the company (Feingold 1998, 155). As mentioned above, he pointed in passing to the uncontextualized decision to have only women in the cast perform a continuing bit of physical schtick in which they, with the dexterity of contortionists, pile into and extricate themselves from a small box. He went on to say, "As its attitude would suggest, Elevator Repair Service isn't always forthcoming about its subject. ERS's standard tactic is dry, unemphatic content, its principal target—the pervasive phoniness of the social structure we inhabit—both slightly facile and rather nebulous. The troupe could reach more daringly far, and grasp more fiercely, without losing its seemingly irrefragable cool" (Feingold 1998, 155). Implicit in this calling out is a challenge to ERS not to overindulge their penchant for a distinctively postmodern "cool," but to be more forthcoming about—or to think more clearly about—the critical implications of their work. It is telling that Feingold locates his criticism in the *content* of the work; this is a significant contrast to the claim by his colleague Brian Parks in his review of *Spine Check* quoted above that ERS's aesthetic approach carried an implicit *formal* critique of "visual-aural-narrative assumptions" (Parks 1993, 88). As if to cement the point, in an otherwise positive review in *Art in America*, Douglas Davis concluded by saying, "ERS lost some of its impact through the relentless use of multiple voices, plots and movement. What we 'follow' in ERS productions is the pure formal brilliance of the ensemble itself" (Davis 1999, 63).

With the door to international touring now open, ERS began to have several shows in repertory in any given season. In addition to *Total Fictional Lie* in the 1998–9 season, the company continued to tour *Cab Legs*, with stops in Ljubljana, Slovenia, and again in Berlin. *Language Instruction* was resurrected and played at the Flea Theatre in New York, and, in addition to its opening in New York, *Total Fictional Lie* was performed both in Berlin and in Houston. As if this weren't enough, they performed a work-in-progress performance at HERE in New York of what at the time they simply called *The Great Gatsby*. The 1999–2000 season saw *Total Fictional Lie* travel to Minneapolis, Columbus, Portland, and Seattle, and the development and premier of a new piece, *Highway to Tomorrow*, again at HERE in New York.

Highway to Tomorrow tackled a text even more daunting than Tennessee Williams's brand of American tragedy: Euripides's *The Bacchae*. The project went through four iterations before it arrived at a final version (as final, that is, as ERS ever gets with a piece). The first iteration involved performers sitting at a table manipulating ersatz puppets—a shoe and a mallet both with sunglasses, for example, and a thermos with a pair of stick-on "googly" eyeballs. The second version replaced Euripides with Fitzgerald's *The Last Tycoon*, which was jettisoned in favor of *The Bacchae* for versions three and four. The thermos remained throughout and opened the show holding a faux book—"Hypnotism for Everyone"—while attempting to bring the audience under its spell. The fact that the puppet was a thermos was another in-joke: they considered it a fortuitous pun on the Greek word "thyrsus," a stock of fennel associated with Dionysus. Although "Thermie," as they dubbed him, made the cut, all the other characters of *The Bacchae* were eventually taken by actors (Bleha 2003, 81–5).

If the challenge that Michael Feingold had issued in his *Voice* review of *Total Fictional Lie* was softened by praise and generosity, his perception of their failure to take it up in *Highway to Tomorrow* was expressed with straightforward pique and impatience. "Whether tragedy should provoke laughter," he wrote, "is a thorny question, which Elevator Repair Service hasn't answered by putting Euripides through its deadpan deconstruction mill. *Highway to Tomorrow*, as ERS retitles it, seems more like the road to nowhere" (Feingold 2000, 79). The terse review ends with Feingold's redoubled critical point:

> As for pity and terror, politics and religion, order and anarchy, and the other antitheses Euripides poured into his great play—don't count on finding them here. Ironically, the great ironist of Greek tragedy is out-ironized by ERS's apathy toward, or maybe suspicion of, the anger behind his ironies. Why, in that case, they wanted to tackle the play is not something I can explain. (Feingold 2000, 79)

Feingold was supported in his impatience by *New York Times* critic D. J. R. Bruckner, who wrote, "The problem is that nothing pulls the fragments here into a comprehensible whole ... [ERS] must notice, as I did, that even with an audience of devotees ready to laugh, there are long stretches of silence when the viewers seemed stunned by their own incomprehension" (Bruckner 2000, E3). The problem for both critics is one of text: if ERS is going to stage a narrative piece, a drama—and a classic one at that—Bruckner demands narrative clarity, while Feingold demands some kind of fidelity to, some communication of, the critical intentions of the play. Neither, it should be noted, asks that ERS change its house style—deconstruction, collage, offbeat humor, and campy choreography—but both place on the company the burden of textual meaning, an attribute often at odds with the ironic detachment of postmodernism, or at least ERS's brand of it.

In its next project, *Room Tone*, ERS shunned the drama in its choice of texts—Henry James's *The Turn of the Screw* and brother William James's *The Variety of Religious Experience*—but very much created a drama in telling the ghostly story of a governess and her two charges contained in Henry's novel. As if to counter accusations of facile irony in their work, the company described the piece as "[a] haunting, humorous, yet sincere meditation on spiritual belief" (Elevator Repair Service)—the operative word being "sincere." The production had all the earmarks of ERS—idiosyncratic dance breaks, absurd humor, an elaborate soundscape—but within a dramaturgical structure more contained and unified than their previous work had demonstrated. *Voice* critic Charles McNulty (Michael Feingold likely recused himself) noticed the departure approvingly: "The ensemble ... is in top form, with disciplined performances that avoid the self-delighted goofiness that has proved something of an occupational hazard for ERS members in the past" (McNulty 2002, 60). At the same time, McNulty, too, pushed the company toward even greater cohesion: "there's still something hermetic about the new piece's vision. Gone, refreshingly, is the insider jokiness ... Surely a more patiently constructed theatrical architecture wouldn't hem in the imagination of one of downtown's loopier collectives. The fertile material deserves not only rigorous eccentricity but eccentric rigor as well" (McNulty 2002, 60).

2004–2012: The Textual Turn

The "more patiently constructed architecture" was soon to arrive, whether or not it was prompted by critical reception. *Room Tone* had first appeared as a work-in-progress in the spring of 2002, opened in the fall of that same year, and was the only production that played in the 2002–3 season, and only in New York. In fact, the last show to have toured was *Total Fictional Lie* during the 1999–2000 season. The *Highway to Tomorrow* run in New York solely occupied the 2000–1 season and toured only to Columbus, Ohio, the following year. The next show to tour would be *Room Tone*, but not until the 2003–4 season, and then only to Washington, DC, Minneapolis, and Burlington, Vermont. In an interview in *Culturebot*, John Collins explained the void in international touring during this period:

We agreed to premiere a show at a really big festival in Europe one time and in retrospect now I know there's no way we could have finished the show in time. We ended up showing something that was short and not very well finished, and I think looked unfinished, and it kind of killed our European touring for a while. But at the time, it was like, they're offering us a lot of money, they want two shows, how could we turn that down? (Horwitz 2004)

Although Collins isn't forthcoming with specifics, the unfinished piece was presumably *Total Fictional Lie*, which played alongside the long-finished *Cab Legs* at the Berlin Festival in 1998.

The absence of touring opportunities during this period afforded ERS more time to devote to their latest project, a version of F. Scott Fitzgerald's *The Great Gatsby*. In 2003, the company began reading the novel aloud to each other in the borrowed office space of the Wooster Group, and from that emerged the idea to stage it in an office setting (Mead 2010). As mentioned above, they had toyed with the idea in a workshop in 1999, but it was not to return until 2004 in another work-in-progress performance, titled simply *Gatsby*, at the Collapsable Hole in New York. The reason for shelving the project for so long was because another stage adaption of *Gatsby* was scheduled at the Guthrie Theatre in Minneapolis, with tentative plans to move to Broadway. Understandably, the Fitzgerald estate made the rights unavailable to other stage versions in New York (Zinoman 2006b, 2:8). Nonetheless, ERS persisted in working on the piece, and days before they were to open in New York in 2005, they were again denied permission (Mead 2010). Rather than abandon the project, they chose to do private workshop showings in lieu of public performances, inviting the directors of prominent international theatre festivals. A bevy of touring offers emerged, and, because permission to perform was denied only in New York, in 2006 they took the piece to Amsterdam, Brussels, Zurich, Oslo, Trondheim, Bergen, and Minneapolis, where it had its American premiere at the Walker Art Center. The show, now called *Gatz*, toured to Vienna, Lisbon, Philadelphia, Portland, and Seattle in 2007; in 2008 to Chicago and Dublin; and in 2009 to Brisbane and Sydney. Finally, in November 2009, the Fitzgerald estate relented and granted the company the rights to perform *Gatz* in New York (Mead 2010). Its official, public New York opening was at the Public Theatre in 2010.

Gatz will be given more attention in the concluding section, but suffice it to say here that ERS, rather than deconstructing their urtext, had, almost inadvertently, finally and fully embraced it. Instead of subjecting Fitzgerald's novel to their will, it had subjected the company to its ineluctable force. And in doing so, it provided the dramaturgical architecture and gravity that so many of their critics had been urging on them. The critical response, in fact, was nothing short of adulation. Ben Brantley, writing for *The New York Times*, called it a "work of singular imagination and intelligence" (Brantley 2010a, C1). At the end of the year, it topped Brantley's "best of" list, and he called it "[t]he most remarkable achievement in theatre not only of this year but of this decade" (Brantley 2010b, AR7). In *New York Magazine*, Scott Brown remarked that whatever trademark ERS irony brought to the piece, it didn't district from the novel: "[I]n fact, it enhances it, exfoliating great gaudy barnacles of accumulated Gatsby kitsch, and forcing a reassessment of our deepest beliefs about ourselves, our culture, our most treasured illusions, literary and otherwise" (Brown 2010). Only Michael Feingold, again writing for the *Voice*, stands out for his faint praise: "Some perception, and much occasional pleasure, comes from the mingling [of book and theatre], but little real illumination, and even less deep connection to the novel's emotional events" (Feingold 2010, 35). Feingold's begrudging attitude was most apparent in his closing remarks: "What intentions fuel ERS's experiments with great American novels remains an open question; whether such experiments are worth pursuing remains a bigger one. But with *Gatz*, particularly given Shepherd's [the actor playing Nick] manifest devotion to this enormous effort, nobody can accuse them of not loving the great works they tackle" (Feingold 2010, 35).[3]

Feingold's last comment makes more sense when one remembers that, although *Gatz* was the first of the literary trilogy created by ERS, it was actually the second to arrive in New York. Between the early workshops of *Gatz* and its premier in October 2010, the company mounted three other projects: the companion pieces of the trilogy—*The Sound and the Fury* and *The Sun Also Rises*, which was the only one that premiered in New York after *Gatz*—and another piece called *No Great Society*. *No Great Society*, which premiered in 2006, was something of a chamber piece, easily the smallest production in scale that ERS had done to that point. The subject was Jack Kerouac, and their source material was recordings of two radically different television appearances: one in 1959 when he recited poetry on the Steve Allen show, the other a 1968 episode of William F. Buckley's *Firing Line* where he appeared drunk and gratingly obnoxious. The entire piece was done with a cast of only four, one actor doubling as both Allen and Buckley, and actress Susie Sokol, playing Jack in a plaid skirt, making no attempt to mimic him physically. Jason Zinoman, writing for *The New York Times*, gave it fulsome praise, calling it "a joy from start to finish" (Zinoman 2006a, B9). At the same time, in what was surely a first for the company, *Village Voice* critic Alexis Soloski essentially accused the show of not being ERS-like *enough*, noting that even Sokol's "remarkable" performance "never quite lifts the show out of the enforced flatness of the interview format" (Soloski 2006, 66). She goes on to say, "[I]t's only in the final moments, when the company breaks wide the chat-show setup and performs a jerking, stomping, rapturous, mostly-seated dance ... that *No Great Society* really surprises and delights" (Soloski 2006, 66).

With a return to "great American novels" came a move to a larger scale of production. Following *Gatz*, the group was a bit stymied as to what to do next. According to Collins, they asked themselves, "'What would we never do?' ... Steve Bodow, half-joking, answered something to the effect of, 'Well, the thing we'd never do is repeat ourselves deliberately, so let's do that'" (Mead 2010). From that came the decision to tackle William Faulkner's *The Sound and the Fury*, this time, however, only the first chapter. The novel spans the thirty-year decline of the Compsons, Mississippi aristocracy who lose both their financial and social standing, as well as the lives of members of the family. Much of the novel takes place outside on the lands of the estate, but ERS's production was contained completely within the Compson home. The company had long eschewed realistic stage sets, only gradually incorporating bespoke scenic pieces until *Gatz*, which re-created in whole its shabby office environment. If that set, as realistic as it was, remained minimal, the set for *The Sound and the Fury* was resolutely maximal. "David Zinn's set," wrote Ben Brantley in *The New York Times*, "is a ravishingly detailed, photo-realist evocation of what an early-20th-century parlor of a once-prosperous Southern home might have looked like" (Brantley 2008, E1). As befitting the grandeur of a Southern estate, it was also large in scale, contributing to the visual impression that this was unlike anything ERS had previously attempted. At the same time, it also implicitly spoke to the issue of production values and budget: the company was given a residency and opened the show in 2008 at New York Theatre Workshop, an Off-Broadway venue with greater resources than the Off-Off venues ERS had played in the past. The designer, David Zinn, was enlisted from outside the company and brought with him an established career on Broadway and in opera, and he created something that could have fit comfortably onto a high-budget Broadway stage. While New York Theatre Workshop was footing most of the bill, clearly the extensive touring of *Gatz* and the increased financial support that comes with increased acclaim had leveraged ERS's production budgets. Whether the budget was leading the company's altered aesthetic or the changed aesthetic the budget is, however, another question altogether.

Like *The Great Gatsby*, Faulkner's *The Sound and the Fury* is another novel of the 1920s—*Gatsby* first published in 1925 and *The Sound and the Fury* in 1929—and, with its Southern setting, offered a regional counterpoint to Fitzgerald's upper-crust East Coast. It is divided into four parts or chapters, and the first, titled "April 7, 1928," is told from the point of view of one of the Compson children, Benjy, a cognitively challenged thirty-three-year old. Seen through his eyes, the narrative is free-associative and impressionistic, and time is rendered disjointed, the past and present eliding one into the other. It proved, undoubtedly, a challenge to translate to stage action. As with *Gatz*, the entire text, verbatim, is spoken aloud, but instead of a single narrator character, it is divided among the cast, and while a physical copy of the book is read from at times, for a majority of the play the actors have memorized their lines. The one radical difference in approach is that the performers rotate through the roles as the performance progresses, the lone exception being Benjy, played by Susie Sokol. The felicitous effect is twofold: with Benjy as the lens through which the audience enters the story, the apparent disjunctions and confusions involved become Benjy's disjunctions and confusions; moreover, reflecting a novel in which all narrators are unreliable, it emphasizes the point that our difference from Benjy is only a matter of degree. Certainly the press saw the point or at least was unbothered by the roundelay of roles from actor to actor. "Watching it, after the first few minutes of resistance," wrote Ben Brantley, "I let myself fall into the shifting swirl of voices and movements. Sometimes it was the stylized, seemingly incongruous elements in this activity that most sharply summoned Benjy's world view" (Brantley 2008, E1). With regard to the overall production, the critics were almost unanimous in their praise, the one exception, in a growing pattern, being Michael Feingold of *The Village Voice*, who again was bothered by ERS's "style" and its failure to illuminate Faulkner's text (Feingold 2008).

ERS teamed again with New York Theatre Workshop for the final piece of their trilogy of 1920s novels, Ernest Hemingway's 1926 *The Sun Also Rises*, retitled by ERS as *The Select*, which opened in New York in 2011. For *The Sound and the Fury*, Dartmouth College was credited along with NYTW for supporting the piece; with *The Select*, the list of sponsors is much longer: the Ringling International Arts Festival, Sarasota, Florida; the Baryshnikov Arts Center, New York; the Philadelphia Live Arts Festival with funding from the Pew Center; ArtsEmerson, Boston; and Festival TheaterFormen, Hannover are all listed as commissioning the work (Elevator Repair Service). It would seem that ERS, after the success of *The Sound and the Fury*, became an even more attractive option for programming venues.

The setting for Hemingway's novel shifts from Paris, to Madrid, to Pamplona, Spain, but its narrator is decidedly American: Jake Barnes, a war vet and journalist, impotent from a combat injury, in love with British Lady Brett Ashley. Brett returns Barnes's affections, but her healthy sexual appetite keeps them tragically apart. Visually, the production would indeed seem aesthetically paired with *The Sound and the Fury*, in part because David Zinn returned to do the design, but also because it utilizes a single interior setting to frame the entire action of the piece, including such exterior scenes as the climactic bullfight. That setting is "The Select," a Paris bar habituated by the characters of the novel, and realized here as an expansive, wood-paneled, linoleum-floored, and not-quite-seedy establishment. Critics were uniformly drawn to the design, both for its realistic detail and its symbolic import. "The stage is littered with bottles," began *Voice* critic Helen Shaw's review. "Rather, the stage is framed in bottles, awash in bottles, clinking in bottles, rolling in them" (Shaw 2011). Insobriety likewise dominates the action, emblematizing Jake's means of escape, Brett's unfettered desires, and the mood of postwar Europe. As with the set, the company approached their work with the text of the novel as they had the previous two but arrived at yet again a different method of translating text to performance. Whereas *Gatz* and *The Sound and the Fury* had kept the text intact and delivered it verbatim, *The Select* became what might be considered, in a sense, a traditional adaptation for the stage. Most obviously, they condensed the story to a three-and-a-half-hour running time on stage, just a little more than half the running time of *Gatz*. Narrative responsibility was, as with *Gatz*, given to the narrator of the novel, Jake, but as a whole the piece was largely dialogic—in performance one might easily have thought that the original text was written for the stage. If there was anything to remind the audience that this was not a "straight" adaptation, it was ERS's trademark dance breaks, not only in their usual idiosyncrasy, but in their anachronistic quoting of contemporary pop-dance moves.

The Select arrived in New York the year following *Gatz*'s belated homecoming and three years after *The Sound and the Fury*. Comparisons, then, were inevitable. While still receiving high praise generally, *The Select* was not favored. "The evidence, though they might not own up to it," argued Ben Brantley, "is that the Elevator Repair folks are 'Gatsby' kinds of guys. 'Gatz' was a soaring hymn to the pleasures of falling under a novel's spell.

'The Select'—which, unlike the verbatim 'Gatz,' compresses its source in the style of a hip Reader's Digest editor—is more flirtation than consummation" (Brantley 2011, C1). In a noticeable reversal, *The Voice* was more positive and more philosophical:

> Hemingway is doomed to be constantly compared to F. Scott Fitzgerald; *The Select* seems doomed to be compared to *Gatz*. In retrospect, Fitzgerald seems as speakable as Homer, while Hemingway's dispassionate journalese resists the messiness of physical representation. Turning *The Sun Also Rises* into something for the stage requires a firmer shoulder, more stagecraft, a subtler intelligence—all of which the company applies to the work in this piece's glorious second half. *Gatz* may still be my sentimental favorite of the two, but there are select moments in this delayed-action riot that held me motionless with awe. (Shaw 2011)

After the epic endeavor of staging three American masterworks and touring them around the world, it is understandable that ERS's next project, *Arguendo*, would choose as a source text something that few in the audience would have a preconceived opinion about or even know.[4] The production was based on the Supreme Court case *Barnes v. Glen Theatre*, which addressed an Indiana law that forbade public nudity and so forced exotic dancers to wear G-strings and pasties. Collins happened upon the case when he was researching copyright law for the *Gatsby* dispute and learned that Supreme Court oral arguments are aurally recorded and available to the public (Sellar 2013).

As with the trilogy, the text was given a verbatim reading with actors taking on and speaking the actual dialogue of the Supreme Court justices and opposing attorneys, action that is interspersed with verbatim interviews done with a variety of interested parties, including an exotic dancer who travelled from Michigan to watch the proceedings. David Zinn returned to design the set and was joined by a video designer, Ben Rubin, who created dizzying arrays of moving text alongside images indicating locale—a notable addition to the mise-en-scène if for no other reason, given the company's Wooster Group influence, than its conspicuous absence previously. Tying themselves in knots with odd and sometimes convoluted hypotheticals, the justices themselves created something of a comedy, which ERS was quick to exploit. But more subtly at work was a meditation on performance itself, a self-reflexivity that avoided postmodern glibness. What is the difference, the court pondered, between expression worthy of First Amendment protection and mere behavior? How can we distinguish between the accepted nudity of a Grecian statue and a pole-dance in Indiana? In its own wild climactic dance, ERS provoked the audience to answer these questions for themselves.

The Dramatic Turn: 2013–Present

Beginning with the tortured rendition of *Summer and Smoke* embedded in *Cab Legs*, through *Room Tone*'s take on *The Turn of the Screw*, to the stage adaptation of *The Sun Also Rises*, ERS had inarguably staged drama. Their "dramatic turn," then, is perhaps not as dramatic as it sounds. What was new for the company was simply performing what was, at a formal level, a true play. Their first, however, was not of an extant script, but one devised in rehearsal with playwright and ERS performer Sibyl Kempson: *Fondly, Collette Richard*, which opened at the New York Theatre Workshop in 2015. The impetus was, as usual for ERS, to do the yet undone. "'We were looking for something that scared us,' said John Collins, 'Deciding we would work with a playwright and do a new play was in some way the scariest thing we could imagine'" (Soloski 2015, AR5). The story they developed was pure Elevator Repair Service: During a quiet dinner at home, the Fitzhuberts are drawn through a mysterious, small door that opens in the living room wall. They emerge in a surreal Alpen hotel, where their adventures lead to a kind of primal awakening. The company maintained the high production values embraced in the literary trilogy and *Arguendo*, engaging what had become its core company designers from those productions, and again the design proved to be one of the notable attractions of the production. Ben Brantley called it "a witty, fastidiously wrought and thoroughly disorienting visual and aural universe in which the solid and the known keep melting at the edges" (Brantley 2015, C1). Reviews were positive, and if critics generally uncovered nothing of great import in the proceedings, they nonetheless appreciated the diversion. "This is a dream," wrote Brantley, "one of the most entertaining you're ever likely to have" (Brantley 2015, C1).

Measure for Measure, which opened in New York at the Public Theatre in 2017, was the company's next challenge of choice. Given the element of ensemble creation in *Fondly, Collette Richard*, Shakespeare's play had the distinction of being the first extant drama produced by ERS, and *Mr. Antipyrine* aside, the first project that wasn't drawn from an American source. The group brought its usual over-the-top physical comedy to the performance, but Shakespeare's language was less amenable to their standard treatment. Actors raced through much of the text at racehorse speed, with the notable exception of the scene between Isabella and Claudio in prison, which was played lugubriously slowly. The rush of words was echoed in projections of the play's text scrolling and careening on the white walls of the set. The effect was similar to that of *Arguendo*, but there the satirical treatment of legalese had emblematic significance; here, despite *Measure for Measure*'s thematic concern with political power and linguistic manipulation, the effect lost its satirical edge. For much of their previous work, such radical tempo choices had had little effect on the understanding of text much friendlier to an audience's ear. With Shakespeare, however, much of the meaning—and story—were surrendered, which critics were quick to point out. Michael Feingold from the *Voice* returned and crafted his review as a conversation between himself and a Martian who had happened upon the performance knowing nothing about Shakespeare. When Feingold remarks that "[o]nly if you come in knowing the play very well can you grasp the intention behind some of their choices," the Martian responds, "That seems a horribly snobbish and outré way to present a play by Shakespeare or anyone" (Feingold 2017). In the *New York Times*, Ben Brantley also pulled no punches: "But if you don't already know 'Measure for Measure'—and it's an uncommonly hard play to know—you'll need NoDoz to stay awake" (Brantley 2017, C5). For the first time in many, many years, the critics panned an ERS production.

Satire would return in *Everyone's Fine with Virginia Woolf*, a blatant parody of Edward Albee's *Who's Afraid of Virginia Woolf?*, which opened in New York at the Abrons Art Center in 2018. The play, written by company member Kate Scelsa, was intended, however, not just as a send-up, but as a feminist corrective of sorts—in a program interview, Scelsa asserted that Martha "must be avenged" (Brantley 2018). Gender roles are reversed, with George now taking Martha's memorable first line from the original: "What a dump!" Martha trails him into the untidy house, saying, "'I'm totes cool with Virginia Woolf ... I like how she was super gay'" (Brantley 2018). The reversal goes so far as to make Nick the victim of a hysterical pregnancy and Martha the seducer of Honey, not, as in Albee's play, Nick. It also adds a character, Camilla, a PhD student and vampire who feeds on human neuroses, who enters late in the play and, in another kind of role reversal, lectures George. Critics generally appreciated the critique of the patriarchal license long taken by male playwrights in creating female characters, were bemused by the sometimes-academic discourse and, by and large, entertained by the oversized, even absurdist, comedy. The one exception was the *Voice*'s Miriam Felton-Dansky, who found something a bit too blithe in the play:

> In a program note, Scelsa explains that, out of love for Albee's original Martha, she wanted to write a version that fixes what Albee got wrong. But this isn't it ... If Virginia Woolf stands in for a whole host of things we need to grapple with as a culture—intellectualism, feminism, queerness—we're not fine, and it looks like we still have a long way to go. (Felton-Dansky 2018)

If any conclusions can be drawn from ERS's foray into staging plays, it is again the burden of textual meaning. Whether it's *Measure for Measure* or *Who's Afraid of Virginia Woolf?*, Michael Feingold or Miriam Felton-Dansky, there has been a critical conscience troubled by what amounts to ERS's appropriation of extant literature. This critical voice, however, isn't univocal, and its counterpoint is clearly on display in Ben Brantley's review of *Everyone's Fine*: "This 'Virginia Woolf' takes place in an age when a text is meant to be mined and ransacked at our higher institutions of learning" (Brantley 2018). The question is, to what extent are we comfortable with a text being mined and ransacked on our stages? It's an old debate, a postmodern debate, and one that won't be settled here. Nor does ERS, in the course of its history, seem to have developed a unified approach to text. Of the many groups that have "deconstructed" extant literature, none has gone further than ERS in their treatment of text as simply fungible material without hierarchical privilege to be used in the creation of live performance. In this way, the company is, par excellence, postmodern. At the same time, with the literary trilogy, they exhibited, if not a reverence for the text, then, as Feingold noted, a love for it. It is hardly a surprise then that their cavalier treatment of the text of *Measure for Measure* provoked such a vituperative critical backlash. Nor is it surprising that the piece that has garnered the most universal and ardent admiration is the one most faithful to its text: *Gatz*.

Gatz: A Closer Look

Like office workers on a Monday morning, *Gatz* begins slowly. Nick, played by actor Scott Shepherd, is the first in, flipping on the light switch to reveal the sad-sack office where he will grind through the day. When his computer fails to start despite protracted efforts, he searches a Rolodex and finds not the number for a repair service, but a copy of *The Great Gatsby*. Between sips of his deli coffee he begins to read aloud, and through the alchemy of theatre becomes not just Nick with the dead-end job, but Nick Carraway, the narrator of Fitzgerald's novel. And just as Fitzgerald's character is "carried away" by his acquaintance with the great Jay Gatsby—whose birth name was, in fact, Gatz—so Nick is carried away by *The Great Gatsby*, as are we, both by the novel and by the shared experience of being carried away. It is an act of reading that transcends, through theatre, the usually solitary transports of great literature.

Nick's colleagues gradually filter in, and their own metamorphosis into the characters of *The Great Gatsby* is equally as gradual and effortless. In fact, it is not until Nick is thirteen pages into the novel that anyone else on stage speaks (Bailes 2007, 509). During this time they are going about their daily routine—filing documents, answering telephones, loafing. Only when one of the workers, a character who will soon assume the role of Tom Buchanan, steals a line straight from Nick's mouth—"Civilization is going to pieces" —are we tipped off to the thoroughgoing transfiguration to come (Bailes 2007, 509). The process whereby *Gatz* slowly but surely hooks the audience through an act of reading mirrors the act of reading itself: we enter the world of a book, as we enter the world of this play, curious but uncertain, engaged in the act of accumulating detail until a picture emerges and accumulating pictures until a world and its people emerge. It is an act of imagination demanded by the novel, but not, in most cases, by the theatre. Of course, this has not always been the case—as Shakespeare's stage and the "O for a muse of fire" speech of Henry V's Chorus make clear—but in the age of realism, the theatre most often dominates the imaginative act. The startlingly simple and powerful thing about ERS's *Gatz* is that it leaves the imaginative labor to the audience.

This is not to say that the production doesn't indulge in mimesis; it does, throughout, and nowhere more thoroughly so than in the party scene from chapter two of the book, a wild bacchanal that on stage becomes an office party gone off the rails—with much cleanup to be done after. It is a purely theatrical moment, and this is what makes *Gatz* more than simply a reading of the book, however well done. As scholar Sara Jane Bailes points out, the reading of the novel and its performance run parallel, at times quite distinct, at times, as in the party scene, fully melded, and at times in playful interplay. "[I]t seems as if a new form of theatre is being discovered, one that charts an unexamined territory constructed out of the interplay of book, stage, and the performativity of the imagination" (Bailes 2007, 509). Key here is her phrase "the performativity of imagination." *Gatz* not only maximizes the pleasure of the novel as a medium, it maximizes the pleasure of theatre as a medium—which is not necessarily in its realist mode. When we see, and accept, a character in *Gatz* begin to play the back of a tacky black-leather sofa as if it were a piano, we experience a kind of frisson, a pleasure at being included in the act of theatrical imagination. We're allowed the vicarious fun of performing, which is what Elevator Repair Service has been after all along.

CHAPTER 8
SITI COMPANY
Scott T. Cummings

In September 1992, a small group of theatre professionals from the United States and Japan gathered on the campus of Skidmore College in upstate New York to announce the creation of the Saratoga International Theatre Institute (SITI), an organization with the ambition to create "a new kind of cultural organization that may help re-vitalize the theater from the inside out." This experiment in international collaboration was spearheaded by two important theatre directors of the day: Tadashi Suzuki, a leading international director from Japan celebrated for his stunning adaptations of Greek tragedy; and Anne Bogart, a notable downtown New York director on the rebound from a one-year stint as artistic director of Trinity Repertory Company in Providence, Rhode Island. Animated by shared ideals about intercultural collaboration and innovative approaches to actor training, they each had practical goals as well. Suzuki was looking to establish a US outpost for a cadre of American disciples who trained with him in Japan, and Bogart was looking to establish a company of actors with whom she could create original work over an extended period of time.

What emerged from the initial convening of the Saratoga International Theatre Institute was the SITI Company, one of the most important American ensembles of the past half century. Their fierce commitment to the ideals and advantages of being a company has resulted in a unique and substantial body of work and an approach to theatre-making and theatre training that has changed American theatre. That training is based on three different practices: the Suzuki Method of Actor Training first developed by Tadashi Suzuki in the 1970s; Viewpoints training as adapted by Anne Bogart and others from the Six Viewpoints first articulated by Mary Overlie in the 1980s; and Composition, a strategy for generating raw performance material that can be combined and shaped into a devised theatre work. The body of work that came out of the training represents Bogart's sustained inquiry into the nature of theatrical perception and the creative process, the value of connecting with tradition and history as a way of moving forward, and what it means to be an American and an artist in the early twenty-first century.[1]

American Theatre Ensembles Volume 1: Post–1970

The Origins and Development of the Company

Born in 1939, Tadashi Suzuki grew up as part of a postwar generation that was alienated by the lingering US presence in Japan. In 1966, with friends from Tokyo's Waseda University, he formed the avant-garde-minded Waseda Little Theatre and began producing work that signaled a departure from the social realism of *shingeki* in favor of the existentialism of Beckett and Sartre and an interest in the ancient traditions of Noh and Kabuki. His historic collaboration with actress Kayoko Shiraishi helped to bring widening attention to his work, including an invitation from Jean-Louis Barrault to perform at his Théâtre des Nations Festival in Paris in 1972. Four years later, Waseda Little Theatre changed its name to the Suzuki Company of Toga (SCOT) and shifted its base of operations to Toga-mura, a remote mountain village in Toyama Prefecture. Here, far from the hustle and bustle of the big city, Suzuki created a destination theatre and idyllic training center with dormitories, studios, dining facilities, an indoor theatre, and a Greek amphitheater on the edge of a small lake with a stunning mountain vista beyond. In 1982, inspired by Barrault, Suzuki launched his own annual international theatre festival in Toga that over the years attracted vanguard theatre companies and visionary directors from around the world, including Yuri Lyubimov, Tadeus Kantor, Ratan Thiyam, Robert Wilson, and many others. Through the 1980s and 1990s and well into the twenty-first century, Suzuki's ever-expanding influence led to leadership positions with the Acting Company of Mito, the International Theatre Olympics Committee, Shizuoka Performing Arts Center, and the Japan Performing Arts Foundation.[2]

The daughter of a career naval officer, Anne Bogart had a peripatetic childhood that included periods growing up in Rhode Island, California, Virginia, and Japan. After graduating from Bard College in 1974, she set out to become a theatre director on the model of such contemporary auteurs as Andrei Serban, Richard Schechner, Richard Foreman, and Robert Wilson, all of whom she wrote about in her 1977 MA thesis at New York University (NYU). Two years later, she began teaching and directing in NYU's newly formed Experimental Theatre Wing. In the 1980s, she experimented with site-specific theatre and directed productions downtown and at NYU, including a controversial production of Rodgers and Hammerstein's *South Pacific* and a collage of Brecht's theoretical writings under the title *No Plays No Poetry*. Eventually, she began directing at resident regional theatres such as the American Repertory Theatre in Cambridge, Massachusetts, and in 1989, she replaced Adrian Hall as artistic director of Trinity Rep, where as a teenager she had been inspired by Hall's environmental staging of *Macbeth*. Conflicts with the board of directors led her to leave Trinity Rep after one tempestuous season.[3] In the early 1990s, she began teaching directing at Columbia University (where she remains head of the directing program) and resumed work as an independent regional theatre director with a reputation as "either an innovator or a provocateur assaulting a text" (Gussow 1994). In 1992, she directed Paula Vogel's *The Baltimore Waltz* at the Circle Repertory Company in New York, earning her second OBIE.

Anne Bogart and Tadashi Suzuki first met in 1988 when Bogart was invited by Peter Zeisler to join a small delegation of American theatre professionals traveling to Japan to meet and exchange views with Suzuki at his isolated theatre compound in the mountains. Zeisler was President of the Theatre Communications Group (TCG), the national service organization of the not-for-profit resident regional theatre, and a champion of Suzuki's work in the United States. By this time, John Dillon and Sara O'Connor of the Milwaukee Repertory Theatre and Sanford Robbins and Jewel Walker of the University of Wisconsin-Milwaukee's professional actor training program had an ongoing collaboration with Suzuki. A small but dedicated group of American actors—including Ellen Lauren, Kelly Maurer, and Will Bond, founding members of the SITI Company—began to travel to Toga-mura in the summers to train with members of Suzuki's company and to observe the world-class artists performing at the annual festival there. Some of them performed in productions that Suzuki toured or staged in the United States, including an all-male, all-American version of his *The Tale of Lear*, coproduced in 1988 by Milwaukee Repertory Theatre, Arena Stage, Berkeley Repertory Theatre, and StageWest in Springfield, Massachusetts.

Bogart and Suzuki met several more times as plans became more serious about launching a joint enterprise that would give her the opportunity to develop an ensemble and provide an artistic home for some of his devoted American protégés. In 1992, without tremendous fanfare, SITI convened for the first time, first in Toga-mura and then in Saratoga Springs with two different productions based on tragedies by Euripides. Suzuki revised his bilingual adaptation of *The Bacchae* titled *Dionysus* with a cast of a dozen SCOT actors and seven American actors (including Ellen Lauren, Kelly Maurer, and Tom Nelis). Bogart directed Charles Mee's manic Gulf War mash-up of *Orestes*, with texts interpolated from William Burroughs, John Wayne Gacy, Elaine Scarry, and *Soap Opera Digest*. At the Skidmore gathering, a panel titled "A Theatre Towards the 21st Century" and a three-page manifesto imagined an organization dedicated to "the growth of individual artists and the development of a new approach to world theatre," one that "would be, for several months a year, a mecca for other artists and interested audiences who would come to exchange ideas, to share work and to be nourished on the work of others" (Bogart 1992). Part theatrical think tank, part international crossroads, part training center, and part summertime development lab, this new institute and its millennial vision were introduced with what the *Village Voice* called a "level of conviction [that] rings fierce, defiant, and, as befits a season with two Greek plays, unfashionably hubristic" (Shteir 100).

Nobody could really know what would emerge from this initial gathering. The partnership was planned to last only a few years, at which point Suzuki would withdraw and leave the fledgling organization under Bogart's leadership to sink or swim on its own. SITI gathered in 1993 for a second summer, first in Toga and then in Saratoga Springs, to present three productions. Suzuki remounted *The Tale of Lear* and also created *Waiting for Romeo* as a showcase for Ellen Lauren, who in addition to her central position in the SITI Company would appear in numerous SCOT productions in the decades to come and become recognized as a master teacher of the Suzuki Method. Also in 1993, Bogart and five actors—Bond, Maurer, Nelis, Mark Corkins, and Danish actress Puk Scharbau—teamed up to create SITI's first original devised piece, *The Medium*, inspired by the writings of media theorist Marshal McLuhan.[4] The year 1993 also marked SITI's first "Summer Intensive" at Skidmore, a rigorous month-long training program that over time also became an incubator for SITI productions. The first Summer Intensive included preliminary work on *Small Lives/Big Dreams*, an original piece inspired by the plays of Anton Chekhov; it then premiered in the summer of 1994, first at the festival in Toga and then in Saratoga Springs. No SCOT production came to Saratoga Springs that summer, a signal of Suzuki's diminishing involvement in what would soon be renamed the SITI Company, with Bogart as artistic director, Lauren as associate artistic director, and a core company of actors that began with Bond, Maurer, and Nelis.

These founding members were soon joined by additional actors. Like Tom Nelis, some of them—KJ Sanchez, Jefferson Mays, J. Ed Araiza, and Barney O'Hanlon—were recruited directly by Bogart, while others—Leon Ingulsrud, Akiko Aizawa, Stephen Webber—came to the company, like Lauren, Bond, and Maurer, through their training with Suzuki or his American surrogates. Sanchez and Mays were integral members of SITI Company in its formative years, but each of them moved on to other professional theatre pursuits in the late 1990s.[5] The other nine actors mentioned here have remained active members of the company right up to the present day. In 2010, they were joined by a new company member, Gian-Murray Gianino, a young actor who they first met in 2001 as an intern-apprentice at the Actors Theatre of Louisville when he was cast as an extra in SITI's *bobrauschenbergamerica*. As with any tight-knit ensemble, the composition of the company became a perennial issue. Over the years, efforts were made to diversify and expand the company by identifying and nurturing younger actors who were talented, compatible, sympathetic to their ideals and committed to their training regimen. While a number of actors worked with SITI on multiple projects—including early associates Susan Hightower, Jeffrey Frace, and Donnie Mather and in the past decade Samuel Stricklen and Eric Berryman—no actor other than Gianino has joined the company as a fully enfranchised member since its beginning. There can be no doubt that the longevity, consistency, and profound familiarity of the company have been a key to their success, but as these individuals have aged and pursued their personal lives, the company has faced many challenges, some of them galvanizing, some quite dispiriting. That so many company members stayed together so long is one of the company's more remarkable achievements.

The annual month-long Summer Intensive on the Skidmore campus played a crucial role in this continuity. It is the cornerstone of SITI Company's identity, vitality, success, and calendar year. For several dozen participants each year (who come from all over the world), it provides a thorough introduction to the Suzuki Method of Actor Training, Viewpoints training, and the Composition work that connects these two practices to the creation of new work. Weekly seminars, workshops by guest teachers, open rehearsals, and often a showcase performance of a current SITI production supplement these daily trainings and make the Intensive an all-encompassing experience. For members of the company, it represents a valuable annual retreat, an opportunity to get away from regular routines and live and work together for weeks at a time; to train together and reconnect as a company; to discuss policies, practices, and future plans under relaxed circumstances; and to lay the groundwork for a new piece or to revisit a piece getting ready to go on tour. Each year, the Composition assignments for the trainees pertain to a SITI project in an embryonic stage of development; students are warned that the company is on the lookout for inspiration or even specific images or staging ideas that might be incorporated into a future SITI creation. Well into the company's third decade, the mission and many specific goals first outlined in the original 1992 SITI manifesto continue to animate and define the Intensive.

Expanding this summer program into a self-sustaining year-round operation has been an ongoing challenge for the company. In 1997, SITI self-produced a season of their first three original pieces—*The Medium*, *Small Lives/Big Dreams*, and *Going, Going, Gone*—at the Miller Theatre on the campus of Columbia University in New York City. This one-time experiment sharpened their focus on a two-pronged strategy of finding sympathetic institutions to host the development of new work and a committed tour management firm to bring that work to performing arts presenters around the United States and abroad. In the 1990s, as SITI developed a network of interest and support around the country, two institutional partners emerged as particularly important. The Wexner Center for the Arts is an interdisciplinary contemporary arts laboratory on the campus of Ohio State University. Charles Helm, director of performing arts there since 1991, commissioned and premiered a number of SITI works, from *Bob* and *Alice's Adventures* in 1998 to *the theatre is a blank page* in 2015. The Actors Theatre of Louisville (ATL) is a large resident regional theatre best known for its annual Humana Festival of New American Plays. Anne Bogart first directed there in 1991, and in 1995 the theatre celebrated her as a "Modern Master" with its tenth Annual Classics-in-Context Festival, which included panels, a keynote lecture, and presentations of her productions of Elmer Rice's *The Adding Machine*, *The Medium*, and *Small Lives/Big Dreams*. At the invitation of three successive ATL artistic directors (Jon Jory, Marc Masterson, and Les Waters), Bogart and the SITI Company returned to the Humana Festival on multiple occasions to create and premiere new work, from *Going, Going, Gone* in 1996 to *Steel Hammer* in 2014.

Actors Theatre of Louisville also provided several key members of the SITI Company. Megan Wanlass stage-managed Bogart's 1995 ATL production of *The Adding Machine* and left Louisville to become SITI's company stage manager for five years and then its executive director for fifteen years. Bogart cast J. Ed Araiza in William Inge's *Picnic* at ATL and then he joined the company as an actor in 1994. Darron West was the sound designer on Bogart's 1993 ATL production of *Picnic*, and this led to an unusual director-designer collaboration when he left Louisville and joined the company. In pursuit of an organic, integrated sound design, West made it his practice to attend rehearsals for each new SITI piece on nearly a daily basis, developing a soundscape in tandem with the actors rather than coming in during technical rehearsals and putting sound cues on top of what the actors had already rehearsed. The integration of West's rich, layered sound designs—almost as if another performer in the piece—became a distinctive signature of SITI's work.

A trio of other designers has worked on the majority of SITI creations. Brian H. Scott began as the protégé and assistant to lighting designer Mimi Jordan Sherin on the first dozen SITI productions, and then starting with *bobrauschenbergamerica* in 2001, he became the company lighting designer; he has designed nearly every new production since then. James Schuette has designed costumes and/or scenery for more than twenty SITI productions, from *Culture of Desire* (1997) to *Chess Match No. 5* (2017). Neil Patel joined the company in 1997 and designed scenery for most SITI productions for the next fifteen years.

While Skidmore College, the Wexner Center, Actors Theatre of Louisville, and in recent years the J. Paul Getty Museum in Los Angeles have been mainstays for SITI Company, Anne Bogart always dreamed of a year-round institutional home for the company, one that would provide stability and make them less dependent on touring to perform or to teach workshops. As the company moved through its second decade, the desire to forge a partnership with a college or university, a large regional theatre or performing arts center, or even a major museum, became more and more explicit, as evidenced by a 2008 *American Theatre* article by Porter Anderson titled "The Search for a SITI State." In that piece (24), Bogart says,

> I have a particular need to bring this group together to magnify the force inwards, and to have people come to us instead of us going to them. We need a theatre to perform in. We need to bring back pieces that were made 15 years ago. We need to have a living repertory, a place people can come to see pieces we made a while back, to look at our archives, a place to house our library. And we need a place where we train for more than two weeks or six weeks, a place where we can take people through a training program in which they've probably performed *with* us before they're done. Then they leave carrying forward something radical and vital in the world of theatre art.

Despite a sustained effort, no suitable and willing host ever emerged. To address the need for a training program that would last more than a few weeks, the company created the SITI Conservatory in 2013, a nine-month training program for twenty artists that operates on an every other year basis out of their small studio space in mid-town Manhattan. As the company entered their twenty-fifth anniversary in 2017–18, they continued to offer a range of training opportunities and to create new work, but touring had become more and more a matter of isolated engagements.

The Trainings: Suzuki, Viewpoints, Composition

The SITI Company is defined as much by their commitment to training as their creation of new work. The goal of the training is to nurture independent self-sufficient actors who take responsibility for their own individual performances and the integration of those performances into the project and the creative process at hand. Like athletes, company members approach training as an ongoing, never-ending process; it is a way to stay in shape or get ready for new work after a dormant period, to hone specific skills and diagnose areas that need attention, to lay the groundwork for a new project, and to warm up and set the tone on any given work day.

When Bogart and Suzuki joined forces to create the Saratoga International Theatre Institute, two approaches to actor training came together that few would have thought compatible at the time: the Suzuki Method of Actor Training that Suzuki had been developing for two decades and Anne Bogart's revision of the Six View Points introduced to her by Mary Overlie in the early 1980s. The Suzuki Method of Actor Training—or Suzuki, for short, where context allows—is pure hard work, most obviously physical work at first encounter but also mental and spiritual work. The Viewpoints are inherently playful insofar as they invite spontaneity and involve elements of improvisation. The SITI Company teaches Suzuki and Viewpoints side by side as two separate and independent practices. There is no attempt to fuse or combine them into a unified system; instead individual actors are left to incorporate the practices and principles behind them into the way that they work. In tandem, Suzuki and Viewpoints aim to develop actors with an undeniable and dynamic presence, one that commands attention, even in stillness, by its energy, concentration, honesty, and interest.

Inspired in part by such ancient Japanese performance traditions as Kabuki and Noh, the Suzuki Method of Actor Training consists of a series of "basic" physical forms—particular ways of standing, walking, squatting, and stomping the feet—that are learned by rote and then repeated with precision again and again to the point of challenging the actor's stamina and focus. While some of these forms have roots in early Suzuki productions, they do not constitute a performance vocabulary in and of themselves. They represent a rigorous discipline, codified by Suzuki and seldom revised over the decades, for training the whole actor. Early on, Suzuki nicknamed this method "the grammar of the feet" because of his conviction that "consciousness of the body's communication with the ground is a portal into a greater awareness of all the physical functions: a point of departure for theatrical performance. The way in which the feet are used is the basis of a stage performance" (Suzuki 2015, 65). But the ultimate focus is the actor's physical center, the area in the lower abdomen and pelvic area that is both the center of gravity and the point of origin of the deepest breath. This center is the root of the speaking voice, the crossroads of the upper and lower bodies, and the wellspring of the actor's power, balance, and what Suzuki refers to as "animal energy." Command of this energy with both rigor and ease is the bedrock of the Suzuki training. In the early stages, mastering the basic forms can turn an actor's focus inward, and so novices are often coached to direct their attention outward onto the horizon or an imagined other in an effort to make contact with something outside of themselves. The goal is to develop, strengthen, and refine the actor's ability to speak with a fully embodied voice.

By her own admission, Anne Bogart stole the Viewpoints from Mary Overlie, a dancer, choreographer, and teacher she met in the Experimental Theatre Wing at NYU. In search of a pedagogy of postmodern performance, Overlie articulated Six View Points—Space, Shape, Time, Emotion, Movement, and Story—as a practical and empowering perspective on the raw materials of dance, theatre, and performance. Inspired by this structuralist approach, Bogart revised, changed, and expanded the Six View Points and then (not without some controversy) used the term "Viewpoints" to refer to nine basic elements of performative movement in relationship to time and space: Tempo, Duration, Repetition, and Kinesthetic Response (the four temporal viewpoints) and Shape, Gesture, Architecture, Spatial Relationship, and Topography (the five spatial viewpoints). These terms provide a simple language for describing basic objective aspects of physical action. That is, what an actor does onstage can be seen to happen at a particular speed and last a particular amount of time. It can be repeated either in immediate succession or intermittently over time. It can be prompted or triggered by something that has come before. Whether in motion or at rest, the physical body of the actor takes specific shapes as a means of abstract expression or purposeful behavior. The arms and other parts of the body isolate themselves in gesture. The actor stands or moves in spatial relationship to other actors and the architecture of the space that contains them (including the objects within it). For an actor charged with the responsibility of creating her own performance, these nine physical Viewpoints constitute a general frame of reference, specific points of concentration, and, in effect, raw materials for the actor's changing presence in time and space.[6] By extension, as a kind of practical phenomenology of the stage, Viewpoints is "a philosophy translated into a technique for (1) training performers; (2) building ensemble; and (3) creating movement for the stage" (Bogart and Landau 2005, 7).

The third component of the SITI Company's training is Composition, a term Bogart borrowed from her Bard teacher Aileen Passloff, a dancer, choreographer, actor, active in the Greenwich Village theatre and dance community in the 1960s. Composition is a strategy for generating bits of performance material by an ensemble that can be refined and combined to make an original piece of physical theatre or dance (or to inform the rehearsal process of an existing script). It is, in effect, a form of collective theatrical writing in three dimensions, a way to explore a subject or theme on your feet, to court discovery and happy accident, to sketch out possibilities without too much time plan in advance. In a classroom or workshop situation, Bogart teaches Composition through a series of assignments, short and simple at first and gradually more involved in terms of length, number of actors, and production elements. Students are given a general topic or theme, a limited set of texts or other sources from which to draw material or inspiration, a designated length of time for the finished piece, and then a list of random ingredients that are somehow to be incorporated into the piece. These ingredients range from physical or verbal actions that are repeated or sustained for a conspicuous period of time (for example, thirty seconds of high-speed talking or gibberish, everybody looking up or walking in circles, singing or stillness) to actions that are abrupt and surprising (a spontaneous kiss or sudden collapse to the floor, the discovery or revealing of an object whose presence was unsuspected, a quick exit or entrance).

Composition assignments are structured to be overwhelming, in a sense. In *The Viewpoints Book*, Bogart and her one-time partner and collaborator Tina Landau talk about exquisite pressure as a strategy for promoting creativity and generating spontaneous play. The pressure of limited time before a piece will be shown—at the end of a single class session, workshop period, or rehearsal process—and the quantity of elements that need to be incorporated requires quick decisions and embracing the impulses of others in the group. Bogart often talks about this in terms of the principle of "one, two, three—go!," which compels actors to leap into action without time to think or plan. From one composition to the next, this approach also tends to leave gaps or incongruities that invite an audience to make associations or look for patterns in the flow of events. For the SITI Company and their original pieces, this has resulted in work that is paradoxically opaque and transparent all at once and that depends on a spectator's willingness, in effect, to complete the process of composition by assimilating often disparate images and forging connections on a personal or individual basis.

Before the SITI Company was formed, Bogart and future members of the company taught the Suzuki Method, Viewpoints, and Composition separately and independently, but with the first Skidmore Summer Intensive and the creation of *The Medium* in 1993, the combination of these practices began to emerge as the unique platform on which the company's work is built. In addition to the annual Summer Intensive, the SITI Company teaches Suzuki, Viewpoints, and Composition in a variety of settings and situations: extended fall and spring sessions in New York, short-term residencies around North America or abroad, one-off workshops and master classes at universities and conservatory programs around the country, and since 2013 in the nine-month SITI Conservatory training program in their New York studio. A number of individual company members also teach on a continuing basis at such schools as Juilliard, NYU, Columbia, Skidmore, and UCLA. Whatever the training situation, both Suzuki and Viewpoints seek to develop the actor's focus outside of the self on a so-called "fiction." Suzuki training starts off more as a private, individual discipline while Viewpoints focuses right away on the surrounding ensemble and the back-and-forth flow of energy and response. When brought to bear on Composition and the creation and rehearsal of a new piece, the two practices have demonstrated a distinct theatrical symbiosis that is the hallmark of the company's work.

Repertoire and Methodology

Over their twenty-five-year history, the SITI Company has created more than forty productions, the majority of which are original pieces conceived and directed by Bogart and created and performed by the company. In tandem with their commitment to training, these original devised works define the company's ethos, aesthetic, and dramaturgy. Their approach is rooted in a method of creating new work that Bogart had been experimenting with since her senior year at Bard when she could not decide what Ionesco play she wanted to direct; instead of picking one play, she took bits and pieces from different plays and staged them as an Ionesco miscellany titled *Knocks, A Collection*. In the 1970s and 1980s, she continued to make postmodern pieces based on an assemblage of texts culled from topically related sources—the plays of August Strindberg, the films of Alfred Hitchcock, the theoretical writings of Bertolt Brecht, the sociology of Erving Goffman, 1930s dance marathons, the Red

Scare in the 1950s—held together in performance with abstract movement, social dance, music, popular song, design, and acting. Bogart has described this strategy metaphorically as a matter of making a nest:

> The notion of scavenging appeals to me. That is what I do. Like a bird that goes and pulls different things and makes a nest. I think it is more a nesting impulse, of taking this and that and weaving it together to make some sort of marriage of ideas. I read a lot and I take little bits of what I read and I put them together into thoughts and ideas. I juxtapose ideas. I like the satisfaction of putting things together like that. (Cummings 2006, 39)

This method was refined in collaboration with the members of the company on their first four original creations: *The Medium* (1993), *Small Lives/Big Dreams* (1994), *Going, Going, Gone* (1995), and *Culture of Desire* (1997). In the conceptual stage, each new work was defined by three givens that provided parameters for the piece and stipulated ground rules for shaping the gathered raw material: "(1) a question or set of questions, which articulated the nature of inquiry, its focus and its curiosity; (2) an anchor, usually an important real-life cultural figure who was seen to embody the question; and (3) a structure, a familiar type of event that was used to organize and arrange performance materials pertinent to the question and the anchor" (Cummings 2006, 96). From one project to the next, the express articulation of these givens might vary, but in practice these three cardinal points established a field of play within which the actors operated with tremendous creative latitude, drawing on their imaginations and their training to generate performance segments that often stood next to each other as theatrical non sequiturs.

The anchor for *The Medium* was Marshall McLuhan, the Canadian professor and media theorist who became a pop culture hero in the 1960s when he argued that advanced telecommunications had created a "global village" in which "the medium is the message." Bogart had a lingering fascination with McLuhan's theory that the technological form of communication shapes, influences, and in a sense determines the actual content of what is communicated. She put the figure of McLuhan at the center of a piece that explored the question of how media in the digital age—from television to the personal computer and even the internet in its early days—were changing the nature of individual psychology and social interaction. The piece borrowed the structure of typical television programs (newscast, talk show, sitcom, game show, etc.) to create a series of segments presented in the manner of hyperkinetic channel-surfing with epigrams from McLuhan and others serving as dialogue. *The Medium* introduced what would become signature traits of the SITI Company's work: the triadic conceptual strategy of question-anchor-strategy; the radical juxtaposition of three coequal performance texts (verbal/textual, physical/gestural, and visual/aural); a nonlinear, often circular approach to theatrical time and space; and a rigorous, aerobic, choreographically precise approach to stage movement.

If *The Medium* presented a reality being propelled helter-skelter into the future by electronic media, *Small Lives/Big Dreams* investigated the question of memory and the lingering effects of a fading past. The anchor for this inquiry was Anton Chekhov, not the playwright himself but his five major full-length plays, each of which was transfigured into a character caught in the middle of an unfolding apocalypse that leaves them dislodged from the world as they knew it and wandering with the others on a metaphysical road to nowhere. Suffused with mourning and a sense of loss, *Small Lives/Big Dreams* reflected Bogart's career-long interest in connecting with the past, be it a theatrical tradition, an historical event or era, or an important cultural figure or work of art from a different period. Such an artwork—Edward Albee's *Who's Afraid of Virginia Woolf?*—was both the structure and the anchor for SITI's next piece, although this was not immediately apparent to an audience. The physical action of *Going, Going Gone*—played out on a nearly bare stage with a white sofa, a glass coffee table, and a shiny cocktail cart—followed the sequence of events of Albee's famous play: two middle-aged hosts, seemingly a married couple, received two younger guests for late-night drinks and conversation. But in place of Albee's text, the dialogue for this encounter was composed entirely of quotations taken from Bogart's reading on quantum mechanics, astrophysics, Heisenberg, and theories about the observer effect. As viewers puzzled out this incongruity, the link between the spoken text and the behavioral text oscillated from absurd to oddly apt until it climaxed with a kind of theatrical Big Bang that made the set and the Nick and Honey characters disappear, leaving George and Martha dancing in the dark against a backdrop of twinkling stars.

The Medium, *Small Live/Big Dreams*, and *Going, Going, Gone* forged SITI Company's identity as an ensemble committed to collective creation with Bogart at the helm. *Culture of Desire* extended this work and initiated a series of pieces focused on major twentieth-century artists, starting with Andy Warhol, the anchor for a fractured meditation on American consumerism that used Dante's *Inferno* as a sub-structure. The piece took as its point of departure the day in 1968 when Warhol was shot by Valerie Solanus, a near-death experience that leads to him being guided by his friend and fashion diva Diana Vreeland on a tour of a brand-name, mass-marketing underworld. With a mix of blank-faced pathos and nerdy charm, Kelly Maurer presented Warhol as "an innocent genius, not a canny manipulator" who seemed to be "a postmodern tramp, a tabula rasa on which American culture projects himself" (Rawson 1997). The goal here, as in the subsequent artist plays, was not to impersonate the actual Warhol or to present a biographical narrative so much as to use the artist-hero as a prism through which to refract a miscellany of texts around the central thematic question.

Much the same intent was at work, though less obviously, when Bogart and SITI took the focus on major artists to another level by creating three solo pieces—*Bob* (1998), *Room* (2000), and *Score* (2002)—each of which showcased a founding member of the company speaking a verbal text drawn from the writings, interviews, or speeches of a single major artist. *Bob* began as a lark when Bogart once asked Will Bond to do an imitation of avant-garde director Robert Wilson, a fascination of hers since the 1970s. This triggered what proved to be a long-term collaboration with Jocelyn Clarke, an Irish writer, dramaturg, and one-time theatre critic who took Bogart's voluminous collection of Wilson's public utterances and fashioned them into a metaphysical portrait of the artist performed by Bond on a simple set using only a chair, a table, a glass, and a bottle of milk. Workshopped in Prague and New York in 1997, *Bob* premiered at the Wexner Center in 1998 and went on to become the company's longest-running and most widely toured production, including a 2016 revival at the Venice Biennale. In a similar fashion, Clarke also assembled the texts for *Room*, which featured Ellen Lauren embodying the elegant writings of Virginia Woolf, much of them from her famous essay "A Room of One's Own," and for *Score*, which featured Tom Nelis as the composer-conductor Leonard Bernstein restlessly moving through a forest of empty music stands as he ruminated on his passion for music. Each of these roughly ninety-minute pieces presented itself ostensibly as a public lecture, but that reality was ruptured by an abstract gestural score as well as expressionistic lighting and sound designs that took the piece beyond the inner roilings of an artist in extremis to ponder the nature of creativity and human consciousness. Conceived as a trilogy about the artistic process, *Bob* and *Room* and *Score* have never been performed together on a single occasion. Still, they can be seen to distill SITI's principles and practices and Bogart's fascination with art and artists down to a simple and elegant form.

In the company's early years, both the success and the challenges of creating original work from scratch catalyzed the desire to collaborate with a playwright sympathetic to their aesthetic; that playwright turned out to be Charles Mee, whose wild take on Euripides's *Orestes* was their first production in 1992. Mee had declined an invitation to work on the Warhol project but then later proposed a piece based on the art-making of Robert Rauschenberg, whose famous sculptural "combines" and "combine paintings" of the 1950s and 1960s represented a very American adaptation of the collage aesthetic pioneered in Europe by Max Ernst, Kurt Schwitters, and others. Mee's offer led to an eighteen-month developmental process that resulted in *bobrauschenbergamerica*, which premiered at the 2001 Humana Festival and became one of SITI's more popular productions, eventually touring to Bonn, Paris, Dublin, New York, and other American cities.[7] Unlike *Culture of Desire* and the three solo pieces, *bobrauschenbergamerica* did not include a surrogate of the artist; instead, it presented eight American archetypes: a working-class trucker (Leon Ingulsrud) and his bikini-clad girlfriend (Akiko Aizawa); a scientist (Will Bond) and an artist (Barney O'Hanlon), who are lovers (and wannabe chicken farmers); a romantic triangle comprised of an uptight guy from Chicago (Danyon Davis), a girl-next-door named Susan (Ellen Lauren), and a homeless man in a dirty trench coat (J. Ed Araiza); and a homespun maternal figure called Bob's Mom (Kelly Maurer), who delivers a series of tender reminiscences about the escapades of her precocious son as a boy. Over the course of forty short, discontinuous scenes, the piece brought these characters together in a series of seemingly random social events—a backyard picnic, a line dance, a yard sale, a game of checkers, a pizza delivery, a square dance, a parade, and so on—that offered a composite portrait of middle America in the second half of the twentieth century. While the piece incorporated some violent aspects of American culture (a beating, an assassination, a tale of homicidal rage), the prevailing spirit was upbeat, carefree, and at moments unabashedly sentimental.

This joyful and invigorating collaboration led to two more theatrical collages written by Mee and based on artists, *Hotel Cassiopeia* (2006) and *Under Construction* (2009), both of which premiered at the Humana Festival. *Hotel Cassiopeia* looked at the art and life of Joseph Cornell, the eccentric twentieth-century artist from Queens, best known for the surreal memory boxes he assembled containing paper cutouts of parrots and constellations, old photographs, wire rings, and a variety of found objects. Similar to the Rauschenberg piece, it sought to theatricalize the spirit and vocabulary of Cornell, although the inclusion of "Joseph" as a character (O'Hanlon) and figures from Cornell's life brought it closer to biography than the other artist plays, albeit in a decidedly impressionistic fashion. *Under Construction* juxtaposed two very different artists, the famous illustrator Norman Rockwell and the renegade installation artist Jason Rhoades who pushed the strategy of assemblage to a new, rambunctious extreme until his untimely death in 2006 at age 41. Inspired by the anarchy of Rhoades, the piece presented a disjunctive cascade of performance bits with a self-conscious irony that deconstructed itself in the making. As the *New York Times* described it, "viewers' eyes and ears are kept busy throughout the almost two-hour show, which maintains a largely manic and tightly wound pace of wordplay, physical romping and set rearranging. But the level of activity stalls at busywork" (La Rocco 2011). *Under Construction* represented the end of a line of investigation for Bogart. It is the last of the artist plays that SITI did with Mee, although they continued to work with him on other projects, including *Café Variations* (2012), which used romantic scenes drawn from various Mee plays as the basis for a music-theatre piece featuring the music of George Gershwin.[8]

Plays by Others

Over the years, interspersed between phases of developing a new original piece, Bogart directed a number of established plays, operas, and musical theatre pieces for a resident regional theatre or opera company, productions that included enough SITI actors in the cast to be considered a company work. For example, in addition to SITI originals that premiered at the Humana Festival, Bogart directed *Miss Julie* (1997), *Private Lives* (1998), and *Hay Fever* (2002) at Actors Theatre of Louisville with mainly SITI actors; Ellen Lauren also appeared in her ATL productions of *Picnic* (1993) and *The Adding Machine* (1995). Bogart worked with the company on productions of Marivaux's *La Dispute* at American Repertory Theatre (2003), Sophie Treadwell's *Intimations for Saxophone* at Arena Stage (2005), and Virginia Woolf's only play, *Freshwater*, with the Women's Project in New York (2009). These productions provided brief periods of full employment for company members and showcased their talents in conventional drama, but only one—their compact eight-actor *A Midsummer Night's Dream* originating at San Jose Repertory Theatre (2004)—was ever seen beyond its initial presentation at the resident regional theatre that sponsored it.

Greek tragedy was always a preoccupation for Tadashi Suzuki, but after SITI's production in 1992 of Mee's adaptation of *Orestes*, the company did not take up the Greeks again until 2009 when they initiated a relationship with the J. Paul Getty Museum in Los Angeles. The company had a series of residencies at the museum's Getty Villa that provided the opportunity to explore, develop, and stage new versions of *Antigone* (2009), *Trojan Women* (2010), *The Persians* (2014), and *The Bacchae* (2018). Two of these—*Trojan Women* and *The Bacchae*—went on to tour nationally, including a stop at Brooklyn Academy of Music's high-profile Next Wave Festival.

In addition to these hosted projects, SITI produced a number of lesser-known scripts from the past on their own. In 1999, Bogart and sound designer/codirector Darron West created a stage version of the H. G. Wells-inspired radio play written by Howard Koch and made famous in October 1938 by Orson Welles and his Mercury Theatre on the Air. *War of the Worlds: The Radio Play* started as a side project related to their collaboration with playwright Naomi Iizuka on a piece about Orson Welles, but it turned into a popular chamber piece that toured extensively after its initial showing at the West Bank Café in New York.[9] In 2004, Bogart directed Ellen Lauren, Will Bond, and Stephen Duff Webber in *Death and the Ploughman*, Michael West's adaptation of a 1401 dialogue in German by Johannes von Saaz about a farmer so bereft over the death of his wife that he engages Death in a passionate argument about why she should be returned to life. And in 2017, co-artistic director Leon Ingulsrud directed SITI actors Akiko Aizawa, Gian-Murray Gianino, and Stephen Duff Webber in his translation of the modern Noh play *Hanjo* by Yukio Mishima. One of the few SITI productions not directed by Bogart, *Hanjo* reflected Ingulsrud's lifelong engagement with Japanese culture and seemed to anticipate Bogart's eventual withdrawal as the company's primary director.

Collaborations with Other Artists and Companies

Collaboration has always been a fundamental principle of the SITI Company's work, but in 2010 Bogart initiated a series of short-term partnerships with major artists and established organizations that took them beyond their normal sphere of operations. This new phase began with *American Document*, a piece created in conjunction with the Martha Graham Dance Company that reinvented Graham's anti-fascist dance of 1938 for the twenty-first century. Bogart drew on film excerpts, written descriptions, and Graham's own notes on the original and then supplemented them with new texts selected by Charles Mee around the thematic question "What is an American?" For SITI, the project was an unprecedented experiment in intercompany collaboration. The cast included ten Graham dancers and six SITI actors performing side by side, prompting the *New York Times* critic to observe, "The ensembles are fully integrated, and it is fascinating to see the SITI actors trying on Graham's striking language, pistoning and pumping through the air with aplomb, even as the dancers try out a few spoken lines" (La Rocco 2010).

Three years later, in January 2013, SITI concluded a challenging nine-month collaboration with Bill T. Jones/Arnie Zane Dance Company on *A Rite*, a hybrid dance-theatre piece commemorating the centennial of Igor Stravinsky's revolutionary ballet *Rite of Spring*. Here again, SITI's approach to theatrical movement rubbed up against the contemporary dance vocabulary of a famous company—with interesting results. As critic Irene Hsiao (2013) described it:

> Jones and Bogart have not attempted to preserve the original narrative of the *Rite*. Instead, they take its themes of sacrifice, loss, and renewal, and consider them in the context of the century that has intervened between the beau monde who broke out in fistfights and riots at Nijinsky's original staging for the Ballet Russes in Paris to the present condition of oversaturated senses, overpopulation, and the greater weight of alienation in an overwhelming universe ... The company rushes in: a mass, a grid, a chaos, a union, a unison, an individual. This vision is repeated throughout, though the form is never the same—it is unsettling and familiar, creating both the order art overlays on a disorderly world and the defamiliarization art insists upon in a world we have learned to perceive in order to survive.

These collaborations with world-class dance companies reflect Bogart's effort to invigorate her company with new challenges and new creative partners even as she continued her decades-long examination of iconoclastic artists and revolutionary works of art from the past.

These same impulses animated SITI's collaborations with composer Julia Wolfe on *Steel Hammer* (2014) and with visual artist Anne Hamilton on *the theatre is a blank page* (2015). *Steel Hammer* began as a song cycle by Wolfe about the legendary African-American folk hero John Henry, celebrated for besting a steam-powered drill in digging a railroad tunnel. Charged with turning Wolfe's music into a theatre piece, Bogart solicited monologues from four African-American playwrights (Kia Corthron, Will Power, Carl Hancock Rux, and Regina Taylor) and recruited two

African-American actors (Eric Berryman and Patrice Johnson Chevannes) to join company regulars Aizawa, Gianino, O'Hanlon, and Webber in a heady, exhausting tour de force. In typical SITI fashion, the piece situated different performance vocabularies—movement *and* dance; music *and* sound design; realistic costumes *and* expressionistic lighting; monologue, dialogue, *and* choral speech—side by side or layered on top of each other without fully integrating them, letting rough edges abrade and sublimating narrative elements to visceral, insistent rhythms. Taking a cue from the elliptical minimalism of Wolfe's music, the piece went in circles, literally and figuratively. Gestures and movement phrases were repeated again and again and performers danced a clog dance or ran in circles around a polygonal wooden platform to the point of exhaustion. The performance was an endurance test for the audience as well, eschewing any hint of folksy populism in favor of a numbing formalism and insistent pile-driving rhythms that for some viewers achieved moments of trance-like beauty. At the heart of it all was the mysterious figure of John Henry, a myth still in the making, a historical cypher in the end, unknowable except by the pure hard labor of Berryman's indelible physical performance. Like earlier SITI works, *Steel Hammer* premiered at the Humana Festival in Louisville and eventually toured to half a dozen cities, including a stop at BAM's Next Wave Festival.

The Wexner Center in Columbus commissioned *the theatre is a blank page* as part of its twenty-fifth anniversary celebration. The piece teamed Bogart and SITI with groundbreaking installation artist Ann Hamilton. Her *event of a thread*, a colossal installation at the Park Avenue Armory in 2012, included SITI actors stationed at desks reading texts. The act of reading—specifically, reading Virginia Woolf's *To the Lighthouse*—was at the center of *the theatre is a blank page*, which invited an audience of less than one hundred into a large auditorium theatre the Wexner's 2500-seat Mershon Auditorium in 2015; UCLA's 1800-seat Royce Hall in 2018—for a hybrid performance-installation that juxtaposed the public, shared, extroverted nature of theatrical experience with the private, often solitary, introverted nature of reading. Upon arrival, spectators were issued a custom-made newsprint copy of Woolf's novel and then guided to different parts of the theatre for different sections of the piece, starting in the back row of the balcony looking down on the stage and ending up onstage lying on the floor looking up into the fly tower. All the while, a Reader sat at a desk and read Woolf's seminal modernist text aloud, not from a book but as printed on an endless silk ribbon pulled through her fingers like a ticker tape and left to pile up on the floor in a Beckettian heap. Larger ribbon-like strips of fabric descended slowly from the flies at one point and actors read the Woolf text from them as well before using them to weave a giant tapestry with the help of the audience. For two-plus hours, the piece examined and played with, as one critic said,

> the texture of words—the way they feel in someone's mouth, in someone's ear, on silk running through your hands, projected in what looks like typewriter script with all the tactile, rhythmic associations that come with that ... this play moves so deliberately that the audience becomes conscious of the breath in its lungs, every shift or cough or creak becomes freighted, and the only way to experience this is to luxuriate in it like a warm bath. You have to let it flow around you; you can't force or command it. (Sanford 2015)

While this venture into installation work added a new dimension to the company's practice, the piece's fascination with the ontology of theatrical time and space and its insistence that a spectator give over to polyrhythms and incongruities and then make of them what they will goes to the heart of Bogart's theatre.

This vision of art-making, for Bogart in particular and the company as a whole, has been greatly influenced by the avant-garde composer and music theorist John Cage, who pioneered chance operations and the principle of indeterminacy through his own compositions and in his famous collaborations with choreographer Merce Cunningham. In 2017, after her experiments with nontheatrical partners in contemporary dance, music, and art, Bogart returned to SITI's tried-and-true methods and created *Chess Match No. 5*, a piece about Cage based on excerpts from a series of his public lectures. As with previous works, the texts were selected by Bogart, arranged into a performance score by Jocelyn Clarke, rehearsed in three hurried weeks of one, two, three—go! composition work, and performed by Ellen Lauren and Will Bond, with designs by James Schuette (sets and costumes), Brian Scott (lighting), and Darron L. West (sound). Conceived as the centerpiece of a large-scale, interdisciplinary Cage project, *Chess Match No. 5* was presented as a series of exchanges, verbal and physical, between two figures identified only as He (Bond) and She (Lauren). Over the course of ninety minutes, they come and go, make toast or coffee, listen to a radio, don silly pointed party hats, line up downstage for a couple of whimsical soft-shoe dances, and sit down again and again at a small table center stage to play chess. All the while, they exchange Cage quotations in the manner of light-hearted, well-mannered conversation. Everything in the production was geared toward heightening the audience's attention to Cage's favorite subject: the sound of silence. Microphones hung down close to the work table made sure that incidental, everyday sounds—toast popping up, the clinking of a spoon, water boiling—were conspicuous and resonant. In the moments of prolonged silence and stillness as He and She stared at the chessboard, the tap of a foot or the slow slide of a coffee mug across the top of table registered as music. Here again, spectators willing to suspend expectations for a structured narrative and give over to the flow of sights and sounds were rewarded with a pleasing tune-up of the senses, one very much colored by the thirty-year working relationship between Lauren and Bond.

Chess Match No. 5's celebration of Cage drew attention to a fundamental principle of the SITI Company's philosophy of performance. As Ellen Lauren put it:

> Just because you don't have a narrative or an Aristotelian sequence of causally related events does not mean you are not getting sensation. That's what acting is: generating and experiencing sensation, and sensation is located in the body. It originates with you. You are receiving the world. Or, as John Cage would say, you are noticing the world. Good acting depends on how expert you can become at noticing sensations, cultivating them, using them to your advantage, and getting the audience to experience sensation because you are … The classic example is Rodin's famous statue of "The Thinker." Nobody sits and thinks like that really, bent over, elbow on knee, chin on the back of the hand. But the shape that Rodin chose for that sculpture generates the sensation of contemplation, just the way that the score of Beethoven's "Ode to Joy" creates the sensation of elation in another human being. Nobody would say that joy sounds just like that. Actors do the same thing. We try to create the vessel or structure or shape of the sensation that we want to make happen in the room. We are not imitating characters or daily life, at least that's not the goal, even if at moments we have to appear as if we are. (Cummings 2018, 171)

This orientation toward performance as an exercise in contacting and stimulating the senses of actor and spectator alike, in attracting and then focusing attention, in being as fully present as possible from one second to the next, has imbued the best of the SITI Company's work over the years with a visceral immediacy that is thrilling, hopeful, and at key moments, sublime.

A Final Note

In May 2017, as part of a four-day symposium on his influential method of actor training, Tadashi Suzuki brought his Suzuki Company of Toga back to Saratoga Springs to perform his version of *The Trojan Women* on the same stage where they performed *Dionysus* twenty-five years earlier. The six-day visit, SCOT's first to the United States in sixteen years, was Suzuki's way of paying tribute to what he and Anne Bogart and a handful of dedicated, daring actors started in Japan in 1992. In the twenty-five years that followed, all of the artists in the SITI Company, to one extent or another, have relied on work outside the company for their livelihoods, yet they have remained together and committed to the ideals and the vision that first brought them together. Very few American ensembles—Lee Strasberg and the Group Theatre; Joe Chaikin and the Open Theater; Paul Sills, Story Theatre, and Second City—have had a wider influence on ensemble theatre-making and professional actor training in the United States. That such a sizable core company of actors—Lauren, Bond, Maurer, Nelis, Ingulsrud, Aizawa, O'Hanlon, Webber, Araiza, and eventually Gianino—stuck together for so long is unprecedented in American theatre. That a core team of designers—Darron West, Brian Scott, James Schuette, and Neil Patel—have collaborated on so many projects with one director is rare. And that one director has sustained the intellectual passion and creative energy to conceive one project after another, nurture its possibility, inspire others with her vision, leave ample room for their contributions, and then, a year or two later, be there on opening night to give notes and push the work forward is remarkable.

As the writing of this chapter concludes in early 2019, the SITI Company anticipates one of its more formidable challenges: the gradual and planned withdrawal of founding co-artistic director Anne Bogart from her central leadership role in the company. The 2011 restructuring of company leadership to include Lauren and Ingulsrud as co-artistic directors and the 2013 creation of the SITI Conservatory represent early steps that anticipated this eventual transition. Change is looming for the company and what new structure and new vision emerge remains to be seen. Whatever that is, SITI's quarter-century record of achievement will remain as a testament to the ideals of American ensemble theatre and in particular to Bogart's conviction that the most exciting, progressive theatre art is created by a company of committed artists working together over time.

NOTES

Chapter 2

1. See for example Filewod (1987); Oddey (1994); Heddon and Milling (2006); Govan, Nicholson and Normington (2007); Britton (2013); Baldwin, Larrue and Page (2008); O'Gorman and McIver (2015).
2. https://www.ensembletheaters.net/about. (accessed December 11, 2017).
3. Indeed, 2013 was a fruitful year for revisionist ensemble theatre scholarship, as it also saw publication of John Britton's collection, *Encountering Ensemble*, and both an edited book of interviews by Radosavljević, *The Contemporary Ensemble*, and the already-cited monograph on new writing and devising, *Theatre-making*.
4. Shannon Jackson finds the origins in the "spectacle of mostly-white participants" performing in the ritual-driven work of the 1960s New York underground scene and suggests this prepared the ground for future ensemble work (2004, 132).
5. Despite several requests for comments from these organizations, I received no responses. Martine Kei Green-Rogers of the Literary Mangers and Dramaturgs of America kindly shared her time and expertise on the subject.

Chapter 3

1. Special thanks is due to company director and playwright John Schneider for making available documents pertaining to the history of Theatre X and participating in interviews essential to preparation of this essay. Theatre X company members—Conrad Bishop, Flora Coker, John Kishline, Victor de Lorenzo, Deborah Clifton, John Schneider, and guest visual artist and theatre artist Jan Fabre, together with Mickery Theatre Director Ritsaert ten Cate—have graciously responded with reflections on their experiences with Theatre X. Their remarks have been edited for length and focus to bring live experiences of the principals into the account of Theatre X offered here. Comments by Ritsaert ten Cate are from "Theatre X: Reflections by Ritsaert ten Cate" (1989, 11). Each has provided helpful insights and information contributing to our understanding of the living experiences that have shaped Theatre X's contributions to experimental theatre.

Notes

2   In 1976 director Sharon Ott joined the company. Later she served as artistic director of the Berkeley and Seattle Repertory Theatres. The company structure evolved to include a board of directors in 1977–8 with diverse members, which included five Milwaukee community leaders including among others Sara O'Connor, Managing Director of the Milwaukee Repertory Theatre; Colin Cabot, Producing Director of the Skylight Opera Theatre; Max Samson, Founding Director of Milwaukee Mask and Puppet Theatre, John Ogden and Leonard Sobczak, long-time Theatre X Board Presidents; and the company members. The positions of managing directors and company manager were established. John Schneider and Sharon Ott were appointed as managing directors and John Kishline as company manager. Others who served in administrative roles: John Sobczak, Managing Director, 1987–90; Pam Percy, Managing Director, 1990–5; Michael Ramach, Producing Director, 1996–9; David Ravel, Producing Director, 2000–2; and Flora Coker, Producing Director, 2002–4. Second-generation members who also contributed to the success of Theatre X would include, among others: Marcie Hoffman, 1982–2002; Wesley Savik, 1984–9; David Schweizer, 1985–90; John Starmer, 1986–96.

3   Despite ongoing successes both national, international, in its Milwaukee home base Theatre X operated on a modest budget. As reported in the *Milwaukee Journal Sentinel* April 26, 1992, Theatre X's projected budget for the season was $125,000 to $200,000 for a season of four to five shows.

4   Additional corporate supporters include The Lynde and Harold Bradley Foundation, The Patrick and Anna Cudahy Foundation, The Gardner Foundation, The Jewish Community Foundation of Milwaukee, The Johnson Controls Foundation, American Medical Services, and Miller Brewing.

5   Writer, producer, and actor of the folk/punk group Violent Femmes, and current member of the cello/drum duo NINETEEN THIRTEEN.

6   From his diaries and shared before his death in 2008.

Chapter 4

1   All quotations by Maleczech are taken from a series of interviews conducted by the author between July 2011 and March 2012.

2   Unless otherwise noted, all quotations by Breuer are taken from a series of interviews conducted by the author between July 2011 and May 2012, and in October 2018.

3   For a thorough account of Mabou Mines's early experiments with Beckett, see Smith Fischer (2012, 28–59 and 99–119).

4   For thorough discussion of the company's founding and its work in the 1970s, see Smith Fischer (2012).

Notes

5   For a fuller examination of *Imagination Dead Imagine* and other productions discussed here including *Dead End Kids*, *Hajj*, *Lear*, and *Lucia's Chapters*, see Brater (2016a).

6   Breuer repeated this technique, albeit with different content, for *Choephorae* at the Patras Festival in Greece (2006).

7   Paracelsus (1493 or 1494–1541) was a Swiss alchemist and physician active in the German medical Renaissance. Lieutenant General Leslie R. Groves was director of the Manhattan Project.

8   Over a span of thirty-five years, Yerxa was the designer for productions directed by Breuer including *The Shaggy Dog Animation*, *The Gospel at Colonus*, *Lear*, and *La Divina Caricatura*. "Alison paints what my soul sees," says Breuer. Lorwin was a producer for ReCherChez, *Sister Suzie Cinema*, *The Gospel at Colonus*, and *Peter and Wendy*.

Chapter 5

1   The Gaffers-tape performance footprint for each piece was designed to fit into the range of live-art black box spaces on the UK circuit, with technical planning similarly tailored. Venues to which Goat Island toured in the UK included, but was not exclusive to, the Center for Contemporary Art in Glasgow, the Ferens Art Gallery in Hull, the Arnolfini in Bristol, Dartington Arts in Totnes, Tramway in Glasgow, and the Nuffield Theatre in Lancaster.

2   Including, though not exclusive to, Sara Jane Bailes, Carol Becker, Jane Blocker, Stephen Scott-Bottoms, Lynda Frye Burnham, Adrian Heathfield, Joe Kelleher, Goran Sergej Pristas, and Alan Read.

3   The Goat Island Archive is maintained in the Libraries and Special Collections at the School of the Art Institute of Chicago. The main archive includes a substantial quantity of materials that reflect the development of the nine performance works alongside the pedagogical and publications activity of the company. The collection includes the working company papers, creative and work development materials with some of the notebooks produced individually by the collaborating member. There is an extensive collection of mainly analog audiovisual documentation, and a sizable quantity of costumes and performance props housed in their original custom-made road cases.

4   *Mr. Roberts*, a play by Joshua Logan, based on a novel of the same name by Thomas Heggen. It would later be made into a film of the same name in 1955. The narrative, based in the South Pacific in the Second World War, challenges the idea of naval life as heroic, offering a realistic and somewhat ironic view of the everyday experiences of confinement and isolation of a group of conscripts.

Notes

5   Correspondence by email between Joan Dickinson and the authors, August 2019.
6   Tim and Greg McCain have a similar physical stature; both are around 6 feet 5 inches tall with large physical builds, whereas Matthew Goulish and Joan Dickinson are more lightly built each at around 5 feet 6 inches tall.
7   *The 39 Steps* (Alfred Hitchcock 1939); *The Harp of Burma* (Kon Ichikawa 1956); *Le Grand Illusion* (Jean Renoir 1937); *Dreams* (Akira Kurosawa 1990).

Chapter 6

1   The author would like to thank Kaitlyn Tossie for her assistance with early research for this essay.
2   The six NU students who were in *Alice in Wonderland* and thus part of the initial conversations about the ensemble were David Schwimmer, David Catlin, Larry DiStasi, David Kersnar, Eva Barr, and Joy Gregory. On February 13, 1988, the company officially formed, adding Andy White and Thom Cox to the initial group for a total of eight founding members.
3   While their initial name separated "looking" from "glass," when a press release typo listed them as Lookingglass Theatre Company, they also elided the two words into one (Catlin 2009, 110–11).
4   For more about Robert Breen's chamber theatre technique, see his manual *Chamber Theatre* (1986). I also discuss Breen, along with Wallace Bacon and the NU-based oral interpretation technique of literary adaptation at length in the first chapter of *Adapturgy* (Barnette 2018).
5   Mary Zimmerman also teaches at NU in the performance studies department.
6   For examples of the kinds of exercises that the ensemble uses to craft their work, see the chapter on Lookingglass Theatre in Johnston and Brownrigg (2019, 99–108).
7   Zimmerman's dissertation, "The Archeology of Performance: A Study of Ensemble Process and Development in the Lookingglass Theatre Production of *The Arabian Nights*," was submitted in December of 1994 to a doctoral committee led by Frank Galati, in the department of Performance Studies at NU.
8   With Northwestern UP, in addition to these two plays, Zimmerman has published her adaptations *The Odyssey* (2006), *Journey to the West* (2011), *Argonautika* (2013), *The White Snake* (2013), and *The Secret in the Wings* (2014). Of these seven scripts, all but two (*Journey to the West* and *The White Snake*) were developed with the Lookingglass ensemble.
9   In 1994, Zimmerman also produced this show at the Manhattan Theatre Club, with two members of the original cast—Jenny Bacon and Chris Donahue as

Notes

Scheherezade and Shahryar, respectively, and the original music director, Bruce Norris—all other roles were played by New York actors cast for this run.

10 Academic critics have not been as forgiving of Zimmerman's adaptation and staging choices in *The Jungle Book*, however—for an example of these critiques of her work, see Clark et al. (2017) and Williams (2014).

11 The whale also appeared in the marketing strategy for the Lookingglass production—on social media outlets, the company used pictures of a giant inflatable white whale "on location" at various sites throughout Chicago to publicize the production, using the hashtag #FindTheWhiteWhale.

12 The other two young men profiled were John Carlile and Dexter Bullard, of Wisdom Bridge and Next Theatre, respectively.

13 Slotnik's films include *Pirates of Silicon Valley*, in which he played Steve Wozniak (1999), *Twister*, in which he played Joey (1996), and *Elevator*, in which he played George Axelrod (2011).

14 As one example of local reviews for *Cascabel*, Chris Jones (*Chicago Tribune*) gave the remounted 2014 production 3.5 stars, calling it "slightly" better than the 2012 version, in part because the Goodman venue allowed for more fly space for the circus acts, but also due to "the inclusion of beverages in the ticket price" (2014).

Chapter 7

1 The company's website provides access to video segments of several of their productions (Elevator Repair Service). For my analysis here, I rely on those videos in addition to personal memory of the many ERS performances I attended.

2 Collins, it should be noted, did not design sound for Elevator Repair Service after their first two productions. Beginning with *Spine Check*, Blake Koh took on that assignment. Still, with Collins at the helm as director, his idiosyncratic approach to sound is easily recognizable.

3 Another connection with the Wooster Group is Scott Shepherd, who, during this same time period, had emerged as one of their leading actors. Just two years earlier, in 2008, he played the title character in their *Hamlet*.

4 In 2011, before *Arguendo*, the company created *Shuffle*, a performance installation at the New York Public Library in collaboration with artist Ben Rubin and statistician Mark Hansen. They describe it as "a site-specific mash-up where the company attempts to read *The Great Gatsby*, *The Sound and the Fury*, and *The Sun Also Rises* simultaneously" (Elevator Repair Service n.d.).

Notes

Chapter 8

1. This chapter is based on twenty years of my research on Anne Bogart and the SITI Company, much of which has reached publication in various forms, including my 2006 book *Remaking American Theater: Charles Mee, Anne Bogart and the SITI Company*. Of necessity, ideas, phrases, and even whole sentences from that earlier writing are recycled here.
2. Book-length studies of Suzuki include Allain (2011) and Carruthers and Yasunari (2004).
3. The split was messy and painful. For one account, see De Vries (1990).
4. When *The Medium* was further developed and presented by New York Theatre Workshop in 1994, Ellen Lauren replaced Scharbau and J. Ed Araiza replaced Corkins. When the piece toured in 1995 and 1996, Bond took over the McLuhan role inaugurated by Nelis and Stephen Webber joined the cast.
5. Both went on to successful careers. Mays became a Broadway actor, known for his tour-de-force roles in *I Am My Own Wife* and *A Gentleman's Guide to Love and Murder*. Sanchez became a director and playwright who heads the MFA Directing program at University of Texas at Austin and runs a documentary theatre company called American Records.
6. The nine Viewpoints articulated by Bogart refer to the physical body in time and space. Eventually, Vocal Viewpoints were articulated and introduced into the training, albeit on a less systematic basis than the Physical Viewpoints. As listed in Bogart and Landau's *The Viewpoints Book*, the Vocal Viewpoints are Pitch, Dynamic, Acceleration/Deceleration, Timbre, and Silence as well as the aural equivalents of Tempo, Duration, Repetition, Kinesthetic Response, Shape, Gesture, and Architecture.
7. For a detailed case studio of the step-by-step development of *bobrauschenbergamerica*, see Cummings (2006).
8. Mee wrote at least one other artist-play for the SITI Company that they never produced, a piece called *Soot and Spit* about James Castle, the outsider artist from rural Idaho.
9. Also titled *War of the Worlds*, the Iizuka/SITI piece featured Stephen Duff Webber as Orson Welles, premiered at the 2000 Humana Festival, and toured briefly to the Edinburgh Festival, BAM's Next Wave Festival, Santa Barbara, and St. Louis. It represents SITI's only direct collaboration with a playwright other than Charles Mee.

BIBLIOGRAPHY

Abarbanel, Jonathan. (1994). "McGurk: A Cautionary Tale." *Back Stage*, 35 (51), December 30: 30.
Abrams, Joshua. (2013). "Review of *Cascabel*, Lookingglass Theatre Company, Chicago, April 8, 2012." *Theatre Journal*, 65 (2): 284–7.
Akalaitis, JoAnne. (2011). Interview by the author. December.
Akeret, Julie. (2012). *Theatre on the Edge: Growing Art and Community at Double Edge Theatre*. USA: Akeret Films.
Allain, Paul. (2011). *The Theatre Practice of Tadashi Suzuki*. London: Bloomsbury/Methuen Drama.
Als, Hilton. (2018). "The Gospel at Colonus." *The New Yorker*. https://www.newyorker.com/goings-on-about-town/theatre/the-gospel-at-colonus.
Anderson, Porter. (2008). "The Search for a SITI State." *American Theatre*, 25 (3), March: 24–7, 81–3.
Anderson-Rabern, Rachel. (2011a). "Efficiencies of Slowness: The Politics of Contemporary Collective Creation." PhD diss., Stanford University.
Anderson-Rabern, Rachel. (2013). "The Nature Theater of Oklahoma." In *Collective Creation in Contemporary Performance*, eds. Kathryn Mederos Syssoyeva and Scott Proudfit, 151–63. New York: Palgrave Macmillan.
Anderson-Rabern, Rachel. (2020). *Staging Process: The Aesthetic Politics of Collective Creation*. Evanston: Northwestern UP.
Archer, Julie. (2011). Interview by Jessica Silsby Brater. November.
Aronson, Arnold. (2000). *American Avant-garde Theatre: A History*. London; New York: Routledge.
Aronowitz, Stanley. (1996). *The Death and Rebirth of American Radicalism*. London; New York: Routledge.
Aston, Elaine. (1999). *Feminist Theatre Practice: A Handbook*. London; New York: Routledge.
Aston, Elaine. (n.d.). "Feminist Theatre." *Drama Online*. https://www.dramaonlinelibrary.com/ (accessed March 14, 2018).
Auslander, Philip. (1994). *Presence and Resistance: Postmodernism and Cultural Politics in Contemporary American Performance*. Ann Arbor: University of Michigan Press.
Austria, Maria. (1998). *Pictorial: Mickery 1965–1987: A Photographic History*. Amsterdam: Stichting Mickery Workshop.
Bailes, Sara Jane. (2002). "This America: A Conversation with John Collins about ERS." *Women and Performance*, 12 (2): 183–200.
Bailes, Sara Jane. (2007). "Gatz." *Theatre Journal*, 59 (3): 508–9.
Bailes, Sara Jane. (2011). *Performance Theatre and the Poetics of Failure: Forced Entertainment, Goat Island, Elevator Repair Service*. London; New York: Routledge.

Bibliography

Baldwin, Jane, Jean-Marc Larrue, and Christiane Page, eds. (2008). *Vies et Morts de la Creation Collective/Lives and Deaths of Collective Creative*. Boston: Vox Theatri.

Banes, Sally. (1993a). *Democracy's Body: Judson Dance Theater, 1962–1964*. Durham: Duke University Press.

Banes, Sally. (1993b). *Greenwich Village 1963: Avant-garde Performance and the Effervescent Body*. Durham: Duke University Press.

Banes, Sally. (2000). "Institutionalizing Avant-garde Performance: A Hidden History of University Patronage in the United States." In *Contours of the Theatrical Avant-garde: Performance and Textuality*, ed. James Harding, 217–38. Ann Arbor: University of Michigan Press.

Barnette, Jane. (2018). *Adapturgy: The Dramaturg's Art and Theatrical Adaptation*. Carbondale: Southern Illinois University Press.

Becker, Carol. (1991). "Goat Island's *We Got A Date*." *The Drama Review*, 35 (4), Winter T132: 53.

Beckett, Samuel. (1981). December 16, Mabou Mines Correspondence. Mabou Mines Archive. Fales Library and Special Collections. New York University. Series IA, Box 1, Folder 8.

Benedict, Stephen and American Assembly. (1991). *Public Money and the Muse: Essays on Government Funding for the Arts*. New York: W. W. Norton.

The Berkeley Rep Magazine. (2008–9). *The Arabian Nights* (program), issue 3.

Berkowitz, Gerald M. (1997). *New Broadways: Theatre across America*. New York: Applause.

Berson, Misha. (1999). "A Rage for the Page: Theatres across the Country Find That Fiction Speaks Volumes." *American Theatre*, 16 (3), March: 53–7.

Bîcat, Tina, and Chris Baldwin, eds. (2002). *Devised and Collaborative Theatre: A Practical Guide*. Ramsbury: Crowood Press.

Bigsby, C. W. E. (1982). *A Critical Introduction to Twentieth-Century American Drama*. 3 vols. Cambridge University Press.

Blau, Herbert. (1964). *The Impossible Theater: A Manifesto*. New York: Macmillan.

Blau, Herbert. (2000). *Sails of the Herring Fleet: Essays on Beckett*. Ann Arbor: University of Michigan Press.

Bleha, Julie. (2003). "A God, a Thermos, a Play: Elevator Repair Service Tackles Euripides' *Bacchae*." *TheatreForum*, 23, Summer–Fall: 79–88.

Boal, Augusto. (2019). *Theatre of the Oppressed*. London: Pluto Press.

Bogart, Anne (2001). *A Director Prepares*. London; New York: Routledge.

Bogart, Anne, and Tadashi Suzuki. (1992). "Towards a New International Theater Center: Manifesto for The Saratoga International Theater Institute." Playbill insert.

Bogart, Anne, and Tina Landau. (2005). *The Viewpoints Book: A Practical Guide to Viewpoints and Composition*. New York: Theatre Communications Book.

Bottoms, Stephen J. (2004). *Playing Underground: A Critical History of the 1960s Off-Off-Broadway Movement*. Ann Arbor: University of Michigan Press.

Bottoms, Stephen, and Matthew Goulish. (2007). *Small Acts of Repair: Performance, Ecology and Goat Island*. London; New York: Routledge.

Bousset, Sigrid. (1993). *Jan Fabre: Texts on His Theatre-work*. Brussels: Kaaitheater.

Bibliography

Bowles, Norma, and Daniel-Raymond Nadon. (2013). *Staging Social Justice: Collaborating to Create Activist Theatre*. Carbondale: Southern Illinois University Press.

Brady, Sara. (2000). "Welded to the Ladle: 'Steelbound' and Non-radicality in Community-based Theatre." *TDR*, 44 (3): 51–74.

Brantley, Ben. (2008). "Faulkner's Haunted Family Moving In and Out of Time." *The New York Times*, April 30: E1.

Brantley, Ben. (2010a). "Borne Back Ceaselessly to the Past." *The New York Times*, November 28: C1.

Brantley, Ben. (2010b). "Hath Not a Year Highlights? Even This One?" *The New York Times*, December 19: AR7.

Brantley, Ben. (2011). "A Lost Generation Drinks Up, Always on Jake Barnes's Tab." *The New York Times*, September 12: C1.

Brantley, Ben. (2015), "A Group Gallop through a Labyrinthine Dreamscape." *The New York Times*, September 29: C1.

Brantley, Ben. (2017). "Finally Taking Shakespeare's 'Measure.'" *The New York Times*, October 12: C5.

Brantley, Ben. (2018). "George and Martha Redux in 'Everyone's Fine with Virginia Woolf.'" *The New York Times*, June 12. https://www.nytimes.com/2018/06/12/theater/everyones-fine-with-virginia-woolf-review.html (accessed October 30, 2018).

Brater, Jessica Silsby. (2016a). *Ruth Maleczech at Mabou Mines: Woman's Work*. London; New York: Bloomsbury/Methuen Drama.

Brater, Jessica Silsby. (2016b). "Ruth Maleczech, JoAnne Akalaitis, and the Mabou Mines Family Aesthetic." In *Women, Collective Creation, and Devised Performance: The Rise of Women Theatre Artists in the Twentieth and Twenty-first Centuries*, eds. Kathryn Mederos Syssoyeva and Scott Proudfit, 115–28. New York: Palgrave Macmillan.

Breen, Robert S. (1986). *Chamber Theatre*. Evanston, IL: Wm. Caxton.

Breuer, Lee. (1976). "Mabou Mines: How We Work." *Performing Arts Journal*, 1 (1), Spring: 29–32.

Breuer, Lee. (1980). "The Funding Game." *Other Stages*, March 20.

Breuer, Lee. (1987). "Performances: *Hajj*." In *Sister Suzie Cinema: The Collected Poems and Performances, 1976–1986*. New York: Theatre Communications Group.

Breuer, Lee. (1989). "Acknowledgments." In *The Gospel at Colonus*, ix, New York: Theatre Communications Group.

Breuer, Lee. (1991). "The Two-handed Gun: Reflections on Power, Culture, Lambs, Hyenas, and Government Support for the Arts." *Village Voice*, August 20, 89–90.

Breuer, Lee. (2002). In *Mabou Mines' Lear '87 Archive*. DVD. Directed by Jill Godmilow, Disk 2, Hour 3. New York: Laboratory for Icon & Idiom.

Breuer, Lee. (2011–12, 2018). Interviews by the author. July–May and October.

Breuer, Lee, Bonnie Marranca, and Gautam Dasgupta. (1979). *Animations: A Trilogy for Mabou Mines*. New York: Performing Arts Journal Publications.

Britton, John. (2013). *Encountering Ensemble*. London: Bloomsbury.

Brown, Kent R. (1973). "Opening on the Education Scene: A Native American Theatre Ensemble." *Journal of American Indian Education*, 13 (1): 1–6.

Bibliography

Brown, Scott. (2010). "A Spellbinding Six-hour Gatz." *New York Magazine*, October 6. http://www.vulture.com/2010/10/theater_review_a_spellbinding. html (accessed October 30, 2018).

Bruckner, D. J. R. (2000). "In This Spinoff of 'Bacchae,' Dionysus Is a Thermos Bottle." *The New York Times*, November 8: E3.

Bull, John, and Graham Saunders, eds. (2017). *British Theatre Companies*. 3 vols. London; New York: Bloomsbury.

Calder, John. (1995). "Obituary: David Warrilow." *The Independent*, August 21. https://www.independent.co.uk/news/people/obituary-david-warrilow-1597292. html.

Callery, Dymphna. (2001). *Through the Body: A Practical Guide to Physical Theatre*. London; New York: Routledge.

Canavan, Claire. (2013). "Created by the Ensemble: Histories and Pedagogies at the Dell'Arte International School of Physical Theatre." In *Collective Creation in Contemporary Performance*, eds. Kathryn Mederos Syssoyeva and Scott Proudfit, 125–36. New York: Palgrave Macmillan.

Cannato, Vincent J. (2009). "Bright Lights, Doomed Cities: The Rise and Fall of New York City in the 1980s." In *Living in the Eighties*, eds. Gil Troy and Vincent J. Cannato, 70–84. Oxford: Oxford University Press.

Canning, Charlotte. (1996). *Feminist Theaters in the USA: Staging Women's Experience*. London; New York: Routledge.

Carroll, Peter N. (1990). *It Seemed Like Nothing Happened: America in the 1970s*. New Brunswick: Rutgers University Press.

Carter, Curtis L. (1993). "Beyond Performance: Re: Jan Fabre." In *Jan Fabre: Texts on His Theatre-work*, ed. Sigrid Bousset, 13–26. Brussels: Kaaitheater.

Carter, Curtis L. (2018). "Interview with John Schneider, July 9." Marquette University, Milwaukee, USA.

Carroll, Noel. (1986). "Performance." *Formations*, 3 (1): 63–80.

Carruthers, Ian, and Takahashi Yasunari. (2004). *The Theatre of Suzuki Tadashi*. Cambridge: Cambridge University Press.

Case, Sue-Ellen, ed. (1996). *Split Britches: Lesbian Practice/Feminist Performance*: London; New York: Routledge.

Catlin, David. (2009). "Curiouser and Curiouser: Reflections from Twenty Years in the Lookingglass (Theatre), or Stealing Borrowing from the Best." *Triquarterly*, 134: 94–122.

Catlin, David. (2015). Unpublished interview with Jane Barnette, telephone. September 16.

Cesare, T. Nikki, and Mariellen R. Sandford. (2010). "To Avant or Not to Avant: Questioning the Experimental, the New and the Potential to Shock in the New Garde." *TDR: The Drama Review*, 54 (4): 7–10.

Chamberlain, Franc. (2007). "Gesturing towards Post-Physical Performance." In *Physical Theatres: A Critical Reader*, eds. John Keefe and Simon Murray, 145–50. New York: Routledge.

Christiansen, Richard. (1990a). "A Fearless New Breed of Directors Hits Town: Their Vision Is Revitalizing Theater." *Chicago Tribune*, December 2: 4.

Bibliography

Christiansen, Richard. (1990b). "Troupe's Fervor Outweighs Flaws of 'The Jungle.'" *Chicago Tribune*, October 5: 28.
Christiansen, Richard. (1996). "So-so 'S/M' Puts Audience in Discomfort Zone." *Chicago Tribune*, January 29: 2.
Clark, Emily, Donatella Galella, Stefanie A. Jones, and Catherine Young. (2017). "'I Wanna Be Like You': Negotiating Race, Racism and Orientalism in *The Jungle Book* on Stage." In *The Disney Musical on Stage and Screen: Critical Approaches from "Snow White" to "Frozen,"* ed. George Rodosthenous, 185–203, London: Bloomsbury.
Cohen, N. (1990). "Essence of Goat." *Arts, Times Educational Supplement*, June 8: 1.
Cohen-Cruz, Jan. (2015). *Remapping Performance: Common Ground, Uncommon Partners*. Houndmills; New York: Palgrave Macmillan.
Cohn, Ruby. (1999). "The Becketts of Mabou Mines." In *Samuel Beckett and the Arts*, ed. Lois Oppenheim, 217–36, New York: Garland Publishing.
Collins, John. (2013). "Elevator Repair Service and the Wooster Group: Ensembles Surviving Themselves." In *Encountering Ensemble*, ed. John Britton, 234–49. London; New York: Bloomsbury.
"Community Engagement." (2019). Lookingglass Theatre Company. http://www.lookingglass.org/community-engagement/ (accessed January 12, 2019).
Connors, Thomas B. (2012). "A Chef of One's Own," *American Theatre*, March: 22.
Coppens, Julie York. (2010). "From Olympus to Neverland: Pure Balance." *Dramatics*, October: 5–10.
Cummings, Scott T. (2006). *Remaking American Theatre: Charles Mee, Anne Bogart and the SITI Company*. Cambridge: Cambridge University Press.
Cummings, Scott T. (2017). "Trans-Pacific Partnership." *American Theatre*, 34 (7) September 2017: 34–6.
Cummings, Scott T. (2018). "Ellen Lauren: The Art of Extreme Acting, an Interview." In *Narrative in Performance*, eds. Barbara Sellers-Young and Jade Rosina McCutcheon, 167–87, London: Palgrave Macmillan.
Curb, Rosemary, Phyllis Mael, and Beverly Byers Pevitts. (1979). "Catalog of Feminist Theatre Parts 1 and 2." *Chrysalis*, 10: 51–75.
Davis, Douglas. (1999). "The Theater of Danger." *Art in America*, 87 (2), February: 61–3.
De Vries, Hilary. (1990). "How a Real-life Drama Came to an Unhappy End." *New York Times*, July 15, 1990: H5.
DeFrantz, Thomas, Renee Alexander Craft, Sandra L. Richards, and Kathy A. Perkins, eds. (2019). *The Routledge Companion to African American Theatre and Performance*. London; New York: Routledge.
Del Signore, John. (2009). "Director Lee Breuer, Mabou Mines' *DollHouse*." *Gothamist*, February 27. http://gothamist.com/2009/02/27/director_lee_breuer_mabou_mines_dol.php.
Dickinson, Joan. (2019). Correspondence by email between Joan Dickinson and the authors. August.
Dolan, Jill. (1991). *The Feminist Spectator as Critic*. Ann Arbor: University of Michigan Press.

Bibliography

Drukman, Steven. (1996). "Shut Up I Tell You (I Said Shut Up I Tell You)." *Artforum International*, 34 (7): 104.

Edgecomb, Sean F. (2007) "History of the Ridiculous, 1960–1987." *The Gay and Lesbian Review Worldwide, Boston*, 14 (3): 21–2.

Ehrman, John. (2005). *The Eighties: America in the Age of Reagan*. New Haven: Yale University Press.

Elevator Repair Service. (n.d.). https://www.elevator.org/.

Evans, Sara M. (2009). "Feminism in the 1980s: Surviving the Backlash." In *Living in the Eighties*, eds. Gil Troy and Vincent J. Cannato, 85–97, Oxford: Oxford University Press.

Faber, Roderick Mason. (1993). "Cameos: American Living Room." *The Village Voice*, September 14: 105.

Favorini, Attilio. (2013). "Collective Creation in Documentary Theatre." In *A History of Collective Creation*, eds. Kathryn Mederos Syssoyeva and Scott Proudfit, 97–112. New York: Palgrave Macmillan.

Feingold, Michael. (1998). "Zombie Aerobics." *The Village Voice*, November 3: 155.

Feingold, Michael. (2000). "A Busch Victory." *The Village Voice*, November 14: 79.

Feingold, Michael. (2008). "Three New Productions Tackle Color Lines." *The Village Voice*, May 6. https://www.villagevoice.com/2008/05/06/three-new-productions-tackle-color-lines/ (accessed October 31, 2018).

Feingold, Michael. (2010). "Tendered Is the Text." *The Village Voice*, October 13: 35.

Feingold, Michael. (2017). "Strictly from Mars: An Extraterrestrial's Take on Elevator Repair Service's Wacky 'Measure for Measure.'" *The Village Voice*, October 18. https://www.villagevoice.com/2017/10/18/strictly-from-mars-an-extraterrestrials-take-on-elevator-repair-services-wacky-measure-for-measure/ (accessed October 30, 2018).

Felton-Dansky, Miriam. (2018). "'Everyone's Fine with Virginia Woolf' Is an Amped-up Riff on Edward Albee's Original." *The Village Voice*, June 19. https://www.villagevoice.com/2018/06/19/everyones-fine-with-virginia-woolf-is-an-amped-up-riff-on-edward-albees-original/ (accessed October 31, 2018).

Filewod, Alan Douglas. (1987). *Collective Encounters: Documentary Theatre in English Canada*. Toronto: University of Toronto Press.

Finkelstein, Avram. (2017). "'Silence = Death': How an Iconic Protest Symbol Came into Being." *Literary Hub*, December 17. https://lithub.com/silence-death-how-an-iconic-protest-poster-came-into-being/ (accessed July 17, 2019).

Fischer, Iris Smith. (2011). *Mabou Mines: Making Avant-garde Theater in the 1970s*. Ann Arbor: University of Michigan Press.

Fiske, John. (1996). *Media Matters: Race and Gender in US Politics*. Rev. ed. Minneapolis: University of Minnesota Press.

Fletcher, Anne. (2016). "From the Center to the Heartland: The Collective, Collaborative Conscience of Jo Ann Schmidman, Megan Terry, Sora Kimberlain, and the Omaha Magic Theatre (1968–1998)." In *Women, Collective Creation, and Devised Performance: The Rise of Women Theatre Artists in the Twentieth and Twenty-first Centuries*, eds. Kathryn Mederos Syssoyeva and Scott Proudfit, 145–60. New York: Palgrave Macmillan.

Fogarty, Sharon. (2007). *Lucia's Chapters of Coming Forth by Day*. Manuscript. Mabou Mines Office Archive.

Fogarty, Sharon. (2011). Interview by the author.
Foley, Helene. (2014). *Reimagining Greek Tragedy on the American Stage*. Berkeley: University of California Press.
Forsgren, La Donna L. (2020). "From 'Poemplays' to Ritualistic Revivals: The Experimental Works of Women Dramatists of the Black Arts Movement." In *The Routledge Companion to African American Theatre and Performance*, eds. Kathy Perkins et al., 250–6. New York: Routledge.
Freeman, John. (2007). *New Performance/New Writing*. Basingstoke; New York: Palgrave Macmillan.
Freeman, Sara. (2006). "Towards a Genealogy and Taxonomy of British Alternative Theatre." *New Theatre Quarterly*, 22 (4): 364–78.
Freire, Paolo. (1970). *Pedagogy of the Oppressed*. New York: Penguin.
French, William W. (1998). *Maryat Lee's EcoTheater: A Theater for the Twenty-first Century*. Morgantown: West Virginia University Press.
Friedman, Dan. (2000). "Castillo: The Making of a Postmodern Political Theatre." *Theater Symposium*, 8: 130–40.
Frieze, James. (2006). "The Mess Behind the Veil: Assimilating Ping Chong." *Theatre Research International*, 31 (1): 84–100.
Frye Burnham, Linda. (1988). "Beating the System." *L.A. Weekly*, August 5–11: 37.
Fuchs, Elinor. (1986). "Presence and the Revenge of Writing: Re-thinking Theatre after Derrida." *Performing Arts Journal*, 9 (2): 163–73.
Fuchs, Elinor. (1996). *The Death of Character: Perspectives on Theater after Modernism*. Bloomington: Indiana University Press.
Fuchs, Elinor. (2004). "Review." *Theatre Journal*, 56 (3), October: 498–500.
Fusco, Coco. (1999). "Elevator Repair Service: Steve Bodow, John Collins, Rinnie Groff." *Bomb* (67), Spring: 50–5.
Galilee, Clove. (2012). Interview by the author.
Garrett, Shawn-Marie. (2001). "The Awkward Age: New York's New Experimental Theater." *Theater*, 31 (2): 45–53.
Gitlin, Todd. (1987). *The Sixties: Years of Hope, Days of Rage*. Toronto; New York: Bantam Books.
Goat Island. (1995). *Goat Island Newsletter*, March.
Goat Island. (2000). *Schoolbook 2*. Chicago: Goat Island and The School of the Art Institute of Chicago.
Goat Island. (2003). "When Will the September Roses Bloom?" Goat Island, Work in Progress, November 8 (Box 5, Miscellaneous papers. Goat Island Archive, John M. Flaxman Library Special Collection, School of the Art Institute).
Govan, Emma, Helen Nicholson, and Katie Normington. (2007). *Making a Performance: Devising Histories and Contemporary Practices*. London; New York: Routledge.
Greenberg, David. (2009). "The Reorientation of Liberalism in the 1980s." In *Living in the Eighties*, eds. Gil Troy and Vincent J. Cannato, 51–69. Oxford: Oxford University Press.
Gussow, Mel. (1976). "Stage: Becketts Creative 'Cascando.'" *New York Times*, April 13. https://www.nytimes.com/1976/04/13/archives/stage-becketts-creative-cascando.html.

Bibliography

Gussow, Mel. (1984). "Theater: 'Pretty Boy' and a Beckett." *New York Times*, June 15. https://www.nytimes.com/1984/06/15/arts/theater-pretty-boy-and-a-beckett.html.

Gussow, Mel. (1986). "Stage: 'Worstward Ho,' a Beckett Monologue." *New York Times*, September 12. https://www.nytimes.com/1986/09/12/theater/stage-worstward-ho-a-beckett-monologue.html.

Gussow, Mel. (1994). "Iconoclastic and Busy Director: An Innovator or a Provocateur?" *New York Times*, March 12, 1994, Arts 11.

Gussow, Mel. (1997). "Intrinsic Avant-gardist Has Crush on Tinker Bell." *New York Times*, February 10. https://www.nytimes.com/1997/02/10/theater/intrinsic-avant-gardist-has-crush-on-tinker-bell.html.

Harding, James. (2013). *The Ghosts of the Avant-garde(s): Exorcising Experimental Theater and Performance*. Ann Arbor: The University of Michigan Press.

Harding, James, and Cindy Rosenthal. (2006). *Restaging the Sixties: Radical Theaters and Their Legacies*. Ann Arbor: University of Michigan Press.

Harding, James, and Cindy Rosenthal. (2017). *The Sixties, Center Stage: Mainstream and Popular Performances in a Turbulent Decade*. Ann Arbor: University of Michigan Press.

Harvey, David. (2005). *A Brief History of Neoliberalism*. Oxford: Oxford University Press.

Harvie, Jen. (2013). *Fair Play: Art, Performance and Neoliberalism*. London: Palgrave.

Harvie, Jen, and Andy Lavender. (2010). *Making Contemporary Theatre: International Rehearsal Processes*. Manchester; New York: Manchester University Press.

Harvie, Jen, and Lois Weaver. (2015). *The Only Way Home Is through the Show: Performance Work of Lois Weaver*. London, Bristol: Live Art Development Agency; Intellect.

Hayes, Jacqueline. (1994). "Representations of Utopia: The Politics of Women's Theatre Groups, 1969–1992." PhD diss., New York University.

Heddon, Deirdre, and Jane Milling. (2006). *Devising Performance: A Critical History*. Basingstoke; New York: Palgrave Macmillan.

Hixson, Lin. (1990). "*Soldier, Child, Tortured Man*, the Making of a Performance." *Contact Quarterly*, Winter: 12–19.

Hixson, Lin. (1997). "Don't Look Down." *Scottish Television Arts Review*, Spring. Video, 11: 04. Goat Island Archive, Library and Special Collections School of the Art Institute of Chicago.

Hobson, Joel. (2018). Unpublished interview with Jane Barnette, Chicago, June 15.

Horwitz, Andy. (2004). "Talking to John Collins of Elevator Repair Service." *Culturebot*. www.culturebot.org/2004/11/265/talking-to-john-collins-of-elevator-repair-service/ (accessed June 3, 2018).

Hsiao, Irene. (2013). "Making It Rite: *Rite of Spring* by Bill T. Jones and SITI." *SF Weekly*, October 14. https://archives.sfweekly.com/exhibitionist/2013/10/14/making-it-rite-rite-of-spring-by-bill-t-jones-and-siti.

Huerta, Jorge. (2006). "The Legacy of El Teatro Campesino." In *Restaging the Sixties: Radical Theaters and Their Legacies*, eds. James Martin Harding and Cindy Rosenthal, 239–62. Ann Arbor: University of Michigan Press.

Bibliography

Hughes, David. (1990). "Locating Goat Island, A Conversation with Lin Hixson and Matthew Goulish." *Performance Magazine*, 61, September: 15.
Hughes, Jenny, and Helen Nicholson. (2016). *Critical Perspectives on Applied Theatre*. Cambridge; New York: Cambridge University Press.
Hurup, Elsebeth. (1996). *The Lost Decade: America in the Seventies*. Aarhus: Aarhus University Press.
Jackson, Julie. (2017). "Not Just Rock 'n' Roll: Chicago Theatre, 1984–1990." *Theatre History Studies*, 36: 75–111.
Jackson, Shannon. (2004). *Professing Performance: Theatre in the Academy from Philology to Performativity*. Cambridge: Cambridge University Press.
Jackson, Shannon. (2011). *Social Works Performing Art, Supporting Publics*. London; New York: Routledge.
Jameson, Fredric. (1991). *Postmodernism, or, the Cultural Logic of Late Capitalism*. Duke University Press.
Jannarone, Kimberly. (2015). *Vanguard Performance beyond Left and Right*. Ann Arbor: University of Michigan Press.
Johnston, Chloe, and Coya Paz Brownrigg. (2019). *Ensemble-made Chicago: A Guide to Devised Theater*. Evanston, IL: Northwestern University Press.
Jones, Chris. (2002). "Zimmerman Touch: With an Alchemy Worthy of Midas, the Chicago-based Director Transforms Classic Tales into Stage Gold." *American Theatre*, March: 19–22.
Jones, Chris. (2014). "Rick Bayless: One Stage at a Time; Chef's Humility Is One of Play's Savory Delights." *Chicago Tribune*, August 6: 4.
Jones, Omi Osun Joni L., L. L. Moore, and S. Bridgforth. (2010). *Experiments in a Jazz Aesthetic: Art, Activism, Academia, and the Austin Project (Vol. 23)*. Austin: University of Texas Press.
Kandel, Karen. (2012). Interview by the author. July.
Kaye, Nick. (1994). *Postmodern Performance*. Basingstoke: Macmillan.
Keefe, John, and Simon Murray, eds. (2007). *Physical Theatres: A Critical Reader*. New York: Routledge.
Kerrigan, Sheila. (2001). *The Performer's Guide to the Collaborative Process: A Practical Guide*. Portsmouth, NH: Heinemann.
Kershaw, Baz. (1992). *The Politics of Performance: Radical Theatre and Cultural Intervention*. London; New York: Routledge.
Khoury, Jamil. (2013). "The Trouble with Mary." *Silk Road Rising*, June 11 (blog). http://www.silkroadrising.org/news/the-trouble-with-mary (accessed January 7, 2019, via *WayBack Machine* internet archive).
Khoury, Jamil. (2013). "Mary Responds: My Interview with Mary Zimmerman." *Silk Road Rising*, June 14 (blog). http://www.silkroadrising.org/news/mary-responds-my-interview-with-mary-zimmerman (accessed January 7, 2019, via *WayBack Machine* internet archive).
Kirby, Michael. (1975). "On Political Theatre." *TDR: The Drama Review*, 19 (2): 129–35.
Kostelanetz, Richard. (1986). "John Cage and Richard Kostelanetz: A Conversation about Radio." *The Musical Quarterly*, 72 (2): 216–27.

Bibliography

Kuftinec, Sonja. (2003). *Staging America: Cornerstone and Community-based Theater*. Carbondale: Southern Illinois University Press.

La Rocco, Claudia. (2010). "Integrating Ensembles to Build a Hybrid Work." *New York Times*, June 10. https://www.nytimes.com/2010/06/11/arts/dance/11graham.html (accessed September 2, 2018).

La Rocco, Claudia. (2011). "Tales From a Hard-hat Zone: The USA." *New York Times*, April 27. https://www.nytimes.com/2011/04/28/theater/reviews/charles-mee-and-anne-bogarts-under-construction-review.html (accessed September 19, 2018).

Leavitt, Dinah Luise. (1980). *Feminist Theatre Groups*. Jefferson, NC: McFarland.

Lee, Esther Kim. (2006). *A History of Asian American Theatre*. Cambridge; New York: Cambridge University Press.

Lehmann, Hans-Thies. (2006). *Postdramatic Theatre*. London; New York: Routledge.

Leonard, Robert H., Ann Kilkelly, and Linda Frye Burnham. (2006). *Performing Communities: Grassroots Ensemble Theaters Deeply Rooted in Eight US Communities*. Oakland, CA: New Village Press.

Lesnick, Henry. (1973). *Guerilla Street Theater*. New York: Bard Books.

Lewis, Ferdinand. (2005). *Ensemble Works: An Anthology*. New York: Theatre Communications Group.

Lewis, Victoria. (2013). "From Mao to the Feeling Circle: The Limits and Endurance of Collective Creation." In *A History of Collective Creation*, eds. Kathryn Mederos Syssoyeva and Scott Proudfit, 209–22. New York: Palgrave Macmillan.

Little, Stuart W. (1972). *Off-Broadway: The Prophetic Theater*. New York: Coward, McCann & Geoghegan.

Lookingglass Theatre Company. (2011). "Lookingglass Theatre Wins Tony Award for Best." *Chicago Examiner*, June 14, n.p.

Lookingglass Theatre Company. (2018a). "Reflecting on Thirty Years, Episode 5: The Legend of Lookingglass," *YouTube*, February 12. http://www.youtube.com/watch?v=QRvlkoX6xTI (accessed January 9, 2019).

Lookingglass Theatre Company. (2018b). "Reflecting on Thirty Years, Episode 9: The Tony Award." *YouTube*, July 24. https://www.youtube.com/watch?v=M24pLfHWfaQ (accessed January 9, 2019).

Lust, Annette. (2003). *From the Greek Mimes to Marcel Marceau and Beyond: Mimes, Actors, Pierrots, and Clowns*. Metuchen, NJ: Scarecrow Press.

Mabou Mines Archive. (n.d.). Production Files. Fales Library and Special Collections. New York University. Series IIIA, Box 9, Folder 368.

Mabou Mines Digital Archive. (n.d.). "Company." https://www.maboumines.org/about/the-company/.

Mabou Mines Digital Archive. (n.d.). "Karen Kandel." https://www.maboumines.org/karen-kandel.

Mabou Mines Digital Archive. (n.d.). "The Red Horse Animation." https://www.maboumines.org/production/the-red-horse-animation.

Mabou Mines Digital Archive. (n.d.). "Suite/Space." https://www.maboumines.org/suite-space.

Mabou Mines Digital Archive. (n.d.). "Summa Dramatica." https://www.maboumines.org/production/summa-dramatica-a-pataphysical-acting-lesson.

Bibliography

Mailik, Gaines. (2017). *Black Performance on the Outskirts of the Left: A History of the Impossible*. New York: New York University Press.

Maleczech, Ruth. (2011–12). Interviews by the author. July–March.

Marks, Peter. (1997). "Peter Pan Is Reborn, and All Go Soaring." *New York Times*, February 7. https://www.nytimes.com/1997/02/07/theater/peter-pan-is-reborn-and-all-go-soaring.html.

Marranca, Bonnie. (1979). "Introduction." In *Animations: A Trilogy for Mabou Mines*, eds. Lee Breuer, Bonnie Marranca, and Gautam Dasgupta. New York: Performing Arts Journal Publications.

Mason, Susan Vanera. (2006). "San Francisco Mime Troupe Legacy: Guerilla Theater." In *Restaging the Sixties: Radical Theaters and Their Legacies*, eds. James Martin Harding and Cindy Rosenthal, 196–212. Ann Arbor: University of Michigan Press.

Matusow, Allen J. ([1985] 2009). *The Unraveling of America: A History of Liberalism in the 1960s*. Athens, GA: University of Georgia Press.

McGinley, Paige. (2010). "Next Up Downtown: A New Generation of Ensemble Performance." *TDR/The Drama Review*, 54 (4): 11–38.

McLeod, Kembrew. (2019). *Downtown Pop Underground: New York City and the Literary Punks, Renegade Artists, DIY Filmmakers, Mad Playwrights, and Rock 'n' Roll Glitter Queens Who Revolutionized Culture*. New York: Abrams Press.

McNeil, Donald G. Jr,. (1994). "On Stage and Off." *New York Times*, December 9: C2.

McNulty, Charles. (1996). "Sound Waves." *The Village Voice*, February 13: 84.

McNulty, Charles. (2002). "The James Gang v. Sophocles." *The Village Voice*, November 5: 60.

Mead, Rebecca. (2010). "Adaptation: Onward and Upward with the Arts." *The New Yorker*, 86 (29), September 27: 44–9. https://www.newyorker.com/magazine/2010/09/27/adaptation-rebecca-mead (accessed October 31, 2018).

Mehrten, Greg. (2011). Interview by the author. July.

Melville, Herman. (1851). *Moby-Dick; or, The Whale*.

Mermikides, Alex. (2013). "Collective Creation and the 'Creative Industries': The British Context." In *Collective Creation in Contemporary Performance*, eds. Kathryn Mederos Syssoyeva and Scott Proudfit, 51–70. New York: Palgrave Macmillan.

Mermikides, Alex, and Jackie Smart, eds. (2010). *Devising in Process*. London: Palgrave.

Metz, Nina. (2005). "'Dollhouse' Hits the Heights." *Chicago Tribune*, November 25. http://www.chicagotribune.com/mmx-051206-stage-review-dollhouse-story.html.

Miller, Douglas T. (1996). "Sixties Activism in the 'Me Decade.'" In *The Lost Decade: America in the Seventies*, ed. Elsebeth Hurup, 133–65. Syracuse: Syracuse University Press.

Miller, Gregory, and Richard Talaske. (2013). "The Isolation of Lookingglass Theatre, or How an Active Water Pumping Station in Chicago Became the Site for an Award-Winning Successful Playhouse." 166th Acoustical Society of America Meeting. http://acoustics.org/pressroom/ and httpdocs/166th/3aAAa3-Miller.html (accessed January 21, 2016).

Miller, Hillary. (2016). *Drop Dead: Performance in Crisis, 1970s New York*. Evanston, IL: Northwestern University Press.

Bibliography

Montgomery, Elizabeth. (1996). "Review of *S/M*, by Mary Zimmerman, Lookingglass Theatre Company, Steppenwolf Studio Theatre, Chicago, February 9, Steppenwolf Theatre, Chicago, March 13," *Theatre Journal*, 48 (3): 373–7.

Morris, Stephen. (2013). "Group Think." https://www.americantheatre.org/2013/03/01/group-think/ (accessed March 11, 2018).

Mufson, Daniel. (2004). "The Burden of Irony, the Onus of Cool: The Wooster Group' Influence on the Cannon Company and Richard Maxwell." In *The Wooster Group and Its Traditions*, Vol. 13, ed. Johan Callens, 263–73. Brussels: Peter Lang.

Murphy, Maiya, and Jon Foley Sherman. (2013). "Lecoq's Pedagogy." In *Collective Creation in Contemporary Performance*, eds. Kathryn Syssoyeva and Scott Proudfit, 111–24, New York: Palgrave Macmillan.

Murray, Simon David, and John Keefe. (2016). *Physical Theatres: A Critical Introduction*. Second edition. London; New York: Routledge.

Network of Ensemble Theatres (NET). "Mission Statement." https://www.ensembletheaters.net/ (accessed December 14, 2017).

Nicholson, Helen. (2014). *Applied Drama: The Gift of Theatre*. Second edition. Houndmills; New York: Palgrave Macmillan.

Oddey, Alison. (1994). *Devising Theatre: A Practical and Theoretical Handbook*. London; New York: Routledge.

O'Gorman, Siobhán, and Charlotte McIvor. (2015). *Devised Performance in Irish Theatre: Histories and Contemporary Practice*. Carysfort Press.

Olsen, Christopher. (2008). "Transformation, Identity, and Deconstruction: Part of the Survival Kit of Collective Theatres in 2007." In *Vies et Morts de la Creation Collective/Lives and Deaths of Collective Creative*, eds. Jane Baldwin, Jean-Marc Larrue, and Christiane Page, 162–79. Boston: Vox Theatri.

Olsen, Christopher. (2011). *Off-Off Broadway: The Second Wave, 1968–1980*. CreateSpace Independent Publishing Platform.

Oppenheim, Lois. (1994). *Directing Beckett*. Ann Arbor: University of Michigan Press.

Overlie, Mary. (2016). *Standing in Space: The Six Viewpoints Theory and Practice*. Self-published.

Parks, Brian. (1993). "Dada's Home." *The Village Voice*, July 6: 87–8.

Peneff, Nicholas. (1988). "High Profile—Lin Hixson and Goat Island." *International Performance Research Center Newsletter*, April, 1988, 8:9–10.

Perlstein, Rick. (1996). "Who Owns the Sixties? The Opening of a Scholarly Generation Gap." *Lingua Franca*, 6 (4): n.p.

Proudfit, Scott. (2013). "Framework for Change: Collective Creation in Los Angeles after the SITI Company." In *Collective Creation in Contemporary Performance*, eds. Kathryn Mederos Syssoyeva and Scott Proudfit, 137–50. New York: Palgrave Macmillan.

Proudfit, Scott, and Kathryn Mederos Syssoyeva. (2013). "From Margin to Center: Collective Creation and Devising at the Turn of the Millennium (A View from the United States)." In *Collective Creation in Contemporary Performance*, eds. Kathryn Mederos Syssoyeva and Scott Proudfit, 13–38. New York: Palgrave Macmillan.

Puchner, Martin. (2006). *Poetry of the Revolution: Marx, Manifestos, and the Avant-gardes*. Princeton: Princeton University Press.

Radosavljević, Duška. (2013a). *The Contemporary Ensemble: Interviews with Theatre-makers*. London; New York: Routledge.

Bibliography

Radosavljević, Duška. (2013b). *Theatre-making: Interplay between Text and Performance in the 21st Century*. Houndmills; New York: Palgrave Macmillan.

Ramírez, Elizabeth C. (2000). *Chicanas/Latinas in American Theatre: A History of Performance*. Bloomington: Indiana University Press.

Rawson, Christopher. (1997). "Warhol's Inferno." *Pittsburgh Post-gazette*, September 12, 1997, Arts & Entertainment 6.

Rea, Charlotte. (1972). "Women's Theatre Groups." *TDR: The Drama Review*, 16 (2): 79–89.

Robinson, Davis. (2015). *A Practical Guide to Ensemble Devising*. London: Palgrave.

Rodosthenous, George. (2017). *The Disney Musical on Stage and Screen: Critical Approaches from "Snow White" to "Frozen."* London; New York: Bloomsbury Methuen Drama.

Royster, Francesca T. (2014). "Experiments in a Jazz Aesthetic: Art, Activism, Academia, and the Austin Project." *Text and Performance Quarterly*, 34 (4): 431–3.

Russo, Francine. (1994). "Cameos: Language Instruction: Love Family v. Andy Kaufman." *The Village Voice*, February 8: 97.

Sainer, Arthur. (1997). *The New Radical Theatre Notebook*. New York: Applause.

Sanford, Richard. (2015). "Theatre Review: Ann Hamilton and SITI Company's *the Theater Is a Blank Page* Dazzles." *Columbus Underground*, April 24. https://www.columbusunderground.com/theatre-review-ann-hamilton-and-siti-companys-the-theater-is-a-blank-page-dazzles-rs1 (accessed September 2, 2018).

Savran, David. (1986). *The Wooster Group, 1975–1985: Breaking the Rules*, Ann Arbor: UMI Research Press.

Savran, David. (1988). *Breaking the Rules: The Wooster Group*. New York: Theatre Communications Group.

Savran, David. (2005). "The Death of the Avant-garde." *TDR/The Drama Review*, 49 (3): 10–42.

Sawyer, Keith. (2003). *Group Creativity: Music, Theatre, Collaboration*. Mahwah, NJ: Lawrence Erlbaum Associates.

Schechner, Richard. (1982). *The End of Humanism*. New York: Performing Arts Journal Publications.

Schechner, Richard. (2008). "An Open Letter to the President of the USA." *TDR: The Drama Review*, 52 (3): 7–8.

Schechner, Richard. (2010). "The Conservative Avant-garde." *New Literary History*, 41 (4): 895–913.

Schneider, John. (1989). "A History of Theatre X." In Theatre X, *Theatre X: 1969–1989*, 3–5. Milwaukee.

Sell, Mike. (2011). *Avant-garde Performance and Material Exchange: Vectors of the Radical*. Houndmills; New York: Palgrave Macmillan.

Sellar, Tom. (2013). "ERSs John Collins Explores a Sexy Supreme Court Case." *The Village Voice*, September 4. https://www.villagevoice.com/2013/09/04/erss-john-collins-explores-a-sexy-supreme-court-case/ (accessed June 6, 2018).

Serrianne, Nina Esperanza. (2015). *America in the Nineties*. Syracuse, New York: Syracuse University Press.

Shank, Theodore. (2002). *Beyond the Boundaries: American Alternative Theatre*. Ann Arbor: University of Michigan Press.

Bibliography

Shannon, Sandra G. (2018). *Modern American Drama: Playwriting in the 1980s: Voices, Documents, New Interpretations*. London; New York: Bloomsbury: 22.

Shaw, Helen. (2011). "The Select (The Sun Also Rises) Guzzles Hemingway." *The Village Voice*, September 14. https://www.villagevoice.com/2011/09/14/the-select-the-sun-also-rises-guzzles-hemingway/ (accessed October 31, 2018).

Shteir, Rachel. (1992). "Enter SITI." *Village Voice*, September 22, 1992: 99–100.

Shyer, Laurence. (1989). *Robert Wilson and His Collaborators*: New York: Theatre Communications Group.

Slocum-Schaffer, Stephanie S. (2003). *America in the Seventies*. Syracuse: Syracuse University Press.

Smith Fischer, Iris. (1993). "Mabou Mines's 'Lear': A Narrative of Collective Authorship." *Theatre Journal*, 45 (3), October: 279–302.

Smith Fischer, Iris. (2012). *Mabou Mines: Making Avant-garde Theater in the 1970s*. Ann Arbor: University of Michigan Press.

Smith, Sid. (1990). "Young Troupe Gives 'Odyssey' a Goofy, Impressive Staging." *Chicago Tribune*, April 20: D28.

Smith, Tim. (2017). "'Alice' Gets a Curiouser Adaptation at Baltimore Center Stage, Featuring Aerials and Demi Lovato Music." *The Baltimore Sun*, December 12. http://www.baltimoresun.com/entertainment/arts/artsmash/bs-wk-alice-review-20171208-story.html (accessed October 21, 2018).

Solomon, Alisa. (2006). "Only Connect: The Living Theatre and Its Audiences." In *Restaging the Sixties: Radical Theaters and Their Legacies*, eds. James Martin Harding and Cindy Rosenthal, 56–76. Ann Arbor: University of Michigan Press.

Soloski, Alexis. (2006). "Just Jack," *The Village Voice*, January 31: 66.

Soloski, Alexis. (2015). "A Collaboration of Wacky and Weird." *The New York Times*, September 6: AR5.

Suzuki, Tadashi. (2015). *Culture Is the Body: The Theatre Writings of Tadashi Suzuki*. New York: Theatre Communications Group.

Swedberg, Anne Kristin. (2006). "Taking It Outside: Community-based Theater and Maryat Lee, 1949–1989." PhD diss., University of Wisconsin-Madison.

Syssoyeva, Kathryn Mederos, and Scott Proudfit. (2013a). *A History of Collective Creation*. New York: Palgrave Macmillan.

Syssoyeva, Kathryn Mederos, and Scott Proudfit. (2013b). *Collective Creation in Contemporary Performance*. New York: Palgrave Macmillan.

Syssoyeva, Kathryn Mederos, and Scott Proudfit. (2016). *Women, Collective Creation, and Devised Performance: The Rise of Women Theatre Artists in the Twentieth and Twenty-first Centuries*. New York: Palgrave Macmillan.

ten Cate, Ritsaert. (1989). "Theatre X: Reflections by Ritsaert ten Cate." In *Theatre X*, 11, 12.

Theatre X. (1989). *Theatre X: 1969–1989*. Milwaukee.

Thompson, Susan Wright. (2007). "*Tout ensemble*: The Actor-creator and the Influence of the Pedagogy of Jacques Lecoq on American Ensembles." PhD diss., Tufts University.

Thompson, Susan Wright. (2013). "Freedom and Constraints: Jacques Lecoq and the Theater of Ensemble Creation." In *Encountering Ensemble*, ed. John Britton, 389–404. London; New York: Bloomsbury.

Bibliography

Tomlin, Liz. (2015). "The Academy and the Marketplace: Avant-garde Performance in Neoliberal Times." In *Vanguard Performance Left and Right*, ed. Kimberly Jannarone, 264–82. Ann Arbor: University of Michigan Press.

Troy, Gil, and Vincent J. Cannato. (2009). *Living in the Eighties*. Oxford: Oxford University Press.

Tsatsos, I. (1991). "Talking with Goat Island. An Interview with Joan Dickinson, Karen Christopher, Matthew Goulish, Greg McCain, and Tim McCain." *The Drama Review*, Winter T132: 66–74.

Valdez, Mark. (2013). "Network of Ensemble Theaters." In *Encountering Ensemble*, ed. John Britton, 209–11. London; New York: Bloomsbury.

Vanden Heuvel, Michael. (1993). *Performing Drama/Dramatizing Performance: Alternative Theatre and the Dramatic Text*. Ann Arbor: University of Michigan Press.

Van Dijk, Bert. (2011). *Devised Theatre: A Practical Guide to the Devising Process*. Plimmerton, NZ: Bert van Dijk.

Vásquez, Eva C. (2003). *Pregones Theatre: A Theatre for Social Change in the South Bronx*. London; New York: Routledge.

Virtusio, Jessi. (2010). "Seeing Is Believing." Daily Southtown, *SouthtownStar*, May 6: FW19.

Wang, Meiyin. (2011). "The Theatre of the Future." https://howlround.com/theatre-future (accessed November 2, 2018).

Weinberg, Mark S. (1992). *Challenging the Hierarchy: Collective Theatre in the United States*. New York: Greenwood Press.

Weiner, Wendy. (1997). "John Collins: Accidents Will Happen." *American Theatre*, 14 (7), September: 48–9.

Weiss, Hedy. (2002). "DANCE NOTES." *Chicago Sun-Times*, May 29: 54.

Weiss, Hedy. (2009). "Lookingglass Grants a Wish—Magic Undimmed in *The Arabian Nights*." Review, *Chicago Sun-Times*, June 1, 31.

Weissmann, David, and Bill Weber. (2002). *The Cockettes*. Strand Releasing Home Video.

Whiting, Frank M. (1988). *Minnesota Theatre: From Old Fort Snelling to the Guthrie*. St. Paul, MN: Pogo Press.

Williams, Joshua. (2014). Review of *The Jungle Book*, adapted and directed by Mary Zimmerman, Huntington. Theatre Company and Goodman Theatre, B.U. Theatre, Boston, September 19, 2013. *Theatre Journal*, 66 (2): 276–8.

Woodson, Stephani Etheridge, and Tamara Underiner, eds. (2018). *Theatre, Performance and Change*. London: Palgrave.

Zeigler, Joseph Wesley. (1994). *Arts in Crisis: The National Endowment for the Arts versus America*. Pennington, NJ: A Cappella Books.

Zimmerman, Mark. (1998). "Some Sort of Awakening." *PAJ: A Journal of Performance and Art*, 20 (2), May: 40–8.

Zimmerman, Mary Alice. (1994). "The Archeology of Performance: A Study of Ensemble Process and Development in the Lookingglass Theatre Production of *The Arabian Nights*." PhD diss., Northwestern University (Evanston: Northwestern University).

Zinoman, Jason. (2006a). "On the TV: Re-enacting Jack Kerouac Interviews." *The New York Times*, February 18: B9.

Zinoman, Jason. (2006b). "'Gatz' and 'The Great Gatsby Vie for Broadway Stages." *New York Times*, July 16. AR8.

INDEX

About Face Youth Theatre 56–7
Actor's Gymnasium 153, 158, 163
Actors Theatre of Louisville (ATL) 201–3, 212
Actor's Workshop 42, 76, 107–8
AIDS crisis 2, 36, 50, 55, 56
Aizawa, Akiko 200, 211, 213, 215, 218
Akalaitis, JoAnne 105–9, 111–13, 111–18, 115–18, 122, 124–5
American Society for Theatre Research (ASTR) 29, 34–5
American ensemble theatre. *See also* collective theatre making
   collective making 2, 21–2
   constituency-based ensembles 47–55
   development-based or educational theatres 57
   discrete styles 21
   ethnic-specific ensembles 47–55
   gay and queer ensembles 55–7
   LGBTQ activism 17, 57
   postmodern 68–81
   second wave 32
Anderson-Rabern, Rachel 29, 35, 81
   Staging Process: The Aesthetic Politics of Collective Performance 35, 81
applied theatre 24, 45, 48–9, 57–65, 67, 159
Araiza, Ed 200, 202, 211, 218
Archer, Julie 116, 119, 122–4, 122–6, 126
Aronson, Arnold 2, 31–2, 32, 69–70
   American Avant-garde Theatre: A History 31
Artaud, Antonin 33–4, 64, 69, 85
   "Theatre of Cruelty" 85
Ashby, Cynthia 133, 145
Aston, Elaine 46, 113
At the Foot of the Mountain (AFOM) 13, 37, 39, 42–4
Auslander, Philip 70
avant-garde style 21, 31–3, 50, 71, 80, 85, 105–7, 198, 216

Bailes, Sara Jane 29, 135, 149, 173, 180, 194–5
BAM Next Wave Festival 68, 119, 213, 215
Banes, Sally 31, 73, 85
Bausch, Pina 68, 136, 144–6
Bayless, Rick 168–9, 171
Beck, Julian 34, 85, 112
Beckett, Samuel 39, 63, 72–3, 73, 88, 92, 99, 107, 111–16, 113–16, 198, 215
Berryman, Eric 201, 215
Bishop, Conrad 83–4, 96–7
Black Arts Movement 48–9, 52
Blau, Herbert 76, 107–8
   The Impossible Theatre: A Manifesto 76
Blue Man Group 38, 168
Boal, Augusto 58, 61
   Theatre of the Oppressed 58
Bodow, Steve 173, 175, 187
Bogart, Anne 39, 110, 197–9, 200, 202–5, 202–18, 218
Bond, Will 199–200, 210–11, 213, 216–18
Bottoms, Stephen J. 30, 112, 134, 140–8
Brantley, Ben 186–93
Bread and Puppet Theatre 23, 37, 67
Brecht, Bertolt 39, 46, 54, 77, 83, 88, 97, 108–11, 125, 132, 177, 198, 207
   No Plays No Poetry 39, 198
Breen, Robert 152, 222 n.4
Breuer, Lee 27, 76, 105–13, 115–16, 118–19, 118–23, 121–3, 125–8, 220 n.2, 221 n.8
Buckley, William F. 16
   Firing Line 186
Builders Association, The 47, 75, 80
Bunraku-style puppet 116, 123
Burnham, Linda Frye 77, 136
Bush, George H. W. 4, 7, 11, 15, 18–20

Cage, John 86, 216–17
CalArts 77–8
Canning, Charlotte 24, 40–1, 43–5, 48
Carroll, Lewis 152, 158, 162, 171

Index

Carroll, Peter N. 1, 71
Carter, Jimmy 4, 6
Castillo Theatre 48, 77
Catlin, David 152–3, 155, 158, 162–4, 170–2, 171–2, 222 n.2
Chaikin, Joseph 31–2
Chekhov, Anton 200, 209
Chong, Ping 32, 51, 70
Christiansen, Richard 153, 166–7
Christopher, Karen 141–2, 144, 148
Circle of the Witch Theatre 42–3
Cirque du Soleil 64, 153, 168
Civil Rights Movement 3, 40, 48
Clark, Jocelyn 124, 210, 216
Clarke, Martha 32, 70
Clifton, Deborah 84, 90, 99–100, 219 n.1
Clinton, Bill 7–9, 11, 14, 17–18, 20
Coates, George 51, 68
Cohen-Cruz, Jan 59–60
Cohn, Ruby 111–12, 114
Coker, Flora 84, 88, 90, 95, 97–100, 219–20 nn.1–2
Cold War 1, 3, 6
collective theatre making 2, 21–2, 40–7. *See also* devised theatre
   collaborative nature 25, 28–9
   collapse or disintegration 38–9
   common chronology 23
   ensemble practice, definition 27
   feminist groups 24
   first wave 57
   group theatres 23–4 (*See also specific examples*)
   "new vaudeville" movement 38
   of 1960s 32, 35, 38, 43, 58–9, 63, 69–70, 72–3, 76–7
   of 1970s 31–4, 38, 40–2, 44–5, 47–8, 50–3, 55–6, 58–62, 65, 69, 72, 77
   second acts 37, 69
   sources of creativity 28
   third-wave companies 39, 69
   UK creative practices 26
   woman's theatre 39
Collins, John 75, 173, 175–7, 175–8, 184–5, 187, 190–1
community-based theatre 48, 62–3, 67
Comprehensive Employment and Training Act (CETA) 47, 53, 60
Crossroads Theatre 44, 47
Curb, Rosemary 41–2

Dafoe, Willem 75, 84, 98–9
Davis, Douglas 182
Davis, Ronnie 76, 108
declension hypothesis 4–5, 32
Defense of Marriage Act 8
Dell'Arte 52, 65–7, 78
Del Signore, John 125
devised theatre 12, 21–3, 25, 27, 31, 33–5, 40, 46–7, 52–5, 57–8, 61–4, 66, 69, 71–3, 76, 79–81, 131, 143, 146, 178, 191, 197, 200, 207
   queer practice 50
Dickinson, Joan 140–2
DiStasi, Larry 153, 222 n.2
Dolan, Jill 14, 46
Doris Duke Artist Award 62, 68
Double Edge 66–7
Downs, David 152, 166

Economic Opportunity Act 60
Elevator Repair Service (ERS) 75, 80
   Arguendo 174, 190–2
   Cab Legs 180–2, 185, 191
   Emperor Jones, The 75, 176
   Everyone's Fine with Virginia Woolf 174, 192
   Fire Extinguisher 173, 175
   Fondly, Collette Richard 174, 191
   Gatz 174–5, 185–90, 193–5
   Great Gatsby, The 78, 174, 182, 185, 188, 194
   Highway to Tomorrow 182–4
   Language Instruction: Love Family v. Andy Kaufman 179, 182
   Measure for Measure 174, 191–3
   Mr. Antipyrine 173–8, 191
   No Great Society 186–7
   plays, staffing of 191–3
   productions 2004–2012 184–91
   Room Tone 173–4, 184, 191
   Select, The 174, 188–90
   Shut up I Tell You 179–80
   Sound and the Fury, The 174, 186–9
   Spine Check 178, 182
   staging approach 175–84
   Summer and Smoke 180–1, 191
   Sun Also Rises, The 174, 186, 188, 190–1
   Total Fictional Lie 177, 181–5
   Turn of the Screw 173, 184, 191

Index

Who's Afraid of Virginia Woolf? 192–3, 209
working methods 173–5
El Teatro Campesino (ETC) 22, 36, 38, 52–3, 55, 58, 96
Endgame 92, 113
Equal Rights Amendment (ERA) 12–14
Etchells, Tim 34, 74

Fabre, Jan 85, 93, 219 n.1. See also Troubleyn theatre company
Falwell, Jerry, Moral Majority 14, 16
Fates 164–5
Feingold, Michael 182–4, 186, 188, 192–3
feminism
    activism 12–15
    second-wave 1, 13, 43–4, 46
    women-focused organizations 13
feminist ensemble theatres 1970–94 40–7
    Alive and Trucking 42–3
    At the Foot of the Mountain 13, 37, 39, 42
    Circle of the Witch 42–3
    Lavender Cellar 42–3
Fiji Company 51, 70
Five Blind Boys 119–20
Fogarty, Sharon 122–7
Ford, Gerald 4, 6
Foreman, Richard 32, 38, 68–70, 72, 74, 176, 180, 198
formalist theatre 32, 35, 38
forum theatre 22, 58
Foucault, Michel 76, 91
Free Southern Theatre 23, 37, 48, 58, 63
fringe theatres, Britain 33–4
Frye Burnham, Linda 77, 136
Fuchs, Elinor 16, 71, 117–18
Fuller, Elizabeth 83, 90
Fusco, Coco 173, 175, 177

Galati, Frank 152, 166, 222 n.7
Galilee, Clove 115–16, 124, 127
Gianino, Gian-Murray 201, 213, 215
Gingrich, Newt 7, 20
Glass, Philip 105, 107, 109, 111–12, 114, 126
Goat Island 34, 73, 75, 77–8
    Can't Take Johnny to the Funeral 130, 135, 141–2
    How Dear to Me the Hour When Daylight Dies 135, 143–4

It's an Earthquake in My Heart 135, 145–6
It's Shifting, Hank 130, 133–5, 142
Lastmaker, The 133, 136, 148–9
Last Night Was Only a Comedy 136, 146–7
legacy and archive 149–50
networks 130–1
performance space 129–35
production phases 135–6
Sea & Poison, The 133, 135, 144–5, 147
Small Acts of Repair 140, 142, 147
Soldier, Child, Tortured Man 133, 135, 137–8, 141
We Got a Date 131, 135, 140–1
When Will the September Roses Bloom? Last Night Was Only a Comedy 136, 146–8
Goldwater, Barry 3, 6
Goodman Theatre 161, 170–2
Goulish, Matthew 133, 136–7, 137, 139–48
Gran Fury 16, 36
grassroots movements 22, 24, 41–2, 48, 58–61, 69, 116
Gray, Spalding 74–5
Great Society principles 7, 11, 19
Groff, Rinnie 173, 175, 177
Grotowski, Jerzy 64–5, 69–70, 72–3, 108, 111, 132, 136, 152
Grotowski's Theatre 37–8, 64, 66, 69–70, 72–3, 108, 111, 132, 136, 152–3
group theatres 23, 32, 47
guerilla theatre movement 21, 42, 56, 60–1, 71
Gulf War 1, 8, 151, 199
Gussow, Mel 51, 112–14, 199

Hangers 77–8. See also Hixson, Lin
Happenings 31, 70–1
Harding, James and Cindy Rosenthal 2, 36, 58, 77
    Restaging the Sixties Radical Theaters and Their Legacies 2, 36, 58
Hartinian, Linda 115–16
Harvie, Jen 34, 46
    Making Contemporary Theatre 34
Hayes, Jacqueline 42–5
Heddon, Deidre and Jane Milling 28–9, 34, 70, 75, 80

Index

Devising Performance: A Critical History 34
Helms, Jesse 16–17, 19–20
Hemingway, Ernest 174, 188–90
Hernandez, Tony 153, 163, 171
historiography of collective creation 4, 31–6, 42
Hixson, Lin 34, 73, 77–8, 130–2, 134, 136–7, 139–42, 145, 147–9
Hoffman, Marcie 90, 220 n.2
Horwitz, Andy 173, 175, 185
Huerta, Jorge 37, 53
Hughes, David 46, 141
Hughes, Jenny 46, 141

Ingulsrud, Leon 200, 211, 213, 218
Irondale Ensemble 68, 75
Irving, Jules 76, 107
Irwin, Bill 38, 76

Jackson, Julie 67, 153, 155
James, Henry 173, 184
Jameson, Fredric 77, 179
Jane Milling 28–9, 34, 70, 75, 80
Jeffery, Mark 143–4, 147–8
Judson Church 31, 70

Kandel, Karen 114, 116, 121–4, 122–4, 127
Kantor, Tadeusz 37, 198
Kate Valk 75
Khoury, Jamil 161–2
King, Rodney 18, 61
King Lear 108, 121
Kishline, John 84, 91, 94–5, 100, 219–20 nn.1–2
Klein, Stacy 66–7
Kramer, Larry 15–16
Krause, Alvina 62–3, 152

La MaMa 39, 52, 86, 106–7, 112, 116, 127
La Rocco, Claudia 212–14
Lauren, Ellen 199–200, 210–13, 216–18
Leavitt, Dinah Luise 42–4
LeCompte, Liz 34, 72, 75
Lecoq, Jacques 65–7, 154
Lee, Maryat 60–1
Leonard, Robert H. 59, 61, 66
Leonard Pitts Mime School 65
Lewis, Victoria 41, 47
LGBTQ activism 17–18

Lilith 41, 42, 44, 45
Living Theatre 2, 21–3, 34, 36, 39, 69, 71–3, 85, 96, 112
Lookingglass Theatre Company 64, 66, 70, 75
  Alice in Wonderland 92, 97, 152, 222 n.2
  Arabian Nights, The 90, 151, 157, 160–1, 163, 167, 169, 222 n.7
  Argonautika 161, 171, 222 n.8
  Cascabel 168–9, 171, 223 n.14
  critical reception 165–9
  founders 152–4
  Hephaestus 158, 163, 168, 171
  improvisation techniques 155–9, 161
  Jungle Book, The 161–2, 223 n.10
  key productions and projects 159–65
  Lookingglass Alice 158, 162, 171
  Metamorphoses 157, 159, 162, 170
  Moby Dick 163–5, 172
  Odyssey, The 154, 161, 165–6, 222 n.8
  performance space 151–2
  significant productions 1997–2017 169–72
  theatrical adaptation 152–3, 158
  1001 Nights 160–1, 162, 169
Lorenzo, Victor De 84, 99
Lorwin, Liza 120, 122, 127
Ludlam, Charles 32, 55

Mabou Mines 28, 32, 68–70, 72–3, 76, 154
  Beckett's work 112–15
  Coriolanus 109–10, 125
  Dead End Kids 116–18
  Dollhouse 114, 125
  Epidog, An 116, 124
  Finnegans Wake 124–5
  Gospel at Colonus, The 119–20
  Hajj 118–19
  Happy Days 88, 99, 115, 121
  inspirations and reverberations 107–12
  Lear 108–9, 114, 121–2, 124
  Lost Ones, The 112–14
  Lucia's Chapters of Coming Forth by Day 123–4
  new works and adaptations 115–26
  Play 111–12, 115
  Peter and Wendy 114, 122–3

Index

Red Horse Animation 105–7, 109, 112, 115–16
Summa Dramatica 116, 121
theatrical innovation 105–7
Macbeth 164, 199
Maleczech, Ruth 105–27, 220 n.1
Malina, Judith 34, 85, 112
Marranca, Bonnie 69, 116
 The Theatre of Images 69
Marshall, Thurgood 15, 18
Mason, Susan Vanera 36, 179
Matusow, Allen J. 4–5
Maurer, Kelly 199–200, 210–11, 218
McCain brothers (Tim and Greg) 136–9, 143
McElduff, Ellen 112–14, 116–17, 121–2
McLuhan, Marshal 200, 208–9
McNulty, Charles 179–80, 184
Mead, Rebecca 185, 187
Mee, Charles 211–13
Mehrten, Greg 110, 117, 119–22
Melville, Herman 163–4, 172
Mickery Theater 88, 91, 219 n.1
Miguel, Muriel 39, 62
Miller, Douglas T. 59, 157
Minimalism 31, 70
Minneapolis companies 42–3
Monk, Meredith 32, 70

National Endowment for the Arts (NEA) 8, 19–20
 four artists (the "NEA Four") 20
 "Ongoing Ensembles Grant" 75
Nelis, Tom 199–200, 210, 218
Network of Ensemble Theatres (NET) 27, 29, 48, 52, 62
Neumann, Frederick 109, 114–17, 126–7
New Deal 3, 7
New Right 3, 14
New Theater Festival 88
New Wave 31, 70
New York Theater Workshop 47, 187–8, 191
Nixon, Richard 2, 4, 18–19, 47, 50
 Watergate scandal 2
"No Child Left Behind" legislation 11
Norquist, John 93–4

Obama, Barack 20
OBIE awards 39, 53, 68, 75, 88, 91, 95, 112, 114, 116, 123, 199

Oddey, Alison 33–5
 Devising Theatre: A Practical and Theoretical Handbook 33
Off-Off-Broadway 21, 30–1
O'Hanlon, Barney 200, 211, 215, 218
Olsen, Christopher 48, 77
Open Theatre 2, 36, 39, 52–3, 218
O'Reilly, Terry 114, 116–17, 123
Otrabanda Company 37, 39
Overlie, Mary 197, 204–5

Parks, Brian 178–9, 182
Paul Getty Museum 203, 213
Performance Group 2, 22–3, 34, 37, 69, 73, 96
physical theatre 64–8
 award-winning documentary 67
 robust traditions 65–6
 sources of inspiration 64
Pig Iron Theatre 40, 65–6, 70
Pilobolus 64, 153
Pomo Afro Homos 50–1
Pop Art 31, 70
Public Theatre 25, 50, 54, 120
Punk music 31, 70

Queer Nation 36, 56

Rainer, Yvonne 85, 136
Raymond, Bill 107–9, 114–17, 121–2, 127
Reagan, Ronald 4–8, 11–12, 14, 16–19, 45, 79
ReCherChez 120, 127
Redmoon Theater 163, 166
regional theatre movement 30–1
Remains Theatre 153, 161
Rohrbacher, Dana 19–20
Roosevelt, Franklin D 3, 11
Rude Mechs 26, 62

Sainer, Arthur 23, 39, 43
 Radical Theatre Notebook 23, 43
Sanchez, Sonia 49, 200
 Sister Son/ji 49
Saner, Bryan 143–4
Sanford, Richard 199, 216
San Francisco Mime Troupe (SFMT) 21–3, 41, 47, 50, 58, 65, 73, 76, 96, 108
 Minstrel Show: Or, Civil Rights in a Cracker Barrel 47

Index

Saratoga International Theater Institute (SITI Company) 26, 28, 75
  actor training methods 197, 199, 201, 204–7, 218
  Adding Machine, The 202, 212
  Bacchae, The 182–3, 199, 213
  Bob 202, 210
  bobrauschenbergamerica 201, 203, 211
  Chess Match No. 5 203, 216–17
  collaborations with other artists and companies 213–17
  Culture of Desire 203, 208–9, 211
  Dionysus 199, 218
  Going, Going, Gone 202, 208–9
  Medium, The 200, 202, 207–9, 224 n.4
  No Plays No Poetry 39, 198
  Orestes 199, 211–13
  origins and development 198–203
  Picnic 202, 212
  plays by others 212–13
  repertoire and methodology 207–12
  Room 210
  Score 210
  Small Lives/Big Dreams 200, 202, 208–9
  Steel Hammer 202, 214–15
  Under Construction 211–12
  Tale of Lear, The 199–200
  theatre is a blank page, the 214–15
  Trojan Women 213, 218
Savran, David 24, 70, 72
  Breaking the Rules: The Wooster Group 24
Schechner, Richard 31, 34, 37, 69, 74, 76, 80, 198
  The End of Humanism 31
Schneider, John 84–5, 87–92, 90–2, 94–5, 97–8, 103–4, 219–20 nn.1–2
Schwimmer, David 152, 166–7, 170, 222 n.2
Second World War 1, 3, 10
Serban, Andre 39, 198
Shank, Theodore 23, 37, 73, 76
  Beyond the Boundaries: American Alternative Theatre 73, 76
  "Collective Creation" 23
Shaw, Helen 189–90
Shepherd, Scott 186, 193
Sills, Paul 155, 218
Sklar, Roberta 39, 42
Snake Theatre 68, 76
Solomon, Alisa 36, 121
Soloski, Alexis 187, 191
Spiderwoman Theatre 39, 45, 62
Split Britches 44–6
Spolin, Viola 24, 155
Squat Theatre 37, 73
Stein, Gertrude 39, 73, 131
Steppenwolf Studio Theatre 153–4, 161, 167, 169
Stewart, Ellen 106–7
Street theatre 36, 39, 60–1, 67
Suzuki, Tadashi 92, 197–201, 204–5, 204–7, 207, 212, 218
Suzuki Company of Toga (SCOT) 198, 218
Syssoyeva, Kathryn Mederos and Scott Proudfit 22, 29, 35–6, 40, 65, 69, 81
  Collective Creation in Contemporary Performance 35
  A History of Collective Creation 22, 35
  Women, Collective Creation, and Devised Performance: The Rise of Women Theatre Artists in the Twentieth and Twenty-first Centuries 35, 40

Tax Reform Bill of 1986 45
Ten Cate, Ritsaert 83, 91–2, 94, 98, 100, 103
Theatre Communications Group (TCG) 30, 48, 199
Theatre de la Jeune Lune 66, 154
Theatre of the Oppressed 22, 24, 58
Theatre X 37, 48, 75
  accomplishments 94–6
  African-American-themes 89–90
  artistic and administrative management 84, 86–7
  audiences 84–5
  CHOMSKY 9/11 94, 99
  cultural diversity 89
  Desire of the Moth for the Star, The 90, 95, 100, 101
  as experimental theatre 83, 85–6
  Fierce Longing, A 88, 91, 99, 101
  History of Sexuality, The 91, 101
  home-city productions 92–4
  international productions 91–2
  Measures Taken, The 83, 88, 97
  methodology 86–8
  mission 84, 88
  My Werewolf 93, 101
  national projects 90–1
  Offending the Audience 92, 100

Index

Razor Blades 88, 91
Sweet Dreams 92, 95
Unnamed, The 88, 91, 98–100
women's role 90
X Communication 83, 92, 96
Thomas, Blair 163, 172
Thomas, Clarence 15, 18
Thomas, Dylan 88
Thompson, Susan Wright 65–6
Title IX Education Amendment 13
ToRoNaDa 121, 126–7
Troubleyn theatre company 85, 93
Trump, Donald 20

United States
    Age of Terror 8–9
    AIDS crisis 16–17
    arts funding 19–20
    economy 9–11
    education 11–12
    politics 2–9
    racial tensions 17–18
    Women's Movement 12–15
Universes 26, 50, 53
Urban Bush Women 49–50

Valdez, Luis 52–3, 55
Valdez, Mark 31, 52–3, 55
Vietnam War 3–5, 19, 63, 94
Viewpoints 197, 201, 204–7

"War on Drugs" 18
Warrilow, David 105–6, 109, 111–21
Water Tower Water Works 156, 162, 165, 169–72
Weaver, Lois 46
Webber, Stephen 200, 213, 215, 218
Weinberg, Mark S. 23, 38, 45, 61
West, Darron 202, 213, 216, 218
Williams, Tennessee 126, 180, 182
Wilson, Robert 32, 38, 68–70, 69–70, 73, 198, 210
Women One Women (WOW) Cafe 46
Women's Experimental Theatre (WET) 39, 45
Women's International Terrorist Conspiracy from Hell (WITCH) 60
Women's Movement 12–15
Woolf, Virginia 210, 212, 215
Wooster Group 24, 32, 34, 37–8, 68–70, 72–6, 77
    international reputation 75

Yerxa, Alison 119–21

Zimmerman, Mary Alice 151, 154–7, 159–62, 165–70, 181
Zinn, David 187, 189–90
Zinoman, Jason 185–7

www.ingramcontent.com/pod-product-compliance
Lightning Source LLC
Chambersburg PA
CBHW072139290426
44111CB00012B/1916